The War on Leakers

ALSO BY LLOYD C. GARDNER

*Killing Machine: The American Presidency
in the Age of Drone Warfare*

The Case That Never Dies: The Lindbergh Kidnapping

*The Long Road to Baghdad: A History of U.S.
Foreign Policy from the 1970s to the Present*

*The Road to Tahrir Square: Egypt and the United States
from the Rise of Nasser to the Fall of Mubarak*

*Three Kings: The Rise of an American Empire
in the Middle East After World War II*

*Iraq and the Lessons of Vietnam: Or, How Not to Learn
from the Past* (co-edited with Marilyn B. Young)

*The New American Empire: A 21st Century Teach-In on
U.S. Foreign Policy* (co-edited with Marilyn B. Young)

The War on Leakers

*National Security and
American Democracy,
from Eugene V. Debs
to Edward Snowden*

Lloyd C. Gardner

THE NEW PRESS

NEW YORK
LONDON

Requests for permission to reproduce selections from this book
should be mailed to: Permissions Department, The New Press,
120 Wall Street, 31st floor, New York, NY 10005.

Published in the United States by The New Press, New York, 2016
Distributed by Perseus Distribution

LIBRARY OF CONGRESS CATALOGING-IN-PUBLICATION DATA

Names: Gardner, Lloyd C., 1934–
Title: The war on leakers : national security and American democracy, from
Eugene v. Debs to Edward Snowden / Lloyd C. Gardner.
Description: New York : The New Press, 2016. | Includes
bibliographical references and index.

Identifiers: LCCN 2015027800 | ISBN 9781620970638
(hardback) | ISBN 9781620970812 (e-book)

Subjects: LCSH: Official secrets—United States. | Government
information—United States. | Leaks (Disclosure of information)—United
States. | Electronic surveillance—United States. | Democracy—United
States. | National security—United States. | BISAC: POLITICAL SCIENCE
/ Political Freedom & Security / International Security. | POLITICAL
SCIENCE / Political Freedom & Security / Intelligence. | HISTORY /
United States / 20th Century. | HISTORY / United States / 21st Century.

Classification: LCC JK468.S4 G37 2016 | DDC 364.1/31—dc23
LC record available at http://lccn.loc.gov/2015027800

The New Press publishes books that promote and enrich public discussion and
understanding of the issues vital to our democracy and to a more equitable world.
These books are made possible by the enthusiasm of our readers; the support
of a committed group of donors, large and small; the collaboration of our many
partners in the independent media and the not-for-profit sector; booksellers,
who often hand-sell New Press books; librarians; and above all by our authors.

www.thenewpress.com

Composition by dix!
This book was set in Electra

Printed in the United States of America

2 4 6 8 10 9 7 5 3 1

For our five grandchildren, Jamie, Dylan, Kyle, Asha, and Naiya

CONTENTS

INTRODUCTION

A building circular . . . The prisoners in their cells, occupying the circumference—The officers in the centre. By blinds and other contrivances, the Inspectors concealed . . . from the observation of the prisoners: hence the sentiment of a sort of omnipresence—The whole circuit reviewable with little, or . . . without any, change of place. One station in the inspection part affording the most perfect view of every cell.

—Jeremy Bentham, *Proposal for a New and Less Expensive Mode of Employing and Reforming Convicts* (London, 1798)

The main theme of this book is the relationship among the so-called intelligence community and the White House and Congress, and how that three-way marriage has developed over the years since World War I. The 1917 Espionage Act has now become the weapon of choice against leakers, but there has always been a campaign against leakers and, inevitably entangled with it, a desire to put leakers and protesters in the same bin as foreign spies and cast enforcement actions in terms of a "balance" between liberty and security. Indeed, no one has put this claim better than President Obama, who declared after the Snowden revelations that it had become necessary to make Americans comfortable with what had to be done. Critics of the intelligence community, on the other hand, see the greatest threat as that posed to U.S. institutions under the Constitution. The battleground has become the indictments under the 1917 Espionage Act, which the Obama administration has invoked more times than any other presidency. The long-standing campaign against leakers has now become a war.

Immediately after the first articles appeared drawing on Edward Snowden's enormous cache of government documents detailing the cooperation of tech companies with government demands for access to metadata, President Obama told a press conference on June 7, 2013, that he had come into office wary of the NSA's eavesdropping program. "I came in with a healthy skepticism about these programs. My team evaluated them. We scrubbed them thoroughly. We actually expanded some of the oversight, increased some of safeguards. But my assessment and my team's assessment was that they help us prevent terrorist attacks." Later in the summer, as what the president called the drip-drop of new revelations challenging his statements that his pre-Snowden investigations got the balance just about right, the president appointed a small panel of experts to advise him on what further changes or reforms might be needed. It did so in December 2013, and we will see that the results were not at all consistent with claims that the program had prevented terrorist attacks.

The reactions of the president to questions about the National Security Agency (NSA) programs, to leaks about the Senate Intelligence Committee's six-thousand-page report on torture of suspected terrorists in the George W. Bush administration, and to the fate of leakers illustrate the second major theme of the book: the effort of the White House not to get caught in a debate between the intelligence community and Congress or between critics and the agencies that carry out the programs. In regard to indictments under the Espionage Act that his Department of Justice put forward in leaker cases, Attorney General Eric Holder explained that many of these cases had orginated under the previous administration and there would be a morale problem if they were called off. It was an odd position to take, at least in some ways, because it suggests that no administration can ever go back over its predecessor's actions and set a new course. Elections, then, could not be about change "you can believe in" in all circumstances. It also suggests, therefore, that since 9/11 there has been a fundamental shift in the balance of power within the federal government and it is necessary now to talk about an "imperial presidency" rather than an "imperial president."

Obama had, in fact, explained that the limitations on a post-9/11 president in managing the imperial presidency obliged him to avoid getting between the intelligence community and its critics. "Part of my job," he said in an interview with ABC News several days before his inauguration, "is to make sure that, for example, at the CIA [Central Intelligence Agency], you've got extraordinarily talented people who are working very hard to keep Americans safe. I don't want them to suddenly feel like they've got to spend all their time looking over their shoulders."[1]

This book will look over a lot of shoulders, going back to the enactment of the Espionage Act in 1917 to discuss how the act was used to suppress dissent. I will also examine how presidents have gradually become more and more dependent on the intelligence community after World War II, by assigning it more and more duties to keep America safe and becoming less independent of its claims to immunity. Finally, this story turns again to the Espionage Act, as the vehicle of choice for enforcing the government's assertions about where the "balance" between security and privacy lies and what punishment should be meted out to leakers (and perhaps tomorrow to recipients and publishers). The symbiosis is visible perhaps best in the close relationship between CIA director John Brennan and President Barack Obama, which began after the 2008 election, developed into a joint worldview, and has set a far-reaching precedent between an elected leader and the heads of the intelligence community.

I am grateful, as always, to Marc Favreau, who has helped to shape this book so that I do not lose myself in the narrative in an effort to cover too much and thereby fail to do justice to the central questions posed below for discussion and debate. An especial thanks to Sarah Fan at The New Press and to Gary Stimeling, whose work will be appreciated by readers as well as the author. Also, I want to again express my debts to Walter LaFeber, Thomas McCormick, Marilyn Young, and Paul Miles for reading parts of the book and for ongoing conversations about concepts of "national security."

Newtown, Pennsylvania
August 2015

1

From the Espionage Act to the National Security State

At the dawn of our republic, a small, secret surveillance committee, born out of the Sons of Liberty, was established in Boston. And the group's members included Paul Revere. At night, they would patrol the streets, reporting back any signs that the British were preparing raids against America's early patriots.

Throughout American history, intelligence has helped secure our country and our freedoms.

—President Barack Obama, January 17, 2014

Obama begins the speech by situating his discussion of the NSA controversies against the activities of the Sons of Liberty and Paul Revere in Boston in revolutionary times. "Throughout American history, intelligence has helped secure our country and our freedoms," he says. It is against this highly favorable background—one in which intelligence is *central to* liberty, not in tension or at odds with it—that Obama mentions the birth of the NSA.

—Benjamin Wittes, *Lawfare*, January 20, 2014

We have grown up as a nation, respected for our free institutions and for our ability to maintain a free and open society. There is something about the way the CIA has been functioning that is casting a shadow over our historic position and I feel that we need to correct it.

—former president Harry S. Truman, 1963

As the debate over NSA contractor Edward Snowden and his revelations exploded into an international cause célèbre, Attorney General Eric Holder Jr. wrote a letter on July 23, 2013, to his Russian counterpart, Minister of Justice Alexander Vladimirovich

Konovalov. "Dear Mr. Minister" began this extraordinary appeal for the return of an American citizen marooned for five weeks in the international transit zone of Moscow's Sheremetyevo airport. Holder promised two things if the Russian government turned Snowden over to American authorities instead of granting him asylum: "First, the United States would not seek the death penalty for Mr. Snowden should he return to the United States. The charges he faces do not carry that possibility, and the United States would not seek the death penalty even if Mr. Snowden were charged with additional death penalty–eligible crimes."

Because it was an urgent matter to get Snowden and his documents back—not only in hopes of recovering still unreleased documents, but also to end the furor he had caused around the world—Holder added an additional promise to reassure world opinion. "Mr. Snowden will not be tortured," he wrote. "Torture is unlawful in the United States." He would not be denied any of the protections citizens charged with other federal criminal offenses enjoyed. Offering such assurances was deeply embarrassing, especially with their implicit references to "enhanced" interrogations in the Bush administration.

Holder listed three different crimes for which Edward Snowden could be prosecuted—theft of government property and two Espionage Act violations, unauthorized communication of national defense information and communication of classified intelligence "to an unauthorized person." This catchall phrase adds yet another issue for critics of the Espionage Act indictments.

The Russian reply to Holder's letter came from spokesperson Dmitry Peskov, who responded in an almost patronizing manner that Russian president Vladimir Putin had expressed his "strong determination" not to let ties with Washington suffer because of the dispute, "no matter how the situation develops." Putin, said Peskov, was not even involved in talks over the fate of Snowden. But, he added, Russia "did not hand over, does not hand over and will not hand over anybody." This was followed by an announcement that Snowden had been granted "temporary" asylum for one year. With nothing changed after one year, Russia granted Snowden three more years of asylum. "I don't think there's ever been any question that I'd like to go home," Snowden said in a television interview in May 2014. "Now, whether amnesty or clemency ever becomes a possibility is not for me to say. That's a debate for the public and the government to decide. But, if I could go anywhere in the world, that place would be home."[1]

There were sporadic rumors of negotiations about possible terms or conditions as the "Snowden story" continued to unfold with additional document releases, and the 2016 presidential campaign brought on new waves of oratory. Possible negotiations about his return sparked strong reactions. "We need to hang him on the courthouse square as soon as we get our hands on him," declared Saxby Chambliss, a former senator from Georgia who had been vice chair of the Senate Intelligence Committee before retiring in 2014. "I hope none of you have any sympathy for him," he told students at the University of Georgia.[2] Always at the heart of the matter was the Obama administration's decision to invoke the 1917 Espionage Act. Indeed, that act had become the central issue in the government's efforts to shut down leaks of classified information about attempts to sabotage Iran's nuclear programs, as well as the extraordinary metadata gathering programs engineered by the National Security Agency. The flip side of the Great War on Terror had become a War on Leakers. And it all began when Woodrow Wilson sought to make the world safe for democracy by using the Espionage Act to suppress dissent at home. That contradiction now stands out as clearly today as it did a hundred years ago.

Why the Espionage Act?

Stymied by the Russian refusal to hand over Snowden, the administration found itself in a predicament as more revelations—about spying on close allies and economic espionage—captured newspaper headlines. President Obama had refused to call Snowden a whistleblower at his August 9, 2013, press conference.

> Mr. Snowden has been charged with three felonies. If, in fact, he believes that what he did was right, then, like every American citizen, he can come here, appear before the court with a lawyer and make his case. If the concern was that somehow this was the only way to get this information out to the public, I signed an executive order well before Mr. Snowden leaked this information that provided whistleblower protection to the intelligence community—for the first time. So there were other avenues available for somebody whose conscience was stirred and thought that they needed to question government actions.

While Obama had not mentioned the 1917 Espionage Act, Holder's letter cited it as the authority for charging Snowden. This was the eighth time the administration had used it against leakers. The surge in Espionage Act cases came as a surprise to many of the president's supporters, as well as to his enemies. When Snowden was charged, the administration had already invoked the Espionage Act twice as many times as had any previous administration, and there were three more years to go in his second term.

In other countries, Snowden might have been charged with violating an official secrets act. The United States has never had an official secrets act like those in Great Britain and other countries, largely out of reluctance to challenge a written Constitution that defends individual rights and protects them against any exaggerated claims made by governments who would use such acts to silence dissent. It is easy to understand why the Obama administration doesn't want an official secrets act on those grounds alone, but there are other reasons as well. The executive branch, especially in the post-9/11 years, desires room for "interpretation" and rejects anything that puts limits on government ability to prosecute leaks to the press. The Espionage Act serves very well in this regard as a powerful deterrent, as it centers on wrongful disclosure of classified information, in comparison to an official secrets act, wherein the emphasis is on the material itself rather than the behavior of the one who supplies the information to the press. It is, therefore, a way around the First Amendment when the government desires to shutter the press without seeming to.

By its very title, the Espionage Act carries weight and conveys impressions to the public that an official secrets act could not. Convictions under the Espionage Act, therefore, always carry the possibility of heavy sentences, adding to the desired deterrent effect. Though it would never be acknowledged as such, use of the Espionage Act is a form of profiling. Even speculation that someone will be charged with crimes under the Espionage Act suggests that the person is disloyal, if not guilty of outright treason. The Constitution contains a specific limited definition of treason—an act of levying war against the United States by aiding an enemy in wartime, witnessed by two people in open court. But the Espionage Act skirts that requirement by requiring only evidence of unauthorized disclosure of classified materials—just as Attorney General Holder said in his letter to Russian authorities.

Before Snowden, the most famous effort to use the Espionage Act to punish a leaker was the 1971 prosecution of Daniel Ellsberg for releasing the Pentagon Papers. Like Snowden, Ellsberg was a former government employee who enjoyed special access to government documents, including the classified study of American policy in Vietnam since the end of World War II. When the Nixon administration failed to prevent the New York Times and other newspapers from publishing excerpts from the study, which Ellsberg had copied in secret, the president ordered Attorney General John Mitchell to proceed with an Espionage Act prosecution against the leaker. It failed, but the reason it failed—the government's evidence was tainted by an illegal break-in of Ellsberg's psychiatrist's office—left the central issue unresolved. Could the Espionage Act be used to punish leakers who had not conspired with agents of an enemy country?

Starting with Debs

The controversies over use of the Espionage Act arose almost immediately, for its primary use during World War I was to suppress dissent. Enacted when America entered the war, it was first used against Socialist Party leader Eugene Debs, sentenced to jail for giving a speech against the war. When Congress voted for war on April 6, 1917, after four strenuous days of debate, not everyone who voted yes understood that they had voted also for mass conscription. Only 75,000 young men stepped forward when President Woodrow Wilson called for volunteers, a disturbing reminder that the debate had not really ended. "Mr. Wilson's War" was not popular in large areas of the country. The administration designated June 5, 1917, as nationwide registration day for the first wartime draft since the Civil War. As the time approached, there was considerable nervousness in the White House about how the day would go. The president urged Americans to put aside differences and make the day one of "patriotic devotion." Every eligible male should seek out his place on "these lists of honor." The day went off quietly enough; nearly 10 million men obeyed the law and registered. Wilson and Secretary of War Newton D. Baker were astonished that it all went so well, with only sporadic and widely scattered resistance.[3]

But while the first day passed without riots or mass protests, the nation remained badly divided over sending troops abroad. Draft resistance spread across various sections of the country. In the South, traditionally considered a stronghold of hawkish sentiment and action, the draft met widespread resistance in rural areas where the progressive Farmers Union was strong. Georgia's Senator Thomas Hardwick observed growing "opposition on the part of many thousands" throughout his state. Moreover, he wrote, "numerous and largely attended mass meetings held in every part of the State protested against it."[4]

Mass meetings with antidraft speeches worried leaders in

Washington. Large numbers of "eligible males" declared themselves conscientious objectors or simply did not show up when called to duty. Wilson then felt compelled to change the tone of his original idealistic call to arms. On Flag Day, June 14, 1917, he warned all loyal citizens to ignore those who appeal "to our ancient tradition of isolation" in order "to undermine the government with false professions of loyalty to its principles."[5] The very next day Congress passed the Espionage Act. When the bill was under consideration, Wilson had asked for additional powers giving him the authority to censor the press. "I have every confidence that the great majority of the newspapers of the country will observe a patriotic reticence about everything whose publication could be of injury," he wrote to Representative Edwin Webb, as Congress discussed an omnibus bill that included press censorship. "But in every country there are some persons in a position to do mischief in this field who can not be relied upon and whose interests or desires will lead to actions on their part highly dangerous to the nation in the midst of war."[6]

Wilson's sense that the American executive would need new powers and new authority to keep secrets was not a product of the Great War, however. Rather, he had in mind the results of the War of 1898 and America's new imperial role in the world, including the administration of "distant dependencies." When foreign affairs become a prominent part in politics and policy, he had written, "its Executive must of necessity be its guide: it must utter every initial judgment, take every first step of action, supply the information upon which it is to act, suggest and in large measure control its conduct."[7]

Despite his appeal to Congress, the president did not get press censorship into the Espionage Act, but the blurring of lines between sedition and dissent began here, and with that blurring came a license for surveillance. As we move through the twentieth century and the small formal empire of the United States became the "Free World" during the Cold War, presidents found it much easier to convince Congress to accept the White House rationale of "national security" to conduct myriad covert operations without much more than token oversight.

Opposition to the World War I draft thus became a particularly suspicious act, and the new law was invoked against speakers at public rallies and those who wrote articles in radical magazines. The assumptions on display in the Flag Day speech, the letters Wilson sent to congressional leaders, and the Espionage Act itself all embody the "agent" theory of dissent. The administration tried to devise a series of "tests" to determine whether or not speeches against the draft or about American war aims derived, however circuitously, from shadowy agents working for the enemy. It soon became the norm to think this way when trying to account for draft opposition, socialist criticism of war profiteers, or supposed failure to understand the true nature of American policy, the reasons for going to war, and White House hopes for a new world order.[8]

During hearings on the Espionage Act, the head of the Women's Peace Party, Helen Thomas, had asserted, "I feel I have a right to interpret my loyalty to my own country in my own terms of citizenship, and according to my conscience, and I do not need any bill to tell me what my love for my country shall represent." At that point several committee members scolded her for such scandalous views. One said, "If your speech goes to the point of being treasonous, you are denied that right and ought to be."[9]

Thomas was never prosecuted for "treasonous" speeches, but President Wilson had counseled the nation in his Flag Day address to be suspicious about the source of unorthodox views. Among the dissidents, however, there were voices not easily called traitorous. Senator Robert M. La Follette of Wisconsin proved an eloquent and prescient voice sounding alarm over the Espionage Act's definition of dissent as disloyalty and treason. In a memo he wrote to himself, La Follette contended, "Treason *cannot* be committed by the *use of language*. Treason must be committed by an *overt act.*" Press censorship might not be specified in the law Congress had passed, but Wilson's intention to use it that way seemed clear to many. And the government did not even have to prosecute individuals to do so. Under the Espionage Act, Attorney General Thomas Gregory claimed he could deny the mails to publications by war opponents and proceeded to wield the law like a weed whacker until nearly all were gone. The president's vague and shifting war plans and purposes, La Follette complained, ranged from resentment about interference with trade one day to prescribing the form of government our enemy must adopt the next, and finally reached the ultimate desire to "make every part of the world safe for democracy." If any of these were grounds for denying American citizens the right to raise questions or speak out, La Follette ended in a ringing statement, then Lincoln was a traitor for opposing the Mexican War.[10]

One line in Wilson's Flag Day speech was particularly alarming, thought Senator La Follette. "Woe be to the man or group of men," the president said, "that seek to stand in our way." Despite his fears about what was happening to constitutional guarantees of free speech and protection against illegal searches, La Follette attempted to walk a fine line, supporting the rights of protesters as perfectly consistent with America's war aims while bemoaning the existence of an international "war party" that operated in the major world capitals. "It is just as arrogant, just as despotic in London, or in Washington, as in Berlin. The American jingo is the twin to the German Junker."[11]

Such speeches brought him a lot of attention, much of it denunciation. Former president Theodore Roosevelt called him "the worst enemy that democracy now has alive." A Wisconsin correspondent for a Seattle newspaper reported on the founding of a Loyalty Legion determined to save the state from the senator's treason, even if it became necessary "to organize vigilantes and lay in a stock of rope." There were efforts to have him expelled from the Senate, but none succeeded. In 1918, however, he began to shift his position: he supported the president's Fourteen Points speech, he said, as a worthy set of guidelines for the peace to come, and criticized Socialist antiwar positions.[12]

One of La Follette's supporters who applauded loudest for his speeches denouncing the war party's aims was Socialist leader Eugene Debs. Debs had already stamped himself as the biggest catch for war zealots out to punish dissenters. He made no bones about his opposition to the war and in his speeches and writings insisted that the draft was unconstitutional. Few were now able to read his diatribes in places like the *National Rip-Saw*, however, for a postal inspector determined that one article contained enough material "objectionable" under the Espionage Act to make it "unmailable" and denied postal service. Debs stood out for government censors as a likely "agent" serving the interests of the enemy, but he was not alone. Wilson's warnings had produced their desired results. An obedient mainstream press followed the campaign of Socialist Morris Hillquit, running for mayor of New York, as if it were trailing genuine spies. "German sympathizers are now working along lines that tend to cover the chances of detection," the *New York Times* explained. "Many of them have joined the Socialist Party, and are preaching sedition under the guise of Socialist Doctrine."[13]

It was only a matter of time before Debs came before a jury. He was arrested after a speech in Canton, Ohio, which a federal prosecutor deemed had violated the Espionage Act. The judge at the trial, David Westenhaver, attempted to clarify what he saw as the only real issue: the defendant was not to be judged for his political views but only for what he intended by his attacks on the draft. It was a clever ruling that spared possible complications with the First Amendment. The prosecution did not have to prove that Debs had actually impeded the war effort, he insisted, but only that he had *intended* to do so by his speeches. As for the defense claim that the Espionage Act was unconstitutional, the judge believed that the question was not for an Ohio jury to decide. "The law was on the statute book, and it was the part of no man to question its authenticity." If he was wrong about that, said the judge, it was up to the Supreme Court to decide. It did, unanimously, with Chief Justice Oliver Wendell Holmes commending Westenhaver's approach, while adding his own codicil to the debate about the Espionage Act. Even if Debs only "indirectly" influenced men to disobey the draft law, he was guilty. In times of peril, the court could only favor the demands of self-preservation over the rights of the individual. "When a nation is at war," he said, "many things that might be said in time of peace are such a hindrance to its effort that their utterance will not be endured so long as men fight and no Court could regard them as protected by any constitutional right." [14]

Westenhaver's ruling foreshadowed a persistent trend in court opinions that sought to avoid challenges to executive authority to conduct foreign policy in secret, culminating in the supine behavior of the FISA Court (established by the Foreign Intelligence Surveillance Act of 1978) after 9/11. In the Debs case, however, the Supreme Court's decision was decided *after* the war ended! Holmes handed down his opinion in 1919, while President Wilson was in Paris attempting to bring about his version of a New World Order. Advised of appeals for clemency on Debs's behalf, Wilson said he was willing to grant "respite" to Debs and others convicted under the Espionage Act if the attorney general saw fit to do so. "I doubt the wisdom and public effect of such an action," he added, thus making it clear he opposed clemency and effectively ending the debate without sustaining any blame for Debs's imprisonment. As we will see, presidents have become very adept at this practice over the years. During the prewar neutrality period, writes historian Ernest Freeberg, the U.S. government uncovered several German attempts to undermine American support for the Allies, and German agents were implicated in a series of explosions at munitions factories. Yet the spy act never netted a spy. "During the war, the Justice Department did not convict a single German spy or saboteur under the Espionage Act." [15]

The Debs case thus set the precedent for the war on leakers. He was not released from prison until President Warren Harding began reviewing the cases of political prisoners as part of his promise to return the country to "normalcy." Many in his cabinet did not agree, but Harding thought simply sending Debs to jail had made the point. There was no purpose served in keeping him there. When he learned he would be released, Debs expected to return to his home in Terre Haute, Indiana, but instead spent Christmas Day 1921 on a train to Washington, D.C. The president had invited him to the White House for a brief interview. Rising to greet him, Harding said, "I have heard so damned much about you, Mr. Debs, that I am very glad to meet you personally." [16]

Harding's friendly greeting could be taken as a public effort to rectify wrongs done to an American citizen by his government. Indeed, Harding said during the 1920 presidential campaign, "It would be a sorry day for this republic if we allowed our activities in seeking for peace in the Old World to blind us to the essentials of peace at home. We want a free America again. We want America free at home, and free in the world." He won in a landslide. [17]

Freeing Eugene Debs played to a general postwar fear of permanent mobilization and what that would mean for personal liberties. Harding's cabinet was by no means unanimous, but the president put aside objections. Why keep a frail old man in jail now that there was no war, no draft, no emergency at all? On the larger issue of whether Congress should repeal the Espionage Act, there was no poll, but many from all points on the political spectrum agreed that the quest to make over the world had proved a corrosive force in domestic politics. Before it ate away any more at the constitutional foundations of the republic, it was time to call a halt.

Almost forgotten for years, the Espionage Act stayed on the books. The act had demonstrated how easily government could push hidden levers to silence dissent. Wartime mobilization inevitably caused a constantly shifting tug-of-war over how to reconcile constitutionally guaranteed civil liberties against the claims of national security. When America formally entered World War II after the Japanese attack at Pearl Harbor, the Espionage Act was there, but antiwar speeeches did not trigger any particular concern in the U.S. government. It was not until near the end of the war that the rapid development of a full-fledged national security establishment, one that had developed out of fear of an atomic Pearl Harbor, started sounding alarms about protecting government secrets.

World War II and the National Security State

A mere two decades after the writing of the Versailles Treaty ending the "Great War," the issue of a peacetime draft once again tested the response to government-mandated military service. Congress voted the first peacetime draft in September 1940 as Hitler's Germany conquered France and seemed ready to leap over the channel to attack the British Isles. Draftees were to serve twelve months. When Roosevelt asked Congress to extend the term of service of draftees to two and a half years in the summer of 1941, the bill passed the House by a one-vote margin. At least that was the official report. Speaker Sam Rayburn swung his gavel before calls for a recount could be recognized. A draft opponent in the House, Thomas H. Eliot from Massachusetts, recalled that shortly after the bill passed, "the Army announced that it was releasing all conscripts over 26, about 200,000 men, none of whom had completed even one year of training. This surprising act of self-disruption may have been caused partly by a shortage of equipment, but the obvious reason for it was the trainees' discontent over the bill's enactment." [18]

Meanwhile, about a year before Pearl Harbor, Hollywood had served up a frothy comedy about the draft, *Buck Privates*, starring a new team, Bud Abbott and Lou Costello. Audiences laughed out loud at their bumbling antics. Eugene Debs was long gone and mostly forgotten, but Roosevelt had to worry about taking a divided nation into a "foreign war." Polls showed that the electorate was deeply conflicted about what it wanted. Big majorities believed it was essential to aid England but did not want to go to war. In the 1940 presidential campaign Roosevelt straddled the polls by promising that American boys were not going to be sent into any "foreign wars." He needed a Fort Sumter to unite the nation. Secretary of War Henry L. Stimson keenly felt the dilemma and wished that the president would be more honest with the public about his intentions.

When Roosevelt began a "complicated series" of maneuvers to ensure that lend-lease aid got through to the British, acts that included reporting the position of German warships to the world, the old Republican statesman Stimson confided to his diary, "I wanted him to be honest with himself. To me it seems a clearly hostile act to the Germans and I am prepared to take the responsibility of it." But Roosevelt resisted forcing a clear-cut crisis, even though a U-boat sank the USS *Reuben James* in late October 1941 as it stood between a lend-lease convoy and German warships.[19]

The lesson seemed to be that while much of the country sensed the likelihood of war, it wanted to believe the president had found a way to win it without actually refighting World War I by sending soldiers to Europe. On December 4, 1941, the *Chicago Tribune* published an article by Chester Manley under the headline "F.D.R.'S WAR PLANS!" Someone in the War Department had leaked Rainbow Five, the plan to defeat Hitler that Roosevelt had ordered drawn up by the army and navy. It called for a 10-million-man army and an expeditionary force ready to invade Europe by 1943.

As a Federal Bureau of Investigation (FBI) investigation set about finding the source of the leak, Republicans and antiwar Democrats immediately seized on the article to accuse the president of willful duplicity for having based much of his 1940 campaign for reelection on promises that he would not send American boys into any foreign wars. Rainbow Five did not say how America would get into the war, but it did envision fighting on European soil. Some in Roosevelt's cabinet demanded that the leaker, when found, be prosecuted under the Espionage Act. The president seemed wary, or even indifferent, about pursuing that idea.

Roosevelt refused to discuss the matter at a press conference on December 5, but his press secretary, Steve Early, while spinning out the usual damage-control stuff about how it was customary for the army and navy to develop plans for all sorts of contingencies, almost as an aside said that the newspapers were "operating as a free press," and had a perfect right to publish material, assuming the story to be genuine. It was the government's responsibility to keep reports secret. Other papers were free to publish such material as well, depending on whether they thought the decision was "patriotic or treason." [20]

Early's comment suggested, on the one hand, that the administration had great faith in the media's ability to know the difference and, on the other, that in a free country the final arbiter could not always be the government. When the Japanese attacked Pearl Harbor two days later, the brief furor disappeared into the smoke rising from the USS *Arizona* before it sank to the harbor floor. [21]

Whatever Early intended to convey, Pearl Harbor became a short way of describing a massive intelligence failure. The Japanese attack accomplished two things: one, the unification of the country in the short term to fight a war against an enemy that had attacked the fleet and, two, a long-term expansion of the intelligence capabilities of the government under a pledge to the nation: no more Pearl Harbors! Nothing became more serious than control of intelligence (or information in general), the supposed sine qua non of wartime national security and the foundation of the postwar national security state. Everything else, it was argued, must yield before its demands.

The question of who was responsible for allowing the Japanese plans for attack to succeed, nevertheless, became an obsession that lasted for years. Part of that obsession was not about intelligence failures but whether the White House had been honest. So at the birth of the national security state there were contradictory interpretations of the results of the investigations. While Roosevelt was accused of leaving the fleet unprepared—or even worse conspiratorial crimes by a few on the fringes—the real outcome proved to be as important to the creation of a national security state as the Great Depression had been to the New Deal. Hunting for a culprit or culprits, the various congressional Pearl Harbor investigations instead eased the way for public acceptance of a vastly increased role for intelligence operations. Plans were already under way for a new agency to fulfill a worldwide role like that of the intelligence services of the old imperial powers of Europe, whose reign was coming to an end.

On July 11, 1941, Roosevelt had named the almost legendary (and legendarily flamboyant) New York lawyer William J. Donovan to a new post, coordinator of intelligence. "Wild Bill" Donovan was a Congressional Medal of Honor winner and head of his own prestigious Wall Street firm. He probably knew more about the goings-on in the back rooms of the major European powers and Great Britain than any other private citizen or, for that matter, most of those in government who dealt with matters of state. FDR had used him as a special emissary to London in 1940, where he was given special briefings on British methods of spying, propaganda, subversion, and commando operations. He worked closely with Sir William S. Stephenson, Britain's intelligence chief in the United States. Donovan's connections in both countries made him a valuable asset all around. He was a natural resource for Roosevelt to tap in providing the U.S. government with a plan to set up an American intelligence operation.[22]

It did not matter that Donovan had run for governor against FDR's man, Herbert Lehman, and that, despite the shellacking he took, he still harbored ambitions to be the first Catholic president of the United States. Nor did it trouble the president that he used all the nasty words Republicans kept handy to describe the New Deal and had even said FDR was "a new kind of red, white, and blue dictator." According to Louis Menand:

By 1940, Wall Street Republicans like Donovan had begun to warm to Roosevelt. They found that they could tolerate the creeping socialism of his domestic programs because they liked his internationalism and interventionism. If there was turmoil somewhere in the world, they wanted the United States to be in the game. This was not just because they wanted access to overseas markets where American investors could enjoy favorable terms—an Open Door policy—although they unquestionably did. They also believed that nations that trade with each other are less likely to go to war against each other.[23]

Never comfortable with the idea of merely being a successor to the British Empire, American elites imagined a grander future for the nation, but, as Donovan's appointment suggested, that did not mean the need for spies or foreign assets would be any the less in this dawning American Century than they had been in sustaining the dominance of European empires and for them to keep tabs on one another. The position of coordinator of intelligence did not last long, as Donovan was made a major general and put in charge of the Office of Strategic Services (OSS). Donovan proposed a new post, an intelligence chief who would report directly to the president. The chief's mission would include espionage, research and analysis, and subversion—everything he had learned from the British bag of tricks. His proposed agency would not have any domestic role, he promised—cross his heart—and he declared that it would *never* seek to take over the FBI's job on the home front or military intelligence's work abroad.[24]

J. Edgar Hoover didn't believe him, and neither did the chiefs of military and naval intelligence. For one thing, Donovan ran the OSS freewheelingly, almost by whim. Although he later became a dedicated Cold War hawk, when he ran OSS he employed as many liberals and leftists as he cared to without worrying about security clearances—the very opposite of the way the military ran the Manhattan Project. On the other side of the fence, "there was virtually nothing that he considered off-limits, from assassinating foreign leaders to engaging in the most sophomoric kind of propaganda." When the CIA later schemed to undermine Fidel Castro's "machismo" by slipping him a potion that would cause his beard to fall out, it was following a path the OSS had pioneered with an attempt to inject Hitler's food with female sex hormones.[25]

The OSS had about thirteen thousand people under Donovan's command—tiny by comparison with later intelligence organizations, but some of those who worked for him and learned their trade became CIA directors, including Allen Dulles, Richard Helms, William Colby, and William Casey. These were the men whose names would come up again and again as having crossed the line with illegal covert activities, including operations conducted against Americans who dissented during the Vietnam War. Donovan had promised that his proposed agency would not cross those lines, but the OSS and then the CIA became, in effect, the president's private army, which under President Obama was charged with the drone campaign to eliminate key figures in lands where no formal declaration of war could be contemplated. Moreover, the OSS and CIA offered plausible deniability whenever someone got caught. Roosevelt's successor, Harry Truman (and all future presidents), might have gained a private army, but it was never free of Donovan's swashbuckling ways, never completely under their control. Plausible deniability worked two ways, after all. When push came to shove, as with the release of the Senate Intelligence Committee torture report in 2014, CIA figures denied that they had kept anything back from their overseers—and who could say them nay? And instead of staying out of domestic concerns, intelligence agencies—all of them—became more deeply involved. It could hardly be otherwise.

But Donovan's original plan wasn't adopted without a struggle. On November 18, 1944, a draft was ready for Roosevelt's approval. It envisioned an independent agency responsible directly to the president and authorized to carry out espionage and counterespionage activities, "subversive operations abroad," and "such other functions and duties relating to intelligence" as the president might assign it, subject only to the restriction that it not operate at home or do domestic police work. (The phrase "other functions and duties" was a blank check that later covered election fixing in Greece and Italy, direct action to topple an elected chief of state in Iran, and dropping bombs in Guatemala to get rid of an unwanted president with a radical domestic program.) Donovan acknowledged that the military chiefs were not happy with his proposal and no doubt suspected that J. Edgar Hoover feared for the FBI's future. Indeed, Hoover probably had a better crystal ball than any of Donovan's other opponents and more reason to fear being shoved aside. When a story by Walter Trohan, a dedicated Roosevelt antagonist, appeared in the press calling Donovan's proposal a New Deal "super spy system" for the postwar world that would "pry into the lives of citizens at home"—a "super Gestapo agency"—Roosevelt hesitated for a moment to rethink the plan.[26]

FDR had resolved his doubts only a week before his death. The "Gestapo" label also alarmed Harry Truman. The unification bill that created the Department of Defense, which Truman sent to Congress on February 26, 1947, also created the National Security Council, the president's top policy making advisory body, and established the Central Intelligence Agency. Congress was ready—fresh from the Pearl Harbor investigation—to approve anything with scarcely a "nay" vote to be found. There was a bit of a rumble over the lack of precision about the new agency's mission. Hoover had many "friends" in Congress. But the vague phrase "such other functions" remained in the bill.

The Agency at Work

President Harry Truman thought he was creating an intelligence agency to prevent another Pearl Harbor. But the 1947 act included the language that allowed the CIA to expand its role by undertaking "such other functions and duties related to intelligence affecting the national security as the National Security Council may from time to time direct." The intervention in the Italian and French elections of the early Cold War thus became the precedent for covert operations of the 1950s to overthrow governments in Iran and Guatemala. Despite his later worries about where all this was heading, Truman had not seen fit to issue orders about what was permissible and what was not. The Russian atomic bomb, moreover, and the accompanying fears of treason with the trial of Julius and Ethel Rosenberg—and, even more frightful, the possibility of large spy rings still undetected—added momentum to a growing sense of national insecurity, and hence to more and more reliance on intelligence agencies as the shield of first resort.

Soon the enemy became not the Soviet Union alone, but the "international Communist conspiracy" that Secretary of State John Foster Dulles had pictured for Congress in seeking funds for aid to Middle Eastern countries after the 1956 Suez Crisis. Foreign affairs almost became counterespionage, a global struggle with an enemy on the dark side of the street. In a later vice president's unforgettable phrase, the gloves came off, and the CIA was ready to go. It was this hidden enemy, the international Communist conspiracy, all of whose members Secretary Dulles claimed not even he knew, that menaced the United States through its agents fomenting revolutions in countries all over the world. Their ultimate objective was to surround the United States boa constrictor fashion. To combat that peril, the CIA had to be "unleashed" to respond in kind. In 1966 Secretary of State Dean Rusk put it this way. There was, he said, "a tough struggle going on all over the world. . . . It's a tough one, it's unpleasant, and no one likes it, but that is not a field which can be left entirely to the other side." This back-alley struggle is "a never-ending war, and there's no quarter asked and none given."[27]

Yet Truman's successors grappled with concerns about the CIA's actions and reputation. Not least there was the worry that having given clearance for covert actions, the president might not always be informed of targets and times. Even Eisenhower felt betrayed by the CIA's insistence on flying U-2 missions over

Russia on the eve of a proposed summit conference in 1960. And John F. Kennedy supposedly vowed after the Bay of Pigs to smash the CIA to smithereens. That didn't happen, of course. Instead, later modifications of the law only decreased the White House's ability to monitor agency activities, just as its headquarters had moved from old World War II Quonset huts on the National Mall to Langley's heavily guarded "campus." Complete with its biblical motto engraved in the floor—"And ye shall know the truth and the truth shall make you free"—the new center was Allen Dulles's dream come true. President Dwight Eisenhower planted the cornerstone at a ceremony attended by five thousand invited guests on November 3, 1959. Inside the cornerstone was a time capsule containing key documents about the agency's creation out of the World War II experiences. News reporters asked what these were. Dulles replied, "It's a secret."

Actually none of the documents was classified, but nevertheless Dulles had indeed spoken the truth about the CIA's relationship with the press—except when it wished its cooperation in *keeping* secrets or to plant stories with favorite reporters making free use of confidential documents in oral conversations with the chosen ones.

President Eisenhower made full use of his private army, a handy weapon that he apparently believed would help keep down the costs of maintaining the nation on a perpetual war footing. He had approved of the CIA's role in toppling the Mossadegh government of Iran in 1953, after it had nationalized the Anglo-Iranian Oil Company, and the Arbenz government of Guatemala the following year when it threatened the United Fruit Company. But when the idea of going after Fidel Castro came up, his major concern was "leakage." The Bay of Pigs proved to be the biggest failure of the new agency—but also, paradoxically, a triumph for those who wanted tighter restrictions on the press. CIA director Allen Dulles presented the agency's plans for rescuing American interests in Cuba by removing Castro from the scene on March 17,

1960. Eisenhower's first response was, "The great problem is leakage and breach of security. Everyone must be prepared to swear that he has not heard of it."[28]

In December 1963, one month after the assassination of John F. Kennedy, Harry Truman wrote an article published in the *Washington Post*. Truman was worried about where things were heading. He began by saying that it was time to take another look at the purpose and operations of our Central Intelligence Agency. He had intended to create an agency to operate "as an arm of the President." It was to provide him with the most up-to-date information possible, particularly the trends of developments and where the current danger spots were located. He wanted raw data, to guard against intelligence information being slanted to conform to the position of a given department and thus leading him into bad decisions. Instead, it had grown into a semiautonomous entity, first among equals in scripting American foreign policy. The rest of the article is worth reproducing as a whole.

For some time I have been disturbed by the way CIA has been diverted from its original assignment. It has become an operational and at times a policy-making arm of the Government. This has led to trouble and may have compounded our difficulties in several explosive areas.

I never had any thought that when I set up the CIA that it would be injected into peacetime cloak and dagger operations. Some of the complications and embarrassment I think we have experienced are in part attributable to the fact that this quiet intelligence arm of the President has been so removed from its intended role that it is being interpreted as a symbol of sinister and mysterious foreign intrigue—and a subject for cold war enemy propaganda.

With all the nonsense put out by Communist propaganda about "Yankee imperialism," "exploitive capitalism," "warmongering," "monopolists," in their name-calling assault on the West, the last thing we needed was for the CIA to be seized upon as something akin to a subverting influence in the affairs of other people.

I well knew the first temporary director of the CIA, Adm. Souers, and the later permanent directors of the CIA, Gen. Hoyt Vandenberg and Allen Dulles. These were men of the highest character, patriotism and integrity—and I assume this is true of all those who continue in charge.

But there are now some searching questions that need to be answered. I, therefore, would like to see the CIA be restored to its original assignment as the intelligence arm of the President, and that whatever else it can properly perform in that special field—and that its operational duties be terminated or properly used elsewhere.

We have grown up as a nation, respected for our free institutions and for our ability to maintain a free and open society. There is something about the way the CIA has been functioning that is casting a shadow over our historic position and I feel that we need to correct it.

Truman's article, according to a CIA historian with access to all the inside sources, "caused considerable consternation in and out of the government."[79] In many ways it was the most important leak in the walls of classification built high around the agency since it was founded. And it makes clear yet again that leaks, or "disclosures" if one prefers, are used by government officials to advance or change agendas or to strike at a rival agency or person. It was an unprecedented disclosure by a former president, with its accusation that his successors had lost full control of the presidency.

While later leaks were said to endanger agents and other individuals, Truman's article was a general call to accounting for what the government had done, and with its allusion to "peacetime cloak and dagger operations" and their ominous "shadow over our historic position," it recalled the fears of a New Deal super-Gestapo. Moreover, Truman's leak actually threatened the life of the agency—especially in the wake of the botched Bay of

Pigs invasion in 1961 and the assassination of President Ngo Dinh Diem of South Vietnam three weeks before the murder of Kennedy. Little wonder that agency officials were stunned. As CIA historian Hayden Peakes writes, "Although attempts would be made to have Mr. Truman clarify his position, the 1963 article proved to be his final written comment on the issue."

In 1964 Truman was visited by former CIA director Allen Dulles, who reminded him that he had signed off on some of the actions the agency had undertaken in manipulating elections to keep the Communists from taking over in vulnerable Greece and Italy. "Yes, he knew all about that," Peakes said he told Dulles and other officials who visited him. "It was important work, and he would order it to be done again under the same circumstances." But he went on to say that the CIA's main duty was to pull together basic information the president needed and had not gotten before from State or the Pentagon. Years later he told another interviewer that it was his successor, Dwight Eisenhower, who allowed the agency to get out of hand. "Why, they've got an organization . . . that is practically the equal of the Pentagon. . . . One Pentagon is too many. . . . Those fellas in the CIA don't just report on wars; . . . they go out and make their own and there's nobody to keep track of what they're up to." [30]

One can argue that Truman was an old man when he made these statements, trying to reconcile his conscience with a faulty memory, or that he was engaged in drawing too fine a line between what he had approved and what now horrified him in the Vietnam years of seemingly perpetual warfare. Even if he had licensed the CIA's charter for covert action, however, his warning has nevertheless not lost its relevance to the post-9/11 world and the role leakers play in keeping track of "what they're up to."

The Heritage: A Summing Up

After World War I ended, Debs was released and the Espionage Act was pretty much forgotten about until 1971, when the Nixon administration tried to send Daniel Ellsberg to prison for giving the Pentagon Papers to newspapers. Ellsberg faced five counts of theft and six of violations of the Espionage Act, for a maximum total of 115 years. That case ended in confusion in 1973 when a judge declared a mistrial because the Nixon administration used former CIA agents to burglarize Ellsberg's psychiatrist's office in hopes of finding damaging information about his mental state.

Whether that trial would have ended in conviction or acquittal is an unanswerable question, obviously, but even though the trial didn't reach a verdict, the Espionage Act has become the government's direst threat against leakers in the post-9/11 years. As in the past, moreover, it has been used not against spies, but against those who expose the secrets of what is now called the intelligence community, in effect a whole new, nonconstitutional branch of government in the United States (legislative, executive, judicial, and covert)—and by far the fastest growing one.

One has to look hard at the decision to invoke the Espionage Act, because from the time of its passage it has been at odds with the self-image of the country as an open society that cherishes the First Amendment. The Debs case was the signifier for the future. Historians and legal scholars have always considered it a notorious example of wartime excess. Charging someone with violating it is a form of profiling, whether or not this fact is recognized or admitted by the Justice Department. The rationale goes this way: Loyal citizens do not act upon their individual judgment about the common good by undermining government efforts to keep secrets that protect the nation. Therefore those who behave this way must be egotistical publicity seekers or agents acting consciously on behalf of another power, or quite possibly both.

Profiling in such a manner starts down the path to a general "agent" theory of dissent. When Edward Snowden fled to Hong Kong, it was alleged that he turned over secret material to the Chinese and then continued to Moscow seeking asylum. He was charged under the Espionage Act. Months later the chair of the House Intelligence Committee, Representative Mike Rogers from

Michigan, told the nation on NBC's *Meet the Press* that Snowden was more than just a thief and that he had some "help." Rogers said, "I believe there's questions to be answered there. I don't think it was a gee-whiz luck event that he ended up in Moscow under the handling of the FSB [Russian intelligence service]."[31] Rogers's counterpart in the Senate, Dianne Feinstein, wasn't quite so sure, but she was a staunch supporter of the NSA data-gathering programs and apparently believed that they deserved her greatest loyalty. When asked if she believed Snowden had Russian help, she replied that he had it in mind from his first day at work "to take as much material down as he possibly could. . . . He may well have [had help]. We don't know at this stage. But I think to glorify this act is to set a new level of dishonor."[32]

Yet Rogers and Feinstein—inadvertently and without noticing the damage to their argument—demonstrate the Espionage Act's big downside: a Newtonian action-reaction effect. First, the great expansion of intelligence capabilities required the hiring of thousands of contractors with top secret clearances, multiplying by several orders of magnitude the likelihood of a leaker acting on his conscience after becoming disenchanted with government behavior or simply seeking fame by telling on everyone. Second, the vagueness of what constitutes an actionable offense under the act, even when the text is read and studied word by word, has produced sharp differences of opinion and prescient criticism from the time the law came into force until the present day. For example, under certain circumstances—such as causing the death of a covert agent—the government could demand the death penalty under the Espionage Act. And yet even that section of the law is not entirely clear, as evidence that lives were lost is difficult to prove in open court. And beyond that line the situation gets much worse.

The Obama administration refused to call Snowden a whistleblower. While it halfway admits that his actions have raised serious questions about government policies, by invoking the Espionage Act it hopes to deter potential leakers in the future. The president appointed a commission that made several recommendations for change, but he tossed the ball to Congress and like all bureaucracies the NSA and CIA played a waiting game. Meanwhile, nearly everyone outside Washington started choosing sides in the ongoing Snowden debate, another unwanted development in the wake of the Russian decision to grant him asylum. Typical of the pained reaching for a "middle ground" was Australia's foreign minister, Julie Bishop, who declared at an international conference, "We welcome President Obama's statement last Friday on your signals intelligence reviews," she said, referring to an announcement that the United States would no longer target friendly leaders' personal communications and would increase oversight of the gathering of private citizens' phone data. But then she turned immediately to condemn Snowden—without whom she wouldn't have known that her e-mails were being read by spies—as a man who was continuing to "shamefully betray his nation while skulking in Russia." She adopted Washington's insistence that the programs had saved lives along with its obsession over convicting Snowden and showed how hard it is for a typical government official to talk about the case without stumbling over her own feet in the process.[33]

2

Where Ellsberg Fits In

We have the rocky situation where the sonofabitching thief [Ellsberg] is made a national hero and is going to get off on a mistrial and the *New York Times* gets a Pulitzer prize for stealing documents. . . . They're trying to get at us with thieves. . . . What in the name of God have we come to?
        —Richard Nixon, White House tapes, May 11, 1973

In his last year as secretary of defense, a very troubled Robert McNamara commissioned a study to inform himself about how the United States had managed to get trapped in the Vietnam quagmire—a reality he had been loath to recognize for such a long time. In 1971 one of the authors of that study, Daniel Ellsberg, secretly delivered copies to the *New York Times* and other newspapers. When the papers began printing excerpts, the White House sought an injunction against further publication. Even though the documents it contained did not reveal secrets about current negotiations, President Nixon and his aides feared others would follow Ellsberg's example, and besides, it was argued, what might happen if each successor had to worry that his secret diplomacy would be revealed within a few years of leaving office?

The effort to stop publication failed, one must conclude, because the war was so unpopular, not because of concern for freedom of the press. The Nixon administration then brought charges against Ellsberg for supposed violations of the 1917 Espionage Act. The outcome of that case was never really decided, however, because of illegal actions by the White House Plumbers (a group of former CIA "spooks" charged by Nixon aides to stop leaks) that caused a mistrial. What was then a spur-of-the-moment effort to dream up a criminal indictment has now become almost routine, as the act has become the Obama administration's weapon of choice against leakers. As noted above, the Justice Department's zealous pursuit of convictions under the Espionage Act—twice as many as any previous administration—has surprised both the president's supporters and conservative critics. But blaming Nixon or Obama for all that has happened is too easy. We should instead talk about the implications of the steady growth of the intelligence community—beginning well before 9/11—and the fact that it now has a reasonable claim to be the most powerful branch of government. Despite the post-9/11 boom in spending and the Lego-like rapid construction of facilities, it did not happen all at once. Even less well understood, however, is the way the president paradoxically is now in danger of becoming a dependent of the intelligence community.

From the early days of the Cold War, Congress—despite a few displays of outrage along the way—has largely agreed that it lacks the expertise and knowledge to carry out its oversight mandates. The courts also fear unwrapping claims the White House makes about national security to see what is really inside. And, in turn, these claims derive from the daily briefings the president receives from the intelligence community.

The first great wave of "national security" censorship followed the dropping of the atomic bomb, which led to the public's acceptance of a "protector" president whose possession of secret intelligence, it was argued, might be the only way to prevent World War III. After the Nixon years, there was a serious reassessment of those beliefs, but they reemerged with greater force (and consequences) after a small group of men using box cutters took control of passenger jet planes and crashed them into the World Trade Center and the Pentagon.

The Obama administration's decision to charge Edward Snowden under the Espionage Act stirred memories of

Daniel Ellsberg's leak of the Pentagon Papers, reminding the public of Richard Nixon's failed attempts to suppress the seven-thousand-page study of how the United States got into the Vietnam War. Release of the Pentagon Papers led to Nixon's ultimate disgrace when a two-bit break-in at the Watergate Hotel complex exposed a shadowy operation that flowed all the way back to the Oval Office. Why the Pentagon Papers had scared Nixon so much, however, goes beyond his well-documented paranoia. The Pentagon Papers and Watergate episodes will be forever linked as instances of government efforts to manage what the public can be allowed to know about national security affairs.

Robert McNamara had felt so strongly about past errors that he commissioned a classified history written by experts inside and outside government. Some argued that it should have remained secret to maintain the people's faith in their government. The very existence of a massive study documenting that the United States had gone to war under dubious pretenses had to be kept secret, it was argued, lest it cause a further loss of faith in the nation's leadership pursuing an unpopular war. So went the rationale for pursuing a conviction of the most famous leaker before Edward Snowden, Daniel Ellsberg. The Orwellian implications of "classifying" history have become as evident as those of using the Espionage Act to deter critics. Both characterize a society obsessed with national security threats, one that has yielded control to agencies who work, as Truman put it, "on the dark side."

There were always those who attempted to challenge the swelling hegemony of the intelligence community. When it appeared for a short time that the Nixon administration might succeed in its attempts to shut down the presses, Alaska senator Mike Gravel used senatorial privilege to read four thousand of the seven thousand pages into the public record. Gravel's action has now become a rallying point for those who demand the uncensored release of the so-called Torture Report detailing the methods the Central Intelligence Agency used against prisoners and terrorist suspects after 9/11. The Senate Intelligence Oversight Committee's staff put together a report of some six thousand pages, which, like the Pentagon Papers, detailed lies the agency told even the White House during the Bush years not only about its treatment of the prisoners but also about the effectiveness of its methods. Completed nearly a decade ago, most of the report still remains secret because the intelligence community insists that it must, using arguments similar to those put forth during the fight over the Pentagon Papers.

The Torture Report involves specific actions policy makers took in the aftermath of 9/11 and justified as protecting the country from more terrorist attacks. When President Obama and the Senate committee came to an impasse over release of even a redacted version of the executive summary of the report, another senator, Colorado's Mark Udall, threatened to follow Gravel's example, demonstrating for critics the continuing lesson of the Pentagon Papers and for classifiers the continuing danger of public debate of national security issues. Udall was cheered on by those who believed Obama had never followed through on promises of greater transparency and had become too close to CIA director John Brennan, his chief adviser on drone warfare during his first term.

From retirement Gravel spoke out in an interview with *Democracy Now*. Yes, Mark Udall should go ahead, he said, and make the full report public. Most members of Congress seem to have forgotten or don't fully understand, he explained, that they have three functions after they are elected: "One is to inform the public. Two is to legislate. And three is to have oversight." The men who served the nation in its earliest years all felt the most important of the three was to inform the people as to what their government is doing. But now only certain senators were allowed even to see copies of the Torture Report but to take no notes. "It just shows you how silly we are, trapped in this unbelievable culture of secrecy that is in the military and has permeated through the rest of our culture."[1]

Udall relented when the executive summary of the report was finally released by the White House, but the tug-of-war between the White House and the committee focused attention on the consequences of President Obama's unwillingness to respond to those who wished him, at the least, to establish a "truth commission" to deal with the accusations of CIA torture of prisoners in locations across the globe. Coming into office in the midst of the worst economic crisis since the Great Depression explains the new president's refusal to make the country even more jittery about its institutions, for it would have ensured a fight with Republicans, who insisted that the Torture Report was a partisan attempt to blacken reputations of men acting in good faith under assurances that what they had done was legal.

Obama feared the consequences of listening to calls for a truth commission. If agents were criminally investigated "for doing something that top Bush administration officials asked them to do and that they were assured were legal," said former top-level CIA official Mark Lowenthal, "intelligence officers would be less willing to take risks to protect the country." That statement itself shows how far we have come, endorsing a "Nuremberg defense" (they were only doing their duty) for waterboarding and other "enhanced interrogation techniques." It is all the more striking, of course, because Obama has called such acts torture. Moreover, Lowenthal assumes that there is no way to condemn torture without undermining the legitimate work of intelligence officers to protect the country. It is all of a piece. Disengaging from one part threatens the whole and risks political embarrassment and defeat. Thus, President-elect Obama told an interviewer, his basic need was to look forward as opposed to looking backward. "And part of my job is to make sure that . . . for example, at the CIA, you've got extraordinarily talented people who are working very hard to keep America safe. I don't want them to suddenly feel like they've got to spend all their time looking over their shoulders."[2]

The fact that Obama could not draw a distinction between the "extraordinarily talented people" working to keep us safe and the specific individuals who carried out such acts of torture as waterboarding really drove home the unacknowledged point that the intelligence community claims immunity and thus power over the White House. The only people who wanted to investigate these issues, said a former White House lawyer and Harvard Law School classmate of Obama's, were the new president's "most extreme supporters," who were "screaming for blood" although "the president himself doesn't seem to share that bloodlust."[3]

From the very outset of his administration, President Obama had to confront issues that went back decades in their origin. Many of these issues are fallout from decisions made on an ad hoc basis that became permanent "understandings" about the way presidents interact with the intelligence community.

The President's Secret Army, from Eisenhower to Obama

Despite his image as the avuncular president of the "quiet" decade, President Dwight Eisenhower played a key role in creating the national security state by using the Central Intelligence Agency to overthrow governments in the Middle East and Latin America before the United States became embroiled in Vietnam. As Harry Truman complained after Kennedy's death, the CIA had already become a policy making branch of government, a rival of other entrenched power blocs in the national security state—the Pentagon, the FBI, the State Department—and, it quickly became apparent, a far more agile player in the game of high-level Washington politics than all the others, especially a sluggish congressional watchdog that only occasionally roused itself to oppose the White House or investigate un-American behavior.

Eisenhower's Cold War gambits proved all too successful, for they gave the Central Intelligence Agency reason to believe that when push came to shove the White House would always have its back—against Congress or any other challenger. With that impression of complete immunity, the men of Langley planned their biggest operation to date—the Bay of Pigs—with Eisenhower's blessing. That fiasco influenced American politics for decades and linked John Kennedy and Richard Nixon in fateful

ways. Much of the Kennedy lore that continues to infuse the national consciousness to this day concerns a supposed change of
heart after the 1961 Bay of Pigs fiasco, in which the CIA promoted
a hapless effort to invade Cuba and overthrow the Communist
government there—assuming that if things went awry, the White
House would intervene to save the day and bail out the agency.
According to various sources, Kennedy was so bitter at the agency
that he wanted to "splinter the CIA into a thousand pieces and
scatter it into the winds."[4] As first steps he fired Allen Dulles, the
original godfather of the CIA, and Richard M. Bissell, the man
who had headed the Bay of Pigs operation. Dulles was replaced
by a Republican, John McCone, Eisenhower's last Atomic Energy
Commission chairman.

Two days after the Bay of Pigs disaster, the president's brother
Attorney General Robert Kennedy presided over a meeting that
launched Operation Mongoose—and turned right back to the
CIA to devise a plan for overthrowing Castro with a $50 million
budget! "No time, money, effort—or manpower is to be spared,"
ordered Bobby. ". . . It's got to be done and will be done." Under
the steady McCone, the CIA used propaganda and sabotage and
even reactivated the Bissell/Mafia efforts to kill the Cuban leader.
Richard Helms, Bissell's successor, told Senate investigators that
the Kennedys had told him "to get rid of Castro," and the man in
charge of Mongoose, Colonel Edward Lansdale, told a newsman
that "acting on orders from President John F. Kennedy, delivered
through an intermediary, he developed plans for removing . . .
Castro by any means including assassination." In a 1964 interview,
however, Bobby sought to conceal Operation Mongoose and specifically denied that there had been any assassination attempts.[5]

McCone also played a central role in Kennedy's efforts to shut
down leaks about all the operations and thereby increased the
role of what authors David Wise and Thomas Ross denoted in
their title *The Invisible Government* (1964), an exposé of CIA activities around the world. McCone snatched galley proofs of the
book from Random House and tried to stop publication. It was

suggested to the director that the agency buy up the entire press run, which would fill out all the bookcases at Langley. Someone pointed out that the publisher could make a lot of money that way, supplying the CIA with a series of new print runs and a need to employ carpenters for new bookcases, so the idea was dropped. McCone also tried to see that the book got bad reviews; his efforts may have helped to keep it in the news, as it is still in print today.

The CIA director had been given a direct order in the summer of 1962 to organize a task force to plug leaks from the Pentagon. Kennedy's action was spurred by the *New York Times* military reporter, the much respected Hanson Baldwin, who wrote a story based on "reliable reports reaching Washington" about the Soviet Union's program of hardening its missile launching sites. The article claimed that various electronic devices, including satellite cameras, had gathered the intelligence data. What was more revealing about JFK's reaction, however, was Baldwin's commentary regarding the missing missile gap that Kennedy had harped on— along with who lost Cuba—during the 1960 election campaign to blame the Republicans for letting the Russians get ahead on ICBMs. Not only were the Russians behind in numbers, reported Baldwin, but they were also well behind in the "strength and diversity of its launching sites." That was the reason they were hardening the sites. Kennedy had known since his first days in office that there was no missile gap. While he allowed subordinates to reveal the truth piecemeal, the president insisted that there was a need for a huge military buildup. As historian Christopher A. Preble put it, "John F. Kennedy's political fortunes were uniquely tied to the missile gap, which was a major factor in Kennedy's rise to political prominence."[6] Here, then, was another instance of the fear of leakers embarrassing the administration: national security as a cover for past political campaigns. It would not be the last instance—the Nixon Watergate crisis would demonstrate that fear to the fullest.

The missile buildup had been sold to the electorate and pundits as part of a generational shift in American politics under the slogan "Let's get the country moving again!" On August 1, 1962, Dr. James Killian, the much-honored former president of the Massachusetts Institute of Technology, now chair of the President's Foreign Intelligence Advisory Board (PFIAB), opened a late afternoon meeting in the White House with a startling statement about Baldwin's article: "We would say to you unequivocally that this has been a tragically serious breach of security."[7] However serious the breach of security might be, it was a greater blow to missile gap politics.

Listening to Dr. Killian's report that day in addition to the president and his brother, the attorney general, were Clark Clifford, Truman's trusted political adviser and one of the authors of the CIA's original charter, and Kennedy's favorite general, Maxwell Taylor, soon to be named chair of the Joint Chiefs of Staff before he went off to Vietnam and became the American ambassador who helped make the decision to escalate the U.S. role in the war during the Johnson administration. Why did Baldwin do it? Kennedy asked. Whatever the reporter's reason, Killian said he had a plan to stop future leaks. The FBI was not really the best answer to leaks of this kind: "We would suggest, therefore, that the director of central intelligence be encouraged to develop an expert group that would be available *at all times to follow up on security leaks*" (emphasis added). That was the most promising recommendation he had heard, said Clifford. Caught up in the moment, the longtime Democratic political adviser apparently forgot that the charter he had helped to write specifically forbade the agency from spying on Americans. "That's a very good idea," Kennedy concluded. "We'll do that." Clifford then added, "To my knowledge it's never been done before and it is long overdue." It was both an astonishing comment about the casual disposition of constitutional questions and a fateful prediction about the ultimate outcome of such "innovations" assigned to agencies like the CIA and later the NSA.

Killian's nine-point program recommended that the president begin by emphasizing his concern over leaks to all government officials, reduce the number of people with access to such information, and require those who did have access to clear all contacts with the press and make memoranda of such conversations. Responsibility for investigating and running down the leaks would be the job of the DCI (director of Central Intelligence) and the director of the Defense Intelligence Agency. But that was not all. The PFIAB report included recommendations for a "confidential policy within the Executive Branch as to the degree of disclosure of intelligence data to be made to Congressional Committees," and—most at odds with traditional American attitudes about government's accountability to the public—"a re-study of possible proposals for legislation to protect official secrets."[8]

An American official secrets act did not result from these proposals, but presidents since Kennedy have found other ways to punish leakers. The Cold War mentality that led a scientist and future Peabody Award winner such as Killian to propose CIA domestic spying explains a lot about the roles people agree to play when they see—or think they see—the *real* stakes of the game from the inside. Having secrets creates not only a temptation to tell someone to reinforce your own importance but also a belief that only those you chose to inform can be considered trustworthy. All the rest, including Congress, are suspect. Together these beliefs bond into a powerful force that builds upon itself and separates society into classifiers and everyone else, all potential leakers or consumers of leaked information.

Three weeks after the Killian meeting, in a half hour alone with CIA Director McCone and General Taylor, Kennedy asked, "How are we doing with that set-up on the Baldwin business?" The CIA director said he had "finally" got a plan "in which CIA is completely in agreement with." The wording here suggests that there might have been some debate about how it could ever square with the original charter. But McCone was ready to set up the task force to investigate leaks, one that reported directly to him. Then a bit later in the conversation, McCone expresses doubts, mumbling his words in some instances so that his meaning is unclear.

"It's clearly a, it's kind of a, of a directive that . . . [to] avoid getting involved, you or your office getting involved . . . [unclear] I can do under the law—there's nothing wrong [with it]—By the National Security Act, I'm charged with [unclear]."[9]

McCone's plan for eliminating leaks was named Project Mockingbird to differentiate it from Operation Mockingbird, a longtime CIA effort to influence media and various transnational organizations. Project Mockingbird was a relatively short-lived taping operation that targeted Baldwin and other newsmen. It began as the Cuban Missile Crisis moved toward a dramatic climax in the fall of 1962. But Kennedy did not have in mind a temporary policy. "I think if they [government officials] begin to think they're going to have to write a report on it," he said in a private conversation before the crisis began, "it's going to have a very inhibiting effect." And in postmortems on press management, Kennedy complained that "we've got to improve our procedures or we're going to find ourselves in bad shape." The objective was to restrict information so that the administration could "put it out in our own way."[10] In short, as Henry Kissinger would say later when Nixon came into office, if there was to be any leaking, he would do it!

In this case, as in others to follow, the PFIAB guidelines themselves were leaked to the press. Pentagon spokesman Arthur Sylvester then admitted on the record that the government had "managed" the news, and an uproar followed, Republicans accusing the White House of selectively leaking information about the missile crisis to make Kennedy look tougher. The leaks did not stop—but Kennedy had set a precedent in using the CIA to perform domestic spying on American citizens.

Nixon and the Hiss "Analogy"

Nixon's well-documented paranoia is usually cited as the culprit in his fight against leakers, and there's no denying his obsessive belief that the combined forces of the media, the Eastern Establishment, and the Washington bureaucracy were out to get him. His determination to centralize all major foreign policy deliberations and initiatives within a tight group in the Oval Office helped to create an impression of unbridled executive power.

Whenever he looked back at his political beginnings, Richard Nixon always pointed to the "Hiss case," to the man he "nailed" as a spy for the Soviets despite the Establishment's disapproving sneers—and he saw himself as the target of its lasting rancor as the outsider who had exposed one of their own. He relished his fate as the underdog who fought through the scorn to reach the top. During the Pentagon Papers episode, Nixon imagined that he would survive—even as Watergate's overflow seeped into the Oval Office—because the public would see Daniel Ellsberg as a traitor, just like Hiss. Over and over again, he repeated the story to his aides about how he caught Hiss out when he claimed he didn't know Whittaker Chambers and that he had not leaked secrets to him for transmission to Moscow in the 1930s.

Alger Hiss was dubbed a special type of leaker for passing secrets to Russian agents. The only documents ever unearthed, however, were the so-called Pumpkin Papers, basically low-level stuff found on ex-Communist Whittaker Chambers's farm outside Washington. But the revelation that Alger Hiss had been at the 1945 Yalta Conference provided Republicans with an opportunity to claim that the Democrats and a dying President Roosevelt had allowed a leaker, Alger Hiss, to furnish the Soviets with government secrets.

Hiss was never convicted under the Espionage Act. He was convicted of perjury yet has gone down in the Nixon legend as a master spy. His presence at the 1945 Yalta Conference gave Republicans enough reason to condemn wartime diplomacy and peacemaking as sellouts to the Russians, regardless of his nonexistent role in decision making. The Hiss case was the first step on the ladder, but Nixon always believed that being right about Hiss meant the Establishment would scrutinize anything he did ever after to bring him down, unlike its treatment of "one of its own," which generally included anyone who graduated from

Harvard. "Kennedy could be as dirty as they come—and my God! He did some outrageous things in there! But he was protected. Johnson—same thing, although to a lesser degree because he wasn't Kennedy. Somehow I made the mistake of thinking or maybe not even thinking—maybe it was an unconscious thing—that I could act like them." [11]

Nixon even believed that the Establishment wouldn't let him end the Vietnam War without denouncing him for failing the so-called Kennedy test—tough-minded courage in the Cuban Missile Crisis that supposedly forced the Soviets to back away from his whip like lions on a circus pedestal. This challenge conditioned Nixon's presidency from the outset. He had won the 1968 presidential race by a hair, defeating Vice President Hubert Humphrey. During the campaign, he pledged a new beginning in presidential candor, a clear reference to the "credibility gap" that Lyndon Johnson's Vietnam policy suffered from even before the 1968 Tet Offensive belied White House assurances that things were going well. "The President has a duty to decide," Nixon said in a radio address, "but the people have a right to know why. The President has a responsibility to tell them—to lay out all the facts and to explain not only why he chose as he did but also what it means for the future. Only through an open, candid dialogue with the people can a President maintain his trust and his leadership." [12]

Nixon was well aware of Johnson's predicament after Tet. Immediately after the battle ended, the Pentagon pressed LBJ to do what the military had been arguing for for at least a year: mobilize the reserves and send General William Westmoreland nearly half again as many troops, to bring the total near 800,000. The plan was thwarted by a newspaper leak. On March 10, 1968, the *New York Times* headline read, "Westmoreland Requests 206,000 More, Stirring Debate in Administration." Neil Sheehan and Hedrick Smith then described the debate under way at top levels of the administration, preventing Johnson from covering the increase in fuzzy statements about all the progress being made. The article alerted both Nixon and his future nemesis Daniel Ellsberg about what leakers could do at critical moments to influence decisions.[13]

To Nixon, the most remarkable thing about the *Times* article was the number of government officials who spoke with reporters. How to avoid the same thing happening in his administration was Nixon's biggest concern. Then at the very end of the campaign, there were some maneuverings by the Republican camp with secret representatives of the South Vietnam regime to encourage them not to agree to peace talks before Election Day. Johnson had access to FBI reports on these meetings but chose not to use them out of concern that doing so would destroy what faith remained in the political system—a brutal if unintended commentary on how divided the nation really was and how desperate the desire not to let on how much the national interest was hostage to domestic politics. Nixon had actually promised Saigon a better deal if he became president. During the campaign, he had implied that he had a plan with statements like "New leadership will end the war." He never actually said he had a secret plan to end the war, but he refused to elaborate on what his policy might be out of supposed concern not to interfere with Lyndon Johnson's efforts to get peace talks started. It reeked of hypocrisy and, arguably, treasonous behavior. That was why Johnson did not act. And it finally brought Nixon to the darkness of the Watergate break-in, with its ruinous aftermath.

Nixon's greatest fear throughout the Pentagon Papers crisis was that someone would reveal what had been said to Saigon through intermediaries. Johnson had decided for the sake of the country not to make known the National Security Agency wiretap that revealed to him what Nixon had been up to, but he called a friend, Republican senator Everett Dirksen, to tell him what was afoot. "I don't want to get this in the campaign," he told Dirksen, but then he added, "They oughtn't to be doing this. This is treason." The senator replied, "I know."[14]

Nixon could never feel comfortable that his "nasty little secret" would remain secret. The release of the Pentagon Papers in 1971 threatened new exposures before the next election, even if there was nothing in the study documenting the secret contacts. Besides, what else might come out if others felt emboldened to act on their own? Once in office, he and his national security advisor, Henry Kissinger, met with the full staff of the National Security Council in the White House basement in early March 1969. His first words to the staffers expressed commiseration for their having to deal with "all those impossible fags" in the State Department. "Ignore the bureaucrats," the president then charged them, providing his own take on international trouble spots. "I want you to handle the rest of the world." Turning to Kissinger, he added softly, "And you and I will end the war."[15] The political stakes were high. "If the war goes on six months after I become president," he had told reporter Harrison Salisbury, "it will be my war." He would not end up like LBJ, holed up in the White House. "I'm going to stop the war—fast."[16]

Kissinger, meanwhile, had warned the NSC group that Nixon insisted that under no circumstances should any of them talk to the press. "If anyone leaks anything, I will do the leaking."[17]

The countdown to six months took a heavy toll on Nixon. His "plan" for ending the war—whether he had used the term during the campaign or not—had come to haunt his early nights in the White House, where at certain times he was drinking heavily and not really in control. Nixon swung back and forth between the illusion that the United States could finally win in Vietnam and the reality of the situation on the ground. He himself called his ultimate ploy the madman theory. "I call it the madman theory, Bob," he told his aide Bob Haldeman. "I want the North Vietnamese to believe I've reached the point where I might do *anything* to stop the war. We'll just slip the word to them that 'For God's sake, you know Nixon is obsessed about Communism. We can't restrain him when he's angry—and he has his hand on the nuclear button.' And Ho Chi Minh himself will be in Paris in two days begging for peace."[18]

The basic trouble with this idea was that Nixon was not *that* irrational; in fact, he was not irrational at all. While Nixon and Kissinger went through options for some initiative to end the war, the joint chiefs of staff presented one of their favorites—bombing the North Vietnamese sanctuaries in eastern Cambodia. Prince Norodom Sihanouk had declared his country neutral, but North Vietnamese forces marched through the border areas to stage their attacks on the South. Sihanouk had struck a bargain that preserved a delicate peace. He would ignore Hanoi's actions, and the North Vietnamese would ignore the indigenous Cambodian Communists, the Khmer Rouge. And on the other side, he would ignore the American raids and bombing across the border.[19]

But the joint chiefs wanted much more—a dedicated program of bombing that would be code-named Menu. It was put up or shut up time. Apart from whatever leverage the president thought he would gain over Hanoi by approving the bombing, he was also concerned to accommodate a military bureaucracy whose support he would need for arms negotiations with the Soviet Union. Nixon also hoped to store up credits for later moves that would seek to transform the Cold War framework so that it would accommodate his and Kissinger's vision of mutual restraint, which would be called détente. Nixon had already concluded that the United States simply could not afford any more Vietnams. Aside from the economic costs, the country would be torn apart.

But to get to that place where negotiations could begin, one had to hopscotch over the deeply embedded Cold War barriers that he himself had helped to put in place earlier in his political career. Kennedy had used his "triumph" in the Cuban Missile Crisis to take tentative steps to dismantle the Cold War ideological monolith that loomed over American politics, but he had also taken responsibility for what happened in Vietnam by increasing the number of U.S. military personnel there tenfold, to fifteen thousand, and even more so by approving (or at least not preventing) the CIA-managed coup against Ngo Dinh Diem. Moreover, he had his own madman theory, an arms policy called mutually assured destruction, or MAD. Speculations about what he would have done in the future hung over his successors for at least a decade.[20]

Secrecy and Foreign Policy

After Cuba, no president could appear to be backing away from a supposed threat, no matter how different the situations actually were. Thus Nixon and Kissinger believed that secrecy was the only way to open up their foreign policy options, to free themselves from the legend and LBJ's war without end. But the way things first appear often trumps the underlying reality, for once the Menu bombings started, the White House became enchanted by a dream of supposed success in weakening the North Vietnamese ability to supply its forces fighting in South Vietnam—so much that the final outcome of the war might change. On March 18, 1969, Henry Kissinger rushed into the Oval Office to declare Operation Breakfast (the first part of Menu) a great success. "He came beaming in," Bob Haldeman wrote in his diary. "A lot more secondaries [explosions triggered by the bombs] than had been expected. . . . Probably no reaction for a few days, if ever."[21]

Sihanouk had kept quiet about the bombing. That was the best part of all. Except for a very few, no one in Washington knew what was going on. The mission was conducted with false coordinates logged in for the pilots, who were not told they were bombing Cambodia. If Hanoi complained, reasoned Nixon and Kissinger, the North Vietnamese would have to own up to the presence of their troops and supplies in Cambodia. And they did not want to do that.

So the bombing went on and on. From March 1969 to April 1970, there were 3,600 B-52 bombing missions that blanketed areas of eastern Cambodia with 110,000 tons of explosives. But those were the figures only for Menu; the total tonnage dropped on Cambodia during the whole war was an order of magnitude higher. These were indeed big numbers, but whatever the damage to Cambodia and the deaths involved, the bombing had no important impact on the Vietnam War. It did, however, set off a civil war in Cambodia that led to the horrors imposed by the Khmer Rouge in the years after the United States disengaged itself from all responsibility for its sometime allies, from 1975 to 1979.[22]

Inside the United States the blowback shattered the president's confidence and once again convinced him that he would not be allowed to end the war his way. On May 9, 1969, William Beecher of the *New York Times* published an article titled "Raids in Cambodia by U.S. Unprotested." Beecher cited "administration sources" for his story about how the White House was willing "to take some military risks avoided by the previous Administration."

Down in Key Biscayne, Florida, Henry Kissinger was reading the *Times* sitting beside a hotel swimming pool while on a short vacation with the president. He flew into a rage about Pentagon leakers. Haldeman and Nixon's other close adviser, John Ehrlichman, had never seen him so mad. "Outrageous! Outrageous!" he shouted about Beecher's article. When he got to Nixon's vacation White House a few blocks away, he continued his rant: "We must do something! We must crush these people! We must destroy them."[23]

Kissinger was sure that the leak came from Secretary of Defense Melvin Laird, or perhaps Secretary of State William Rogers, rivals for influence who wished to discredit him. He had already phoned Laird, who was on the golf course at Burning Tree Country Club near Washington. He got out just "You son of a bitch" before Laird hung up on him. The defense secretary had been to Vietnam and was preaching his own version of the way out of the morass—Vietnamization. He had no quarrel with bombing Cambodia but wanted it as part of his own plan, not as part of a cantilevered scheme involving rewards and punishments for the peripheral players. But would he go so far as to leak?

Responding to Kissinger's tirade, Nixon quipped that instead of Mel Laird, "You should look at your own people"—all those Ivy Leaguers on the NSC staff, that was where the leak had sprung. Kissinger decided he might be right and called J. Edgar Hoover three times before noon. Hoover's notes of the conversations include the words, "National security . . . extraordinarily damaging . . . dangerous . . . destroy whoever did this."[24] They talked about putting wiretaps on one person—Morton Halperin— who had traveled to Florida with the White House entourage and was Nixon's best guess as the leaker, and on another, Colonel Robert Pursley, Laird's Vietnam adviser, who was Kissinger's best guess if Laird hadn't done it. The phones of several NSC aides were then tapped for reasons having naught to do with national security but rather in order to find out what they might be telling their contacts in the intellectual establishment.[25]

Next came wiretaps on several news reporters, including Henry Brandon of the *London Times*, who actually was a frequent outlet for Kissinger's leaks designed to influence news stories about the administration's foreign policies. When the Watergate scandal flooded the White House, Kissinger testified to a congressional committee that perhaps the Brandon tap was actually aimed at him, portraying himself as both a victim of Nixon's obsessions and (perhaps more realistically) not always aware of how far this clearly illegal wiretapping went. Returning the favor, Nixon later put the blame on Kissinger. Tapes revealed during the impeachment hearings record Nixon saying, "I know that he asked that it be done. And I assumed that it was. [Anthony] Lake and Halperin. They're both bad. But the taps were, too. They never helped us. Just gobs and gobs of material: gossip and bullshitting—the tapping was a very, very unproductive thing."[26]

In his memoirs, however, Nixon laid out a general case for secrecy as essential to his later achievements in foreign policy: "I can say unequivocally that without secrecy there would have been no opening to China, no SALT agreement with the Soviet Union, and no peace agreement ending the Vietnam War." This is among his most candid statements about his national security concerns. His successes depended on keeping knowledge away from the public, knowledge that would divide his camp and

provide political enemies with arguments to use against him, possibly paralyzing his initiatives.

A year after the wiretaps ended, however, the Supreme Court
ruled in 1972 that national security taps on American citizens
must be authorized by a court-ordered warrant if the subject had
no "significant connection with a foreign power, its agents or agencies." The opinion was written by Associate Justice Lewis F. Powell, known as a moderate and a consensus builder on the court.

> History abundantly documents the tendency of Government—
> however benevolent and benign its motives—to view with sus-
> picion those who most fervently dispute its policies. Fourth
> Amendment protections become the more necessary when
> the targets of official surveillance may be those suspected of
> unorthodoxy in their political beliefs. The danger to political
> dissent is acute where the government attempts to act under so
> vague a concept as the power to protect "domestic security."
> Given the difficulty of defining the domestic security interest,
> the danger of abuse in acting to protect the interest becomes
> apparent.[27]

The case was actually about the wiretapping of suspects accused of destroying government property, not the exposure of
government secrets. But it was broad enough to stop the Nixon
administration from engaging in any more of the FBI-organized
taps on officials and reporters. The decision came a year after the
court had ruled against the government's efforts to halt the publication of the Pentagon Papers, the biggest leaking case of the
twentieth century, and two days after the Watergate break-in by
the Plumbers operating out of the White House. However, Watergate had not yet metastasized from a back-page story to the
headlines that would bring down Nixon and all the president's
men—except Henry Kissinger.

While the Beecher article didn't stir up a firestorm in the
media, it was far from forgotten. During the 1974 impeachment

hearings in the House of Representatives, Elizabeth Holtzman sat on the Judiciary Committee. She drafted a resolution of impeachment to hold Nixon accountable for concealing from Congress the secret bombing of Cambodia. Unfortunately, the committee did not approve it, because, she later wrote, it might appear political—something that stemmed from "opposition to the war instead of the President's abuse of his war-making powers." As Holtzman rightly observed thirty years later, disentangling Nixon's wiretapping from the war was not really possible. "I think the interesting thing is that, if you go back to Watergate, a lot of it stemmed from the Vietnam War and the Cambodia bombings. The President had an enemies list. . . . Who were these enemies? These were people who opposed his policies on the war in Vietnam." Or who held secrets he did not want revealed.[28]

Holtzman saw the same connections in the George W. Bush administration's behavior after 9/11, in policies adopted that halted serious debate—in fact prevented it altogether—about the existence of weapons of mass destruction in Saddam Hussein's Iraq. Impeachment was necessary once again, she argued, because, "Otherwise, the record can be rewritten. The history can be changed. You cannot change a vote." In both cases, she argued, secrecy and lies were connected to wars. The tendency of presidents to see their policies as inherently protected by the national security imprimatur and to view their opponents as scarcely less dangerous than outright traitors is a constant theme in American political history and is not peculiar to Richard Nixon. Justice Lewis Powell's opinion on behalf of a unanimous Supreme Court is worth repeating: "History abundantly documents the tendency of Government—however benevolent and benign its motives—to view with suspicion those who most fervently dispute its policies." It's remarkable that this sentence was written at a time when the Cold War defined international politics and supposedly defined good citizenship.

The Beecher wiretaps proved to be the beginning of a broad justification in the Nixon administration for any measure believed necessary to protect the public from open discussion of foreign policy questions, not simply to guard military secrets. Nixon and leaders of the CIA and National Security Agency all believed that the public was not to be trusted, in part because the Vietnam-era protests had so divided the country. Having engaged the nation in what had become at best a stalemate with no end in sight, no elected leader could bring the conflict to a close without risking the wrath of outraged voters from one side or the other. Indeed, the entire Cold War ideological foundation had been put at risk by the torment Vietnam engendered. Vietnam, it was argued by Cold War councils of wise men, must not start an unraveling of the hard-line status quo maintained in large part by the secret fourth branch of government, the intelligence community. In this atmosphere of fear, the division of American society between classifiers and leakers began to shape executive decisions about what constituted national security.

After National Guardsmen fired on protesting college students at Kent State in 1970, killing four and wounding nine, it did seem that the country had entered a spiral of rage and protests. Many citizens thought the black nationalist movement had overtaken the civil rights movement following Martin Luther King Jr.'s assassination. There is no doubt that fears of a breakdown of the social order spread across the United States and provided justification and rationalizations for those engaged in spying on "radicals"— without too much concern for civil liberties. On the other side, there arose a number of dedicated groups such as the Citizens Commission to Investigate the FBI, inspired by a Catholic peace movement, which carried out a nighttime raid to force open FBI files on spying at the low-security federal building in Media, Pennsylvania, near Philadelphia. The documents the raiders distributed to the press proved that the FBI had undertaken surveillance of college campuses and other secret infringements on civil liberties and coercive behavior carried out against Vietnam protesters. The first story based on the pilfered documents appeared in the *Washington Post* on March 24, 1971, "Stolen Documents

Describe FBI Surveillance Activities," after Attorney General John Mitchell had warned that lives would be put in danger by the leakers and by those who published the documents. It was essentially the Nixon administration's defense for any and all disclosures on domestic or foreign policy matters, aka the national security card. The Media gang was never caught, and just three months later came the Pentagon Papers.[29]

The Biggest Leak of All, Before WikiLeaks

All the foregoing is background to understanding the administration's reaction to the sudden appearance on a Sunday morning in June 1971 of the first installment of documents from McNamara's commissioned study of the origins of American involvement in Vietnam all the way back to World War II. The Pentagon Papers, like the Snowden documents, were an unfolding story, occupying front-page headlines for days and weeks at a time. It was the biggest release of secret papers until the documents that an army private supplied to Julian Assange, the founder of WikiLeaks.

Ironically, argues Ken Hughes, an expert on the Watergate tapes, Ellsberg's release of the Pentagon Papers in June 1971 came at a very delicate moment, a time when Nixon and Kissinger really had given up on Operation Menu and incursions into Laos and Cambodia and wanted to find a way out of the war, a time when they feared exposure of its origins almost more than any other thing. Mistrust of the public tempts national leaders to see constitutional restraints as the greater of two evils. More than the secrets in the Pentagon Papers were at stake. Nixon saw the 1972 presidential campaign through a lens that looked back to the days of the Hiss investigation and its aftermath. All the wiretapping he approved in 1969, the effort to stop publication of the Pentagon Papers, the break-in at the Democratic headquarters in the Watergate complex in Washington—all were part of the same battle.[30]

It was immaterial to the president that the Pentagon Papers revelations were not about *his* lies, and though he saw in Daniel

Ellsberg's actions yet another effort to bring him down, the Establishment's attempt at a knockout blow, there were many who agreed that his efforts to stop the newspapers from printing the documents were justified so as to protect future presidents' ability to conduct foreign policy. He was just stuck with a bad war. He tried to solicit comments from foreign countries to that effect, then present them as evidence that our allies were disheartened by the revelations, indicating an inability to keep negotiations confidential. He was not unique in this effort, as the Obama administration's reaction to the WikiLeaks documents followed a similar path, with little more success.

The story of the Pentagon Papers leaker begins with the disenchantment of a Cold Warrior. The reason Daniel Ellsberg acted was not just Vietnam, although the McNamara study was his cri de coeur about where American policy was headed. Indeed, the raid on the FBI office in Media, Pennsylvania, and the secret documents made public about FBI efforts to pressure college administrators into providing information on Vietnam protesters played a part in influencing him to risk prison because he feared where the country was heading.[31] Ellsberg had begun his military career as a hawk, heading to Vietnam as a marine officer after receiving his PhD from Harvard. He put in a stint at the Department of Defense, working on counterinsurgency questions, then spent more time in Vietnam in the mid-1960s working under the fabled "Quiet American," Colonel Edward Lansdale.[32]

It was during this tour in Vietnam that Ellsberg really began to feel doubts that Vietnam was the right place to work the wonders of counterinsurgency. "I was still a cold warrior, looking for lessons in our Vietnam experience that could help the United States defeat Communist insurgencies *elsewhere*," he wrote in his memoirs. But escalating the war and sending more troops to Southeast Asia was not the way to demonstrate it could be done. The size of the disaster was the only thing that would grow from Lyndon Johnson's policy. When he returned to the United States on leave, he was on a flight with Secretary of Defense Robert McNamara, who asked him to settle a debate. McNamara had been hearing reports of progress in pacification, he told Ellsberg, that he didn't believe could be true. "I say things are *worse* than they were a year ago. What do you say?" Ellsberg hesitated to be so sure. Maybe they were about the same, he suggested. But McNamara quipped, "That proves what I'm saying! We've put more than a hundred thousand more troops into the country over the last year, and there's been no improvement." Surprised by the defense secretary's frank assertions, Ellsberg was taken aback further after the plane landed and McNamara strode over to the microphones to issue another upbeat report: "Gentlemen, I've just come back from Vietnam, and I'm glad to be able to tell you that we're showing great progress in every dimension of our effort."[33]

The very next year, however, McNamara ordered the study that became the Pentagon Papers. Ellsberg was among those invited to take part in providing the secretary with a detailed study of the decision-making process going all the way back to World War II. Supplemented with contemporary documents, the narrative revealed all too clearly the miscalculations and skewed judgments that had led to the present stalemate. Throughout the writing of the Pentagon Papers, Ellsberg was in contact with Morton Halperin, who, as Nixon had rightly guessed, opposed attempts to escalate pressure on Hanoi by attacking targets in Cambodia and Laos. While not a whistleblower or leaker, Halperin certainly encouraged Ellsberg's developing sense that leaks were the only remaining hope of changing policy. If advocates of "staying the course" could resort to planned leaks or go to the press with falsely optimistic predictions of "progress," Halperin reasoned that then it became the duty of true patriots to inform the public of the actual facts. After the articles about General Westmoreland's troop requests came out in 1968, eventually leading to LBJ's decision not to seek reelection, Ellsberg took up that cause, went to the reporter who had written those pieces, Neil Sheehan, and offered him additional information about where the troop request stood and how the military analyses of enemy troop strength had been deliberately underplayed to show "light at the end of the tunnel." Ellsberg later wrote, "My thought was to expose and subvert the very process of presidential lying about war policy."[34]

Ellsberg had seen what one leak about Westmoreland's troop requests could do in the early days of 1968, and what Beecher's leak about the secret bombing of Cambodia could not do a year later. At that point, he began to think about the McNamara study in his safe at the RAND Corporation, the U.S. Air Force–sponsored think tank in California. In October 1969, he and five colleagues at RAND wrote an open letter to the *Washington Post* opposing the war. A month later, he went to Washington and spoke with Senator J. William Fulbright about getting the Pentagon study declassified. The chair of the Foreign Relations Committee, a longtime opponent of the government's strategy (and victim of LBJ's manipulations to obtain the 1964 Gulf of Tonkin Resolution that launched the American phase of the war in earnest), contacted Defense Secretary Melvin Laird to see if the study could be released. Laird promised to provide the committee with information about policies but not the study, which had been constructed from "contributions provided on the basis of promises of confidentiality." Ellsberg also approached Senator George McGovern, who seemed willing to push ahead with an effort to get out the documents, but then decided against challenging the classifiers.[35]

Ellsberg then turned to newspapers, especially to Neil Sheehan of the *Times*, to whom he gave a set of the papers. With the aid of an antiwar veteran, Anthony Russo, Ellsberg had managed to take copies of the papers out of his RAND office section by section. His last encounter with Kissinger came at a conference held at MIT at the end of January 1971. The national security advisor opened the conference with a speech describing the background of President Nixon's Vietnam policy, which he insisted was winding down the American participation in the war as fast as possible. It was filled with references to the "tragedy" of revolutionary movements, their destabilizing impact on international politics, and the need to deal with them forcefully. Nevertheless, he said, "We are trending down the war in Vietnam, and I assure you that the war will continue to trend down." Kissinger had told delegations of former Ivy League professors much the same thing in his Washington office, always with the admonition to pay more attention to what the administration was doing than to what was being said to the press. At the time of the MIT conference, Kissinger told a group of colleagues at Harvard that by the time the United States finally pulled out of Vietnam, "you'll have nothing to criticize us for except that we didn't do it sooner."[36]

With a knowing nod, he implied that complete withdrawal was a foregone conclusion and that the pace had been slowed only by the need to appease the hard-hat constituency. Shortly after the MIT conference, Nixon made a statement indicating that full withdrawal was still a highly conditional proposition, and the administration launched another disastrous military excursion, this time into Laos. Kissinger's former Harvard colleagues "felt deceived and angry."[37]

Ellsberg had directly challenged Kissinger at the conference by asking if he had any estimate of the number of Vietnamese who would die as a result of American bombing policy over the next twelve months. The question left Kissinger struggling for a way to answer, while attacking Ellsberg for accusing him of racism and asking if he had anything different to suggest? Months later in the Oval Office, as the New York Times published the first installment of the Pentagon Papers, Kissinger used their "debate" at MIT as proof that Ellsberg was a deranged person who had called him a "murderer."

The Times publication of the Pentagon Papers began on Sunday, June 13, 1971, the day after Nixon's daughter Julie married David Eisenhower on the White House lawn. Kissinger's assistant Colonel Al Haig called the president shortly after noon that day. Nixon asked Haig to tell him the latest information on American casualties, hoping it would be fewer than twenty over the past week. Haig thought that might be the case. "Nothing else of interest in the world today?" asked the president. "Yes sir, very significant, this, uh, Goddamn *New York Times* exposé of the most highly classified documents of the war." But Haig's concern was not shared at first by the president, especially after he told Nixon that it really was a "tough attack on Kennedy," showing that American military participation in the war really began in 1961. Haig added, "They're gonna end up in a massive gut fight in the Democratic Party on this thing." [38]

Nixon was of course glad to hear that the likely result of the Pentagon Papers would be to divide the Democratic Party, which it certainly did. One could argue that the Pentagon Papers tipped the balance in favor of George McGovern's nomination in 1972, driving a wedge between key groups in the old New Deal coalition and rending it beyond repair. When Kissinger called later that day, he essentially repeated Haig's point that the McNamara study put all the blame on Kennedy and Johnson. By this time, however, Nixon was beginning to have some second thoughts about what it could do to him—and to future presidents. And what else might be revealed? The secret negotiations over the visit to China? The tilt to Pakistan in its war with India? All the other secrets that could be leaked brought back his old feelings that the press was out to get him. Nevertheless, his mind was already outlining ideas about how he could benefit from exposure of Johnson's maneuvers for the 1968 bombing halt, the context of Kennedy's Bay of Pigs fiasco, and even Roosevelt's deceitful "road to war" in 1941. At one point, Nixon even declared that, if played right, the Pentagon Papers could mark the end of the Democratic Party! "Well," he told Haldeman, "we're going to expose them. God, Pearl Harbor and the Democratic party will—they'll have gone without a trace if we do this correctly. Who would you put in charge, Bob?" [39]

Here was a strange, backhanded admission that the Pentagon Papers actually *did* threaten the policy consensus based on historical myths—that the United States was reluctantly forced into World War II, that the Bay of Pigs invasion was only an attempt to help Cuban exiles reclaim *their* revolution, and that LBJ was actually trying to secure peace in Vietnam with his bombing halt at the end of March 1968. Nixon wanted the Democrats "gone without a trace," but they were the party of the Marshall Plan, the Berlin Blockade triumph, etc. It is necessary to keep in mind that destroying the Cold War consensus was actually what scared policy makers the most about leakers, not the revelation of past military secrets.

Already the word was out that the culprit was Daniel Ellsberg. It might have come as no surprise to Henry Kissinger, but it was certainly unwelcome news. In an Oval Office meeting, Kissinger lost no time in lashing out against his former student. He said Ellsberg had weird sexual habits, used drugs, and while in Vietnam had enjoyed flying around in a helicopter taking potshots at Vietnamese below. "Henry said he was the most dangerous man in America today," reported Charles Colson, who heard one of Kissinger's tirades. "He said he must be stopped at all costs."[40] The pattern of denouncing leakers as outliers did not begin here, but the accusations against Ellsberg as an egotist who deemed himself beyond normal restraints was essentially the same set of charges made against Snowden four decades later.

Nixon's first move was an attempt to stop the New York Times from publishing any more excerpts from the McNamara study. And that task he assigned to Attorney General John Mitchell. Mitchell sent Times publisher Arthur Sulzberger a minatory telegram demanding that the paper cease publishing the Pentagon Papers: "FURTHER PUBLICATION OF INFORMATION OF THIS CHARACTER WILL CAUSE IRREPARABLE INJURY TO THE DEFENSE INTERESTS OF THE UNITED STATES. . . . I RESPECTFULLY REQUEST THAT YOU PUBLISH NO FURTHER INFORMATION OF THIS CHARACTER AND ADVISE ME THAT YOU HAVE MADE ARRANGEMENTS FOR THE RETURN OF THESE DOCUMENTS TO THE DEPARTMENT OF DEFENSE."[41]

The respected Times reporter/columnist James Reston was dining that night at the home of Robert McNamara, the instigator of the Pentagon Papers, and heard about Mitchell's telegram there, along with the paper's initial response that it would obey a court order. McNamara tipped his own hand, suggesting to Reston that the paper should obey only a Supreme Court order, not one from just any court. Reston passed the suggestion on, the *Times* continued to publish, and the case went to court.[42] No one in Mitchell's Justice Department really had any idea what was in the McNamara study, and it was equally unlikely that anyone in Defense had read much of it in the original version.

Mitchell's telegram also argued that the Pentagon Papers contained top secret documents. "As such, publication of this information is directly prohibited by the provisions of the Espionage Law, Title 18, United States Code, Section 793." In the absence of an official secrets act, this was as close as the government could come to declaring that newspaper publication was illegal. The problem for the government was that the First Amendment was more fundamental to American understandings of the role of the press than the World War I Espionage Act, a hastily drafted piece of legislation that began in controversy and actually had no provisions that referred to publication. It was the first time in 150 years, the papers would argue, that the government had attempted to use prior restraint to shut down the presses. This did not mean, of course, that there had been no instances when the press had voluntarily withheld publication of sensitive stories—most recently, of course, in the Cuban Missile Crisis. In World War I, the Espionage Act had been successfully used to shut down criticism by throwing Eugene Debs into prison. But Debs's invitation to the White House in 1921 had effectively repudiated such use of the act—up until the administration sought an injunction against Ellsberg and the *Times*.

The government injunction was argued before Judge Murray Gurfein, who could find nothing in the Espionage Act that applied to the Pentagon Papers publication. The only applicable law, he said, was the First Amendment, which guarantees freedom of the press against prior restraint. Then he addressed the real reason why the government wanted to shut down the presses. "If there be some embarrassment to the Government in security aspects as remote as the general embarrassment that flows from any security breach, we must learn to live with it. The security of the Nation is not at the ramparts alone. Security also lies in the value of our free institutions. A cantankerous press, an obstinate press, an ubiquitous press must be suffered by those in authority in order to preserve the even greater values of freedom of expression and the right of the people to know."[43]

What is remarkable here, one should add, is that Gurfein had no up-close knowledge of Nixon's personality and the president's obsession with the Establishment as a force determined to bring him down. His point was the more general one and speaks to the effort by some to set out Nixon as an exception, whose behavior should not condition the response to Snowden's illegal and dangerous actions. Instead, Gurfein highlights that governments hate to be embarrassed by leaks and hide behind walls of "national security" to prevent open debate. Gurfein's ruling was not the final word, nor were the *Times* excerpts the only place where the Pentagon Papers appeared. When the *Washington Post* and the *Boston Globe* began their own series of articles, government lawyers found themselves running from one city to another to try to stanch the flow. Ultimately, the Supreme Court ruled 6–3 that the government could not prohibit the newspapers from printing the information. But the controversy did not end there, as Chief Justice Warren Burger could not achieve a consensus about what the majority opinion (or the minority opinion) should say, at least not in the time he had to finish the ruling, so there were nine separate opinions in the Pentagon Papers case. In many of the opinions, there were harsh words for the newspapers as well as the administration. Perhaps the most significant thing about the ruling was that during the questions put to the newspaper lawyers, the point was made that the death of a hundred soldiers or the sinking of a troopship did not meet the standard of "immediate" damage to national security. In other words, the personal tragedies involved (if there were any, and it would be impossible to demonstrate the Pentagon Papers had endangered a single person) did not constitute a reason for abandoning the First Amendment. Justices Hugo

Black and William O. Douglas joined their opinions. Black said there could be no breaching of the First Amendment at all. The press had a duty, he insisted, "to prevent any part of the government from deceiving the people and sending them off to distant lands to die of foreign fever and foreign shot and shell. I believe that every moment's continuance of the injunctions against these newspapers amounts to a flagrant, indefensible, and continuing violation of the First Amendment."[44]

The Trials of Daniel Ellsberg and Richard Nixon

The Supreme Court settled the publication issue—but nothing else. As if Nixon needed any urging, Kissinger kept on the theme that Ellsberg was a danger to national security because he had in his possession secret information about American nuclear strategy and other vital defense secrets. John Ehrlichman argued in his memoirs that without Kissinger's constant fanning of the flame, Nixon might have brushed off the whole thing as LBJ's worry, not his. And all through the first weeks after the newspaper articles, the president looked upon the Pentagon Papers as an opportunity to "get" the Democrats, going all the way back to Pearl Harbor. "In view of this case," he said the day after the Court ruled, "I want . . . recommendations with regard to what can be done about World War II. What can be done about Korea. . . ." Where were all those papers? "And these are the things that will embarrass the creeps. Put it out."[45]

Nixon did not rest there. He now wanted Ellsberg treated like Alger Hiss—the man he exposed as an alleged Communist spy in the case that had launched his career. On June 28, two days before the Supreme Court decision, Ellsberg surrendered to arrest at the federal courthouse in Boston, even as a grand jury in Los Angeles was indicting him on charges of theft and espionage. On July 1, 1971, in the Oval Office, President Nixon told Haldeman, Colson, and Ehrlichman, "We're through with this sort of court case. . . . I don't want that fellow Ellsberg to be brought up until after the election. I mean, just let—convict the son of a bitch *in the press. That's the way it's done.* . . . Go back and read the chapter on the Hiss case in *Six Crises* [Nixon's memoir written after his 1960 defeat to John F. Kennedy] and you'll see how it was done. It wasn't done waiting for the Goddamn courts or the attorney general or the FBI. . . . We have to get going here."[46]

Colson came away from the meeting assuming that he had received his marching orders. He contacted E. Howard Hunt, who prepared a memorandum titled, "The Neutralization of Ellsberg." His idea was to build a file of damning information about Ellsberg to destroy his credibility. The plan was discussed at a meeting of the Plumbers, the special operations group set up in the White House in the wake of the Pentagon Papers to find the sources of leaks and plug them. Although it was not widely known for some time, one of the Plumbers served as liaison with the CIA, another instance of domestic spying on Americans that the agency's charter specifically forbade. It was becoming a commonplace practice. At the August 1971 meeting, Hunt presented the gist of his memorandum: a covert operation to get a "mother lode" of information about Ellsberg by breaking into the office of his psychiatrist, in Beverly Hills, California. Present at the meeting besides Hunt were G. Gordon Liddy, a former FBI agent; David R. Young Jr., a member of the national security staff; and Egil Krogh, a deputy assistant to the president. Liddy told the group that the FBI "frequently carried out such covert operations" in national security investigations, and that he had done some himself. Krogh remembered, "I listened intently. At no time did I or anyone else there question whether the operation was necessary, legal or moral. Convinced that we were responding legitimately to a national security crisis, we focused instead on the operational details: who would do what, when and where."[47]

Young and Krogh then sent a memo to Ehrlichman recommending a covert operation to obtain Ellsberg's medical files. The president's assistant approved the plan, writing in longhand

on the memo, "if done under your assurance that it is not trace-
able." When the plot was uncovered later, Krogh was the first of
the "president's men" to be convicted, after pleading guilty to
criminal conspiracy in depriving Dr. Fielding of his civil rights,
specifically his constitutional right to be free from a warrantless
search.[48] From the standpoint of the Bay of Pigs veterans—Hunt
and Liddy and other members of the Plumbers unit who broke
into Democratic headquarters at the Watergate complex the next
year—Fielding had asked for it. He had refused the FBI's request
for an interview.

The burglary was not the only strategy in Hunt's program to
defame Ellsberg. The plan also included a proposal to interview
Ellsberg's first wife, as well as the owner of a Saigon restaurant he
had frequented. The memo also called for CIA assistance in providing a "covert psychological assessment/evaluation on Ellsberg."
Director Richard Helms supplied one, but it was not of much use.
Well briefed on the Hunt plan, Nixon had even phoned J. Edgar
Hoover to complain about the FBI's apparent indifference, saying
he was "having to resort to sending two people out there" to Fielding's office.[49] The break-in apparently revealed no files worth the
effort, and the burglars left the office in a mess to suggest that a
desperate drug addict had perpetrated the crime. Ehrlichman was
appalled at the results. He had expected Hunt to pull off a James
Bond–style caper, leaving no trace.

The government case against Ellsberg, meanwhile, was growing and reached a peak when the indictment was expanded in
December to fifteen counts of theft and espionage. If convicted,
he could have been sentenced to 105 years in prison. Nixon would
have been surprised by the lack of support for Ellsberg in Establishment circles. When *Times* lawyers approached Cy Vance,
secretary of the army under Kennedy and Johnson, seeking a statement in support of what Ellsberg had done, he said, "I'd better not
do that." Reston called McGeorge Bundy, who turned him down
coldly: "Your problems are not mine."[50] That in the end Ellsberg faced no convictions had little to do with liberal resistance

or public pressure. These reactions are no longer surprising to anyone studying the growth of the national security state even without 9/11 as a powerful stimulant.

By this time, as John Dean would put it in a memorable comment to Nixon about the 1972 Watergate break-in, there was a cancer growing on the presidency. The president was fortunate, as he campaigned against Senator George McGovern that year, that the press investigation of Watergate's sponsors in the White House had yet to find the mother lode of information "Deep Throat" possessed and later passed on to Carl Bernstein and Bob Woodward of the *Washington Post*. McGovern's "Come Home, America" rallying cry did not resonate with enough Americans to give him a real chance in the election.

But soon enough, Watergate overtook Vietnam as the major crisis facing Nixon's White House. The 1964 Tonkin Gulf Resolution had already been repealed in January 1971, and then in 1973 a Watergate-disturbed Congress passed the War Powers Resolution, which required the president to seek legislative authority for large-scale military actions after sixty days. Nixon vetoed the resolution, but Congress easily overrode the veto. Presidential aides, especially Henry Kissinger, later argued that the war was lost because of the shortsighted focus on Watergate. Yet such alarmist responses could not prevent the Pentagon Papers from bolstering arguments that presidential power had grown such widespread roots during the Cold War that they threatened to choke the Constitution.

For Nixon, the key argument in favor of going after Ellsberg was not that his revelations threatened the lives of individuals or the success of specific diplomatic initiatives, however much the administration wished to make that case, but rather that the Pentagon Papers breached the walls of the national security state. "Now," Nixon told Charles Colson when the first articles appeared, "they're running with the line [the] . . . 'right to know.' . . . That's of course a Goddamn code word: right to know, the public has no right to know secret documents." Colson expanded on the president's opinion: if it were the battle plans for the withdrawal of troops next week, there would be no argument about it. But there were no battle plans about next week in the Pentagon Papers. Instead, one had to argue, "Now the integrity of the system as a whole is at stake." "That's right," said Nixon.[51] In other words, the logic of protecting "the system as a whole" required a pretense that the Pentagon Papers revealed secrets the public had no right to know. What the whole drama revealed, perhaps more than anything else, was the tendency—indeed, presumption—that anything that exposed mistakes or even bad judgment had to be kept from the public. And this would be the case whether it was Richard Nixon or any of his successors.

The trick was to make a jury believe. Opening arguments in the second trial of Ellsberg and Anthony Russo began on January 17, 1973. Ellsberg writes in his memoir, *Secrets,* that during the time he copied and leaked the McNamara study, he had not really thought about the relevance of the First Amendment to his revelations and the government's movements against him. The newspapers had relied on the Constitution in their defense of the publication, but Ellsberg had not believed he could claim protection for his acts. "I worked in the executive branch for the president, on military and foreign policy. I didn't think that the Constitution or congressional laws applied to me in what we were doing. In that respect, I was exactly like the various White House officials who testified later during the Watergate hearings that they believed—in the words of their boss, President Nixon—that 'when the president does it, it is not illegal.' "[52]

That would be the very same defense voiced on behalf of those accused in the Torture Report, a defense that President Obama chose not to challenge. Ellsberg's lawyer Leonard Boudin tried to convince his client, meanwhile, that he had not actually broken any law. But, added Boudin, when the government goes into a courtroom and presents twelve felony counts, you can't be sure you'll walk out a free man. The odds were maybe fifty-fifty. Ellsberg then testified, "I knew that not a page [given to the press] could injure the national defense if disclosed to anyone, and had I believed otherwise I would not have copied it." His purpose in passing on the papers was to give Congress the self-confidence to end the war.

How the trial would have ended will never be known. On April 27, 1973, the presiding judge turned over to the defense a memo from Watergate prosecutor Earl Silbert to Assistant Attorney General Henry Peterson that revealed the break-in at Dr. Fielding's office. The judge demanded to know if the White House had ordered E. Howard Hunt and members of the Plumbers to carry out the raid. It had. Three days later, Nixon announced the departures of John Ehrlichman and H.R. Haldeman in a desperate effort to keep his presidency afloat in the swirling rapids of Watergate.[53]

On May 11, the judge ruled on a defense motion to dismiss the case, saying "bizarre events have incurably infected the prosecution of this case." The courtroom erupted in roars and laughter. In the White House, Nixon was outraged: *"What in the name of God have we come to?"* It was a good question. The Ellsberg case was the first attempt to proscribe the printing of leaked documents in the press by using the 1917 Espionage Act as the equivalent of an official secrets act. When Nixon demanded action against the press, Attorney General John Mitchell came up with the idea of using the act to back an injunction. The government lost that case but pursued Ellsberg under the same rationale. Whether it would have lost again without the wrongdoing by the Plumbers remains an unanswered question.

3

The Great Transformation

Given the history of abuse by governments, it's right to ask questions about surveillance—particularly as technology is reshaping every aspect of our lives.
—Barack Obama, August 9, 2013

If you are outside of the intelligence community, if you are the ordinary person and you start seeing a bunch of headlines saying, U.S.—Big Brother looking down on you, collecting telephone records, et cetera, well, understandably, people would be concerned. I would be, too, if I wasn't inside the government.
—Barack Obama, August 9, 2013

Reflecting on the Pentagon Papers analogy, critical commentators like to point out that there are great differences between Daniel Ellsberg and Edward Snowden, beginning with the age of the leakers. Ellsberg was a forty-year-old war veteran with high-level experience in government; Snowden, still in his twenties, had little experience outside computer screens. Ellsberg's decision was taken after long deliberation and years as a policy maker; Snowden's, after a short time as a contractor. Ellsberg's decision was part of a coherent approach; Snowden's actions stemmed from immaturity and naïveté about the needs of national defense after 9/11. Ellsberg's revelations were about past decisions; Snowden revealed current secrets essential to national security. The list goes on, and it reveals the important links between past and present.

Ellsberg, now in his mid-eighties, has been quick to join the debate, dismissing Snowden's critics with a broadside against the Obama administration's continued use of the Patriot Act to justify his right "to kill anyone anywhere in the world, here or elsewhere, including American citizens." Perhaps the most important thing, he argues, is that he remained free on bail while the events surrounding his trial for violating the Espionage Act played out. He could argue against the war at public rallies even as the government tried to put him in jail. Snowden is in enforced exile in Russia, a situation that abets unrelenting criticism for his "flight from justice." Without doubt the Vietnam era was very different from the post-9/11 years: the executive summary of the bipartisan National Commission on Terrorist Attacks made public in August 2004 minced no words about the failures of intelligence and the new national mood after the tragedy: "At 8:46 on the morning of September 11, 2001, the United States became a nation transformed."

Ellsberg commented on the main effect of that transformation for leakers:

> All the things that were done to me then including [the] CIA profile on me, a burglary of my former psychiatrist's office in order to get information to blackmail me with, all of those things were illegal, as one might think they ought to be. They're legal now, since 9/11, with the Patriot Act, which on that very basis alone should be repealed. . . . Snowden . . . shows very dramatically the dangers of the Patriot Act used as it is. So the fact is that all these things are legal. And even the one of possibly eliminating him.[1]

Almost as if to confirm the lopsided changes since 9/11, National Intelligence general counsel Robert Litt told a New York conference on secrets and security, "People who leak classified information commit crimes, and if we can catch them, which is not always easy, we ought to prosecute them and they ought to go to jail."[2] There seems little room to maneuver between these views.

In the Vietnam years, Americans came to believe they were

fighting someone else's war. The trauma of 9/11 has still abated only a bit, despite the failed wars in Iraq and Afghanistan that resemble nothing so much as the Vietnam stalemate after an even longer period. And now, just as there came a call for reform of the methods employed by the National Security Agency in collecting metadata and spying on Americans, the Ebola crisis in Africa and the rise of the Islamic State in Iraq and al-Sham (ISIS) have once again chased away the threat to the power of the intelligence community. For how long? Edward Snowden's revelations and those of other leakers go to the heart of the national security state's claims much more than the Pentagon Papers did. It is hard to see where that debate will end. The tortuous twists and pivots made by administration spokespersons—and even the president—indicate just how hard it is to wage a war against leakers on national security grounds without getting tripped up by embarrassing questions. In part this is because the White House does not always know exactly what is happening in the operations it has authorized.

Where Are We Heading?

On May 23, 2013, two weeks before the bombshell Glenn Greenwald detonated with the Snowden documents, President Obama had given a major speech on the state of the world and American military policy at the National Defense University. He talked about the fragmentation of Al Qaeda since Osama bin Laden's death, about the importance of drones where no other weapon can be used successfully, and, far along into the speech, about the Department of Justice and the investigation of national security leaks. There were challenges to finding the right balance between our security and our open society, he acknowledged, but "as Commander-in-Chief I believe we must keep information secret that protects our operations and our people in the field."

Speaking as commander in chief nearly always foretells a hard line. Thus, "to do so, we must enforce consequences for those who break the law and breach their commitment to protect classified information."

On the other hand, "a free press is also essential for our democracy. That's who we are. And I'm troubled by the possibility that leak investigations may chill the investigative journalism that holds government accountable." Therefore he recommends leaving reporters alone but going after their sources.

> Journalists should not be at legal risk for doing their jobs. Our focus must be on those who break the law. And that's why I've called on Congress to pass a media shield law to guard against government overreach. And I've raised these issues with the Attorney General, who shares my concerns. So he has agreed to review existing Department of Justice guidelines governing investigations that involve reporters and he'll convene a group of media organizations to hear their concerns as part of that review. And I've directed the Attorney General to report back to me by July 12th.

But by July 12 everything had changed. Whether that "group of media organizations" ever met or not, the headlines were now filled with Snowden's exposés of what many were calling government overreach. So the president's May 23 speech at the National Defense University was already as dead, the saying goes, as yesterday's news. But even so, even if there had been no Snowden event, the speech reads as a defense of administration investigations that had pursued a record number of convictions for leaking under the 1917 Espionage Act. It is actually a syllogism of sorts, with a major premise that there must be consequences for those who breach their commitment to protect classified information, a minor premise that investigative journalism must not be chilled, and a conclusion that journalists should not be at "legal risk for doing their jobs." But the conclusion depended upon the administration's definition of their jobs.

Perhaps the most telling indicator of where this was all going could be found in the contemporaneous prosecution of a State Department adviser, Stephen Kim, who told a Fox News reporter, James Rosen, that American intelligence believed North Korea would respond to additional sanctions with more nuclear tests. Kim passed this information to Rosen, who published it—and Kim was brought up on charges of violating the Espionage Act. The case did not involve secret documents, nor did Kim's actions include passing information to an enemy state. More than that, the FBI actually charged Rosen with being an abettor "and/or co-conspirator." Obama's talk about a shield law at this very time suggests that his definition of the legal job of a reporter differs considerably from the First Amendment guarantee. The DOJ accused Rosen of encouraging Kim to disclose classified information by using a secret system of passing along messages via e-mail. When have investigative journalists *not* used such methods to coax out information from nervous sources? asked Glenn Greenwald. Writing in *The Guardian* three days before Obama's speech, the man who would soon break the Snowden story talked about "this newfound theory of the Obama DOJ—that a journalist can be guilty of crimes for 'soliciting' the disclosure of classified information."[3] The theory, said Greenwald, amounted to "criminalizing the act of investigative journalism itself." He then cited recent warnings issued by James Goodale, the *New York Times* general counsel during the Pentagon Papers fight. "The biggest challenge to the press today is the threatened prosecution of WikiLeaks, and it's absolutely frightening."[4]

The American public had had little idea before Snowden of the unseen presence of the NSA endlessly watching and sifting data into patterns to be interpreted on call if needed—until the first week of June 2013. Using top secret documents supplied by Snowden, journalist Glenn Greenwald published his initial *Guardian* article online under the title, "NSA Collecting Phone Records of Millions of Verizon Customers Daily." A little known special court established in 1978 by the Foreign Intelligence

Surveillance Act (FISA), wrote Greenwald, had ordered Verizon to supply the National Security Agency daily with electronic copies of "all call detail records or 'telephony metadata' created by Verizon for communications between the United States and abroad," as well as "wholly within the United States, including local telephone calls." A copy of the secret court order was attached to the article. It expressly forbade the company from disclosing to the public either the existence of the mandate or the court order itself. *The Guardian* had approached the NSA, the Justice Department, and the White House for comments in advance of publication, and all were offered the opportunity to raise specific security concerns regarding the publication of the court order.[5] None did.

But the administration had actually had a great deal to say—in private. When *The Guardian US's* foreign editor Spencer Ackerman informed National Security Council spokesperson Caitlin Hayden about the story it intended to publish, she responded that she had a proposal he would want to hear, via a conference call with top officials, including deputy FBI director Sean M. Joyce, deputy director of the NSA Chris Inglis, and NSA general counsel Robert Litt. These were top guns. Their mission was to shoot down the story by persuading *The Guardian US's* editor Janine Gibson that the story about Verizon was far from impartial. They would also offer Gibson an invitation to the White House for a cozy chat. As usual, the subtext was, *You don't really understand how things work.*[6]

Gibson deflected the proposal adroitly, countering that she believed there was an overwhelming public interest in the story. She was open to listening to their concerns. After twenty minutes, the White House team was getting very frustrated. They could not discuss specific concerns, because even to discuss the secret Verizon document on the phone would be a felony. Gibson recalled that as the conversation went on, her accent became even more starchily British, until she sounded like Mary Poppins. That produced an outburst from one of the team in a thick cop-show accent, "You don't need to publish this! No serious news organization would publish this!"[7] Gibson replied in an icy tone, "With the greatest respect, we will take the decisions about what we publish." Attempts were also made to pressure *The Guardian's* parent company in London—to no avail. The White House still couldn't quite believe they were not in control of the situation. A few minutes after the story went live, Hayden sent a note to Ackerman, "Are you guys going ahead?"

The worst of it was the White House had no idea of the scope of the leak, apparently believing that the story about Verizon's forced compliance was a one-off event. The next day, however, the *Washington Post* published a second article, by Ellen Nakashima, "Verizon Providing All Call Records to U.S. Under Court Order." The article described "tens of millions of American customers" being covered, which made it clear that the program was not simply about calls *to* the United States. Administration officials spoke a little more publicly to the *Post* than they had to *The Guardian*, confirming that the court order was authentic before repeating the standard assertion that such information "has been a critical tool in protecting the nation from terrorist threats." The White House official added that "all three branches of government are involved in reviewing and authorizing intelligence collection," not just the secret court or the White House. Congress was "regularly and fully briefed" on how the information is used.[8]

At a congressional hearing, Senator Ron Wyden, a Democrat from Oregon, had asked James Clapper, director of national intelligence (DNI), about a recent statement by the director of the NSA, General Keith Alexander. Wyden quoted the statement: "The story that we have hundreds of millions of dossiers on people is completely false." Wyden had served on the committee for a dozen years, and he really did not know what a dossier was in the context of Alexander's assertion. So could Director Clapper give him a simple yes or no answer to one question: does the NSA "collect any type of data at all on millions or hundreds of millions of Americans?"

CLAPPER: "No, sir."

WYDEN: "It does not?"

CLAPPER: "Not wittingly. There are cases where they could inadvertently perhaps collect, but not wittingly."

Wyden thanked him for the answer but added that he would have additional questions to give him in writing. After the hearings, Wyden told reporters he'd wished to give Clapper a chance to amend that statement before it was locked in as his testimony. For a time, the director's office stonewalled Wyden on follow-ups, but after *The Guardian* and *Washington Post* articles, that was not possible. In an interview with NBC's Andrea Mitchell, Clapper offered an explanation. "I responded in what I thought was the most truthful, or least untruthful manner, by saying no." But he admitted his answer was "too cute by half." Still, he maintained that the real matter at issue in the exchange turned on the question of what was meant by *collection*. There were obvious differences over the meaning of such words. "When someone says 'collection' to me, that has a specific meaning, which may have a different meaning to him."[9]

Too cute by half was not enough. Calls for Clapper's resignation forced the president's advisers to come to his defense. National Security Council spokeswoman Caitlin Hayden said the president had " full faith in director Clapper and his leadership of the intelligence community." Press Secretary Jay Carney was even firmer in declaring Obama's support. The president, he said, "certainly believes that Clapper has been straight and direct in the answers that he's given, and has actively engaged in an effort to provide more information about the programs that have been revealed through the leak of classified information." Indeed, Carney went on, Clapper had been "aggressive in providing as much information as possible to the American people."[10]

Obama had appointed Clapper to the position in 2010; now he stepped back and allowed his advisers to respond to demands that the director resign. He took a similar backseat role when

questions arose about whether Edward Snowden should be prosecuted. Obama apparently feared that the Snowden affair was in
danger of becoming a personal attack on him. "These leaks are
released drip by drip, one a week," he complained, "to kind of
maximize attention and see if they can catch us at some impreci-
sion on something." Obama seemed to suggest that Snowden and
his journalist conduit, Glenn Greenwald, were out to get him personally, as much as they claimed to be acting on behalf of a public
that had been left in the dark by its government. There was even
a distant echo of Nixonian agonizing about the motives of the
Snowden-ites using the affair to undermine his presidency and a
corresponding belief that his own actions were carefully thought
out to protect the "presidency" from debilitating and malicious
attacks.

Instead of "change you can believe in," Obama's famous campaign slogan, a growing number now thought it was "continuity
you had to live with." In 2008 Senator Obama had been one of
three Democrats to vote for an amendment to the FISA law, an
addition that granted explicit legal immunity to telecommunica-
tion firms that participated in bulk surveillance, a policy President
George W. Bush had initiated as a lawless secret. It would now become a base from which to project the NSA's overseas collection.[11]

For a time it seemed that all hell had broken loose with sul-
fur fumes pouring into the skies over Langley, Virginia, and
NSA headquarters at Fort Meade, Maryland. Obama's popularity
ratings dropped 7 percent in the first week after the Snowden-
Greenwald revelations, and 17 percent among Americans under
thirty, African Americans, and independents—the key segments
of the president's electoral coalition. Still worse, in some ways,
because of the ongoing nature of the Snowden story, 61 percent
of those in a CNN poll gave Obama a thumbs-down about his
handling of surveillance, while only 52 percent had disapproved
of George W. Bush's practices.[12]

Greenwald's constant stream of interviews over the next twelve
months celebrated such reactions as major achievements in

challenging government overreach: "It's been universes stronger than what we a year ago hoped to achieve, even under our best case scenario."[13] And Greenwald promised that even after a year there was more, much more, in the "huge archive" now in his possession. His greatest worry, he told an interviewer, was how to "get that reported relatively quickly so that the world can have knowledge that they should have, and have that factor into the debate." As matters stood, he said, there was a "huge disconnect between public opinion and the way these systems continue kind of unmolested, and it's very undemocratic and dangerous, and I am concerned about that a lot."[14]

Obama's worst fear was that he and his administration would become the *subjects* of the public debate, instead of appearing to be disinterested *participants* in the search to find ways to reconcile presumed national security needs with respect for civil liberties. Hence the president announced the appointment of a committee, a high-level group of experts to review "our entire intelligence and communications technologies." That was not the same, obviously, as saying there would be major changes in policy. In fact, it seemed even milder than the proposals he made in the quieter pre-Snowden days. The stated goal gave away the change: it was to make Americans more "comfortable" with the NSA programs.

The president's first reaction to Snowden's revelations had been a hurried claim that the NSA was not actually listening in on phone conversations but simply gathering metadata. "In the abstract," he had said on June 7, 2013, two days after the first articles appeared, "you can complain about Big Brother and how this is a potential program run amuck, but when you actually look at the details, then I think we've struck the right balance." The right balance now meant that Obama was no longer seen simply as the anti-Bush candidate who had ridden the crest of antiwar feelings all the way into the White House. He was now the man who had stepped up the war in Afghanistan and had sent hundreds of drones on controversial killing missions to Pakistan and Yemen. The president found himself constantly trying to strike a balance not just about investigating reporters who had been given secret documents or information but also about a wide range of issues raising national concerns about an imperial presidency, now suddenly challenged by both Republicans and Democrats over spying on Americans by its intelligence agencies.[15]

Consequently, whenever he spoke about the NSA programs for sweeping up telephone and Internet communications, the president sounded an ambiguous note, halfway between justifying them and admitting that we *should* be worried. "Collect it all" had been NSA director General Keith Alexander's command—and his boast. Once a comforting assurance, such a claim now appeared to be an ominous sign of what the future might hold—no matter how much faith one had in one president's intentions.

Obama's Predicament

Alexander's statements and boasts were no longer abstract; the reality was the source of the president's dilemma. Positioned uneasily between his personal commitment to more transparency and openness on the one hand, and on the other the momentum created by the growth of the intelligence agencies (CIA, NSA, FBI, and all the others) not just since 9/11 but since the end of World War II, Obama entered the White House precisely at the moment these agencies commanded technological resources that brought a previously unimaginable ability to pinpoint an individual's location and study that person's behavior undetected. It was a bit like watching a huge Google map of the world swoop in on an individual house—if one added in the ability to know exactly what was going on inside that house at any time of day.

In an appearance with popular TV interviewer Charlie Rose, the president seemed defensive about his acceptance of universal espionage. Some people were saying, he told Rose, " 'Well, you know, Obama was this raving liberal before. Now he's, you know, Dick Cheney.' Dick Cheney sometimes says, 'Yeah, you know? He took it all, lock, stock and barrel.' " But that was never his objective, he said; rather it was to strike the right balance, to make sure the government was "making the right trade-offs." Rose persisted, however: "So I hear you saying, 'I have no problem with what NSA has been doing.' " He did not, the president affirmed, because actual wiretapping required a FISA Court order. Rose still pursued his point by focusing attention on a different aspect of the situation: "But has FISA Court turned down any request?"

Put off stride by the question, Obama hesitated before formulating a careful answer. "The—because—the—first of all, Charlie, the number of requests are surprisingly small . . . number one. Number two, folks don't go with a query unless they've got a pretty good suspicion." Unsure of his footing, he quickly pivoted into a long discussion of the misinformation about what the programs did and did not do. While admitting that mistakes had been made in not allowing the public to know more about the way they worked to protect American security without harming citizens' right to privacy, people are, "not getting the complete story," he said. It was yet another formulation of "if you knew what I know."

Rose refused to be deflected and picked up on that point: "Let me just ask you this. If someone leaks all this information about NSA surveillance, as Mr. Snowden did . . . did it cause national security damage to the United States, and therefore should he be prosecuted?" Once again Obama ducked: "I'm not going to comment on prosecution. . . . The case has been referred to the DOJ for criminal investigation—and possible extradition. I will leave it up to them to answer those questions." [16]

Obama's hesitancy about prosecution—who would bring the indictments and what they would be—demonstrated unease about the First Amendment concerns involved, as well as fear of losing his base of supporters. Putting the Department of Justice out in front was damage control. The president knew very well what his attorney general, Eric Holder, was planning. It was in this charged atmosphere that the pursuit of Edward Snowden became the biggest controversy, or at least the longest-lasting front-page story, of the Obama years. One week after the first article appeared detailing the NSA's forced arrangement with Verizon and other telephone companies, the Department of Justice filed charges against Snowden in the U.S. District Court for Eastern Virginia.

Justice attorneys had asked the court to seal the document, but it quickly became apparent that that approach would only exacerbate fears the government had something to hide. The court document charged Snowden with conveying classified information to an unauthorized party, disclosing communications intelligence information, and theft of government property. The first two charges came under the 1917 Espionage Act, which the administration had already stretched into the equivalent of an American official secrets act—one with even more severe penalties than the British version.

Who Is Edward Snowden?

Snowden's audacious acts divided the country. He was denounced by congressional leaders in both parties. South Carolina's Lindsey Graham tweeted on June 10, 2013, "I hope we follow Mr. Snowden to the ends of the earth to bring him to justice." But Graham was playing on Snowden's ball field by using Twitter, and his tweet brought on a shower of protests that perhaps surprised the senator. The effort to demonize Snowden was getting off to a very bad start, as the users of Twitter and Facebook are largely from the same generation as the fugitive.

"I've always thought this was a treasonous act," declared Senator Bill Nelson, a Florida Democrat. "Apparently so does the U.S. Department of Justice. I hope Hong Kong's government will take him into custody and extradite him to the U.S."[17] Another Democrat, Senator Dianne Feinstein, chair of the Intelligence Committee, fully agreed with Nelson, as did a parade of other political figures, including Condoleezza Rice and Hillary Clinton. "I don't look at this as being a whistleblower," said Feinstein. "I think it's an act of treason." Snowden had violated his oath to defend the

Constitution, she said. "He violated the oath, he violated the law. It's treason." [18]

But was that so? The charges filed against Snowden did not include treason. Under the Constitution, treason is defined as waging war against the United States, "adhering" to the enemy, or giving "aid and comfort" to the enemy, and conviction requires two witnesses or a confession. Supplying classified information to the nation's enemies could obviously fit under some definitions of treason. But because he supplied the information not to any specific enemy but to everyone on earth, there were problems with using the Constitution to indict Snowden—the First Amendment issues. Even those who most wanted him prosecuted couldn't ignore the complication.

Feinstein herself raised the issue in a roundabout manner, as journalists queried her about the duties of the chair of a watchdog committee. She was asked if she would look into Snowden's accusations about the NSA programs. "I'm open to doing a hearing every month, if that's necessary," she told ABC News. But she added, "Here's the rub: the instances where this has produced good—has disrupted plots, prevented terrorist attacks, is all classified, that's what's so hard about this." [19]

So the two sides were drawn up. On one, Snowden's supporters wished to focus on the actions of the National Security Agency; on the other, critics wanted to focus on the nerdy computer analyst with a grandiose vision of himself. The best that could be said, apparently, was that Snowden was an enigma—a perfect description perhaps for someone working on codes and secret messages. He was born on June 21, 1983, the son of a career Coast Guard officer, and grew up in Maryland, actually not far from Fort Meade, the home base of the National Security Agency, the supersecret arm of the intelligence community that hires more mathematicians on a yearly basis than any other organization in the United States. The NSA is part of the Department of Defense and is always headed by a high-ranking military officer. Its original mission was signals intelligence (sigint), but the telephone and Internet data it now gathers takes it over into human intelligence (humint).

Snowden did not graduate from high school, as a result of an illness that kept him out of class for several months. He attended a community college, however, and quickly found his métier in computers. He also found a name for his Internet posts; he would sign on as TheTrueHOOHA. Over the next few years, he posted hundreds of messages on all sorts of subjects under that name, creating his own webserver. The Internet was for him "the most important event in human history."[20]

Snowden's computer skills eventually brought him into government, where, as he said on his website, experience counted for more than a high school diploma or college degree. Parallel to Daniel Ellsberg's intellectual journey, Snowden began as a hawk. In 2003 he was a cheerleader for the American invasion of Iraq and decided to enlist. He wanted to fight in the war because, he said, "I felt like I had an obligation as a human being to help free people from oppression." He did sign up, but during infantry training he broke both legs in an accident that soon led to a medical discharge. From there he moved into jobs where his Internet skills finally secured him a position in the CIA in Geneva, Switzerland.

His views on such things as Social Security and other liberal policies had not changed, as he took Thoreau's fierce individualism as a model, both for opposing government intervention in the economy and for viewing the CIA as a dangerous and growing menace to American freedoms. "Society really seems to have developed an unquestioning obedience towards spooky types," opined TheTrueHOOHA in February 2010. "Did we get to where we are today via a slippery slope that was entirely within our control to stop? Or was it a relatively instantaneous sea change that sneaked in undetected because of pervasive government secrecy?"[21]

Snowden's 2008 candidate had been Ron Paul, but hearing Barack Obama's presidential speeches had made him think that some of the policies he had come to fear would be changed if the Illinois senator won. But following Obama's election, he quickly grew disillusioned as his new work as a computer analyst for a defense contractor gave him a good observation post for viewing the growing surveillance state. "I watched," he wrote, "as Obama advanced the very policies that I thought would be reined in." In December 2012, he sent a short anonymous e-mail to Glenn Greenwald, an author and columnist for *The Guardian*. That was the beginning of a correspondence that eventually led to the meeting in the Mira hotel in Hong Kong. But it was not an easy path, not at all. In fact, Greenwald largely ignored this overture, in part because his mysterious correspondent wished him to install special software to protect his communications, and Greenwald was not a computer software guy. A month later, Snowden turned to Laura Poitras, a documentary filmmaker, with much the same message, but she had had experience with encryption software and was more ready to meet his demands for ultrasafe security. She was told to devise long passwords: "Assume that your adversary is capable of a trillion guesses per second."[22]

Once communications were established, Poitras began receiving messages that outlined a number of surveillance programs, not just the Verizon story. She had heard of only one of them. About each program, her correspondent wrote some version of "This I can prove." Poitras had produced documentaries about the Iraq War that had not pleased the government and had moved her base of operations to Berlin after several unpleasant experiences with security when she reentered the United States. She worried now that she was falling into a trap set by government agents who wanted to trick her into disclosing information about the people she had interviewed for a recent film, including the founder of WikiLeaks, Julian Assange. "I called him out," Poitras recalled. "I said either you have this information and you are taking huge risks or you are trying to entrap me and the people I know, or you're crazy."[23]

Finally, she decided to take a chance by contacting Greenwald and agreeing to fly with him to Hong Kong. Aboard the flight, she showed Greenwald a thumb drive with thousands of the documents, a collection that revealed the scope of the surveillance programs. They both trembled with excitement at the prospect of meeting this person, presumably a top-echelon intelligence official with years of experience who had finally become fed up with the whole business. Instead, they met a slim young man in casual clothes, who greeted them in the hotel with a Rubik's Cube in his hand.

Snowden's Facilitators

Snowden had long planned the release of the documents and (as he told a Hong Kong newspaper, the *South China Morning Post*) had sought a position with the management consulting firm Booz Allen Hamilton three months earlier in order to gain the widest access he could to collect proof of the NSA's surveillance programs. He also told the *Morning Post* that he had found evidence that the NSA was hacking into computers in Hong Kong and on the mainland. He may have hoped that by granting this interview after going public, he could give the authorities there some reason not to accede to demands that he be extradited to the United States. From what he had seen of the government's treatment of Bradley (now Chelsea) Manning, the source of embarrassing WikiLeaks documents about the war in Iraq and a wide range of diplomatic matters, he apparently felt that his best protection was to seek asylum before he was arrested. If that was his plan, it worked. The *Morning Post* reporter who interviewed Snowden wrote, "His admission [about Booz Allen] comes as US officials voiced anger at Hong Kong, and indirectly Beijing, after the whistle-blower was allowed to leave the city on Sunday."[24]

This interview with the Hong Kong newspaper added insult to injury by exposing American hacking in China at a time when the U.S. government was charging Beijing with conducting a hacking campaign against U.S. businesses. When Washington asked to have Snowden extradited, Hong Kong authorities passed the request on to Beijing. The infuriating response was the American request could not be acted upon because the document did not spell his name correctly. Hong Kong justice secretary Rimsky Yuen said that discrepancies in the paperwork filed by the U.S. authorities were to blame. Hong Kong immigration records listed Mr. Snowden's middle name as Joseph, but the U.S. government used the name James in some documents and referred to him only as Edward J. Snowden in others. "These three names are not exactly the same, therefore we believed that there was a need to clarify," said Mr. Yuen. Besides that, he added, the U.S. authorities did not provide his passport number.[25]

It was all a sham, of course, a big put-down of the arrogant superpower. Charging Snowden with violations of the Espionage Act might have been the best strategy at home to satisfy Obama's political needs, but these comments showed that it ran the risk of not getting him back from Hong Kong, which enjoys semiautonomous status from China and whose extradition treaty has an exception for political crimes. The third charge against Snowden—for theft of government property—was a backup, presumably to get around such exceptions. Indeed, when a DOJ official was asked about American hopes that Hong Kong authorities would move swiftly to arrest Snowden, he refused to elaborate on the efforts, but said only, "The U.S. and Hong Kong have excellent bilateral cooperation on law enforcement matters."[26]

Angered by the deliberate procrastination that gave Snowden his chance to get away, the White House now said it would damage Chinese-American relations. A Justice Department spokeswoman scoffed at Hong Kong's excuse for not stopping Snowden from leaving the country. "The fugitive's photos and videos were widely reported through multiple news outlets. That Hong Kong would ask for more information about his identity demonstrates that it was trying to create a pretext for not acting on the provisional arrest request."

Worse still, Edward Snowden's critics were losing the PR

battle—and badly. Appearing at a joint press conference with Angela Merkel, the German chancellor, whose personal phone the NSA had tapped, the president tried to go on the offensive.

We know of at least 50 threats that have been averted because of this information not just in the United States, but, in some cases, threats here in Germany. So lives have been saved. And the encroachment on privacy has been strictly limited by a court-approved process to relate to these particular categories. Having said all that, what I've said in the United States is what I shared with Chancellor Merkel, and that is that we do have to strike a balance and we do have to be cautious about how our governments are operating when it comes to intelligence. And so this is a debate that I welcome.

But the White House did not speak with one voice. Set against Obama's desire to reach out to his critics, there was the usual "unnamed senior Administration official," who questioned Snowden's motives. Where he sought asylum was supposedly a dead giveaway: "Mr. Snowden's claim that he is focused on supporting transparency, freedom of the press, and protection of individual rights and democracy is belied by the protectors he has potentially chosen: China, Russia, Cuba, Venezuela, and Ecuador. His failure to criticize these regimes suggests that his true motive throughout has been to injure the national security of the U.S., not to advance internet freedom and free speech."[27]

Snowden soon became a national, indeed international, preoccupation, "escaping" from Hong Kong, where he had first met with Greenwald, eluding efforts to apprehend him, and finally landing in Russia seeking asylum. He was already the world's most famous fugitive: depending on your viewpoint, a truth teller forced into exile by a government that was violating its own Constitution or an egotistical saboteur, a folk hero or a traitor. Obama deeply resented Snowden's actions not only for revealing the betrayal of his base by his approval of the spying but also for the way the gradual revelations forced him back on his heels, trying every week to answer new gotcha questions for which there's no acceptable answer.

While the administration debated against itself, the public debated Snowden's motives with Senator Feinstein's conundrum in mind: how is it possible to have an open conversation about national security issues when the documents are classified and the claims for success cannot be seen?

The Debaters

Daniel Ellsberg quickly became a vocal champion of Snowden. He readily agreed that there were big differences between the 1970s and the second decade of the twenty-first century. He wrote that the United States was obviously not now a police state, but that the extent of the electronic and legislative infrastructure in place boded ill for democracy. "If, for instance, there was now a war that led to a large-scale anti-war movement—like the one we had against the war in Vietnam—or, more likely, if we suffered one more attack on the scale of 9/11, I fear for our democracy. These powers are extremely dangerous." [28]

Over and over again during the next twelve months, Ellsberg would stress that while he was under indictment in 1972, he was free to speak out and defend his reasons for acting. That would never be the case with Snowden, as Senators Graham and Feinstein more than intimated in their comments. His treatment would be more like that handed out to Chelsea Manning, the army specialist (a rank equivalent to corporal) who provided Julian Assange with the huge numbers of secret documents that WikiLeaks released. In the military, it was easy to arrest, incarcerate, try, and sentence Manning with no opportunity for her to reach a public audience. Her trial was going on at the time that Snowden's documents were being revealed, and he cited her example as a reason why he would not risk coming back from exile in Russia. [29]

The issue came up in one of the articles posted online by Marcy Wheeler, an Internet journalist and commentator whose postings struck home time and again. She zeroed in on State Department spokesperson Jen Psaki in an exchange with reporters over Snowden's access to the press in a Russian airport while he awaited a decision on being granted asylum. Psaki was rocked back on her heels several times by questions about the State Department's position that Russia had given the man accused of crimes a propaganda platform by facilitating access to him. She kept repeating that Russia ought to do the right thing by sending him home. Unlike presidential press conferences, where the atmosphere or aura of the White House discourages combative exchanges, Psaki did not enjoy the same sort of immunity.

She was asked by Associated Press reporter Matthew Lee, for example, about the United States position that freedom of speech is an absolute right, in the pursuit of which the State Department often cites with favor the activities of human rights organizations around the globe. How was it different when the same groups supported Snowden's right to speak out? Psaki tried to suggest that there was a difference in that he was not "a whistleblower or a human rights activist." At this point, the exchanges became testy.

QUESTION: I just don't understand. I think this is an incredibly slippery slope that you're going down here, that the U.S. Government is going down here, if you are coming up and saying to us that you're trying to prevent an American citizen—albeit one who has been accused of serious crimes—from exercising his right to free speech. You don't agree with that?

MS. PSAKI: I believe that what I've conveyed most proactively here is our concern about those who helped facilitate this event [a news conference] . . . and make it into a propaganda platform. . . .

QUESTION:—the propaganda platform aside, free speech covers propaganda. Last time I checked it covers a lot of things. . . .

MS. PSAKI: Well, Matt, this isn't happening . . . in a vacuum. And this is an individual, as we all know, who has been accused of felony crimes in the United States. We have expressed strongly our desire to have him returned. . . .

QUESTION: But as you have also said, he is a U.S. citizen.

MS. PSAKI: He is, yes.

QUESTION: He remains a U.S. citizen, and he enjoys certain rights as a U.S. citizen. One of those rights, from your point of view, is that he has the right to come back and face trial for the crimes he's committed. But the rights that you're not talking about are his right to free speech, his right to talk with whomever he wants. . . . I don't understand why those rights are—why you ignore those and simply say that he has—that he's welcome to come back to the United States and exercise his right to be tried by a jury of his peers. Why is that the only right that he gets, according to this Administration? [30]

If there were now to be categories of free speech and propaganda, Wheeler's article commenting on Psaki's performance pointed out, beyond what had been the historic "rule of reason," where did that leave the Constitution? Of course the administration's position hinged—somewhat as it had in the drone killing of Anwar al-Awlaki, an American citizen living in Yemen—on justifying the murder based on the "imminence" of the threat he posed to "national security" so as to waive his Fourth Amendment right to a jury trial. In Snowden's case, free speech, the First Amendment right, was trumped by concerns vaguely called "propaganda," just as in al-Awlaki's the Fourth Amendment was trumped by vaguely defined "imminence." [31]

It is of some interest that the Justice Department's Office of Legal Counsel (OLC) memorandum justifying the killing of al-Awlaki was kept a close secret by the administration until a federal court ordered its release in June 2014. Even then, large portions dealing with the circumvention of the Fourth Amendment had been redacted. American Civil Liberties Union deputy legal director Jameel Jaffer commented, "The release of this memo will allow the public to better understand the scope and implications of the authority the government is claiming."[32]

The NSA and OLC both made claims to extraordinary authority for what the government was doing. Defenders of the Bush and Obama administrations' insistence that their policies were warranted by 9/11 often cited the Supreme Court's 1979 decision in *Smith v. Maryland* that a telephone subscriber did not have a Fourth Amendment right to privacy about telephone numbers he dialed since he had voluntarily given his approval to the phone company to track numbers called for billing and other purposes. Extrapolating from that decision, proponents said the government's program was no more intrusive than what Verizon did.

It was a demonstrably false comparison, as retired executive editor Max Frankel wrote in the *New York Times* on June 22, 2014. The issue was not how we balance personal privacy with police efficiency, as the Supreme Court decision had been interpreted, he argued. He wrote, "We have long since surrendered a record of our curiosities and fantasies to Google. But Google and Amazon do not indict, prosecute and jail the people they track and bug. The issue raised by the National Security Agency's data vacuuming is how to protect our civil liberty against the anxious pursuit of civic security. Our rights must not be so casually bartered as our Facebook chatter. Remember 'inalienable'?"[33]

President Obama and his team repeated almost endlessly that the data vacuuming had prevented several dozen potential terrorist attacks, "with elliptical references to threats against New York City's subways and stock exchange." "Even if true and satisfying," Frankel went on, they are being publicized only because "this huge data-gathering effort could no longer be denied": "As those of us who had to defend the 1971 publication of the secret Pentagon Papers about the Vietnam War have been arguing ever since, there can be no mature discussion of national security policies without the disclosure—authorized or not—of the government's hoard of secrets." As for the supposed watchdog FISA Court, it

was no court in the customary sense, operating in secret and without "any real challenge to the evidence, [its judges] function more
as a grand jury than a court. Mr. Obama conceded that only a few
warrants have ever been turned down (a few have been modified),
a success rate he attributes to government restraint." But the opposite was more likely the case, as the court acted as a facilitator
for the NSA to protect it against legal actions. Frankel pointed out
that FISA judges were like "members of Congress, who pose as
watchdogs but melt when they hear appeals to patriotism from the
managers of the intelligence service."[34]

What ought to compound skepticism, Frankel concluded, was
the news that there was money to be made in the mass approach.
Much of the snooping was farmed out to profit-seeking corporations with great appetites for government contracts secured by executives who enriched themselves by shuttling between agency
jobs and the contractors' boardrooms. "We have privatized what
should be a most solemn government activity, guaranteeing bloat
and also the inevitable and ironic employ of rebellious hackers
like Mr. Snowden," he wrote.[35]

Max Frankel was a voice from past wars over the Pentagon Papers; not all of his colleagues in the mainstream media rushed to
defend Snowden's actions. Indeed, NBC's David Gregory pursued
a different line on *Meet the Press*, asking Greenwald, "To the extent that you have aided and abetted Snowden, even in his current
movements, why shouldn't you, Mr. Greenwald, be charged with
a crime?"[36] It was more a prosecutor's than a reporter's question.
Greenwald shot back, "I think it's pretty extraordinary that anybody who would call themselves a journalist would publicly muse
about whether or not other journalists should be charged with
felonies." Gregory backed off a step or two but did not abandon his
position, citing "lawmakers" who had raised points about Greenwald's claims. "Well, the question of who's a journalist may be up
to a debate in what you're doing. And of course anybody's who's
watching this understands I was asking a question; that question

has been raised by lawmakers, as well. I'm not embracing anything. But obviously, I take your point."

Not even Richard Nixon had gone so far in the Pentagon Papers case as to assert what was and what was not journalism under the First Amendment. Clearly, 9/11 had transformed the nation, fostering the intelligence community's growth into a Leviathan true to Thomas Hobbes's famous description of the state. The Snowden affair did not happen in isolation but was part of a much larger war being waged against not only leakers but investigative journalism of both traditional and nontraditional modes. We must turn now to the bigger picture.

4

Front Lines—Leakers and the New (Old) Journalism

What bothers me the most is we've allowed ourselves to become terrorized. And we've done that to ourselves.

—James Risen, October 19, 2014

Rather than be too aggressive about publishing these stories, I think we have been too meek. I frankly regret my decision back in 2003 to withhold from publication a story by Jim Risen about Iran's nuclear program.

I've come to believe that unless lives are explicitly in danger . . . almost all these stories should be brought out in public.

—Jill Abramson, former managing editor of the
New York Times, December 3, 2014

God forbid we wake up tomorrow and ISIL is in the United States.

—Senator Marco Rubio, November 19, 2014

Edward Snowden was called out by his critics for making it easier for terrorists to evade apprehension before they carried out new attacks on the West. The British spy agency GCHQ seemed the most alarmed of all—and the most certain about the damage done by the American who leaked the documents to *The Guardian's* Glenn Greenwald. The current spymaster, Sir Iain Lobban, said the leaks had had a devastating effect on counterterrorism operations, as well as those against organized crime. "We have actually seen chat around specific groups . . . discussing how to avoid what they now perceive to be vulnerable communications methods, or how to select communications which they now perceive not to be exploitable."

Asked whether these overheard discussions related directly to the Snowden revelations, Sir Iain replied, "It is a direct consequence. I can say that explicitly."[1] Alan Rusbridger, the editor of *The Guardian*, took all such comments in stride. The Snowden File stories had played out very differently in various countries, he said. In Germany they stirred bad memories of the Stasi listeners taking down every word East Germans spoke even in the privacy of their homes. "And so it doesn't require much imagination as a journalist to see the danger of the state having extraordinary, intrusive power into citizens' lives." But the British are different. "They think of their spies as James Bond or the Enigma machine, so we quite like our spies." Aside from people like Sir Iain, however, the "Brits were a bit complacent."[2]

Journalism, Rusbridger insisted, was an essential thing needed for a society to function. From its beginnings in the early nineteenth century, he said, *The Guardian* had aimed at exposing government wrongdoings. "I think of journalism as like a fire service, or like a water utility. . . . It doesn't have to be a printed thing, but a resilient organization with professional training and standards, [so] that when it comes under ferocious attack, [it] can defend its journalism." Terrorism was a threat, but if fear of terrorism "is going to be used to trounce 300 years of civil liberties, that's a disaster for the rest of the world."[3] Glenn Greenwald was a perfect example, Rusbridger argued, of the new journalism "that was going to be created in the future by people who were not just journalists." At the time *The Guardian* hired Greenwald, for example, "he had an avid following of about a million of his own people. . . . We thought he was an interesting figure and we wanted to harness that."[4]

One of those million was Edward Snowden. When asked why he had decided to contact filmmaker Laura Poitras and Glenn Greenwald instead of the *New York Times*, he said that the newspaper at the center of the Pentagon Papers challenge to government overreach had faltered in recent times by refusing to print James Risen and Eric Lichtblau's 2004 story on warrantless domestic eavesdropping. After *The Guardian* and *Washington Post* shared the Pulitzer Prize for public service, the *Times*'s new executive editor, Dean Baquet, told an interviewer, "It was really painful. There is nothing harder than, if you are the *New York Times*, getting beat on a big national security story—and to get beat by your biggest overseas competitor and your biggest national competitor, at the same time. It was just painful."[5]

"I am much, much, much, much more skeptical of the government's entreaties not to publish today," added Baquet, "than I was ever before." When Baquet made this comment, journalists' discontent with the Obama administration had reached a level never experienced before even during the last years of the Bush presidency. Immediately after inauguration day in January 2009, Barack Obama had taken steps to ease the process of declassification of documents under the Freedom of Information Act and ordered agencies to wield the confidential or top secret stamp with less frequency and more concern for openness in government. But these intentions were countered by increasing pressure from the intelligence community to shut down leaks. Obama's first director of national intelligence, Dennis Blair, had noted that in the previous four years 153 national security leaks had been referred to the Justice Department as "crime reports," but the FBI had investigated only 24—and no leaker had as yet been prosecuted.[6]

According to Blair, the *New York Times* reported, all that changed after Fox News reported in June 2009 that American intelligence had gleaned word from within North Korea of plans for a nuclear test. Blair then met with Attorney General Eric Holder Jr., and they coordinated a more aggressive approach for producing speedy prosecutions, explaining, "We were hoping to get somebody and make people realize that there are consequences and it needed to stop."[7] The Justice Department indeed "got somebody"—a low-level State Department contractor, Stephen Kim, and sent a powerful message about "consequences" to reporter James Rosen. In a secret subpoena for Rosen's phone records and personal e-mails, it stated that "there is probable cause to believe that the reporter has committed or is committing a violation" of the Espionage Act—"at the very least, either as an aider, abettor and/or co-conspirator."[8]

Later it was discovered that the government had secured secret subpoenas for the telephone records of the Associated Press in the Bush administration going back to 2002, as well as the personal records of another reporter, James Risen, by invoking the mantra of national security. Attorney General Holder reacted to these discoveries by insisting that the subpoena for the co-conspirator charge was warranted, while testifying to Congress that the focus should be on the leaker, and then had a Justice Department spokesperson issue a statement (or claim) that reminded critics of the argument in the Middle Ages about how many angels could dance on the head of a pin: "Saying that there is probable cause to believe that someone has committed a crime and charging the person with that crime are two different things."[9]

Three days later, the president said in a speech at the National Defense University that he was "troubled by the possibility that leak investigations may chill the investigative journalism that holds government accountable." But his administration continued to invoke the Espionage Act as justification for secret subpoenas. "This kind of puts us into the deep freeze," commented one of Edward Snowden's attorneys, Jesselyn Radack. "I feel like we're back to the Dark Ages." Using the Espionage Act to get access to reporters' e-mails was setting a dangerous precedent. It was "beyond chilling."[10]

The debate ranged from whether Rosen's "flattery" of Stephen Kim to get a story was a criminal act, to the question of what was journalism and what was theft of government property. The debates and the cases blurred into one another throughout Obama's presidency from its earliest days.

Michael Hastings and the "New" Journalism

Perhaps no figure better represents the "new" journalism of the Internet Age than Michael Hastings, whether one admires his courage or loathes his methods. He is approximately the same age—a little older, actually, but far more flamboyant—than Edward Snowden. The day after Greenwald's first article appeared online, Hastings titled his article on BuzzFeed "Why Democrats Love to Spy on Americans." Like Snowden, Hastings had supported Barack Obama in 2008, and like the disappointed analyst who went to Hong Kong to meet with reporters, Hastings had grown deeply disillusioned.

At one time, he had believed that the military had forced Obama's hand in 2009 when the new president ordered a "surge" of thirty thousand troops in Afghanistan. It was under that impression, and the apparent belief that he could help Obama with his brand of journalism, that Hastings ingratiated himself with the new commander in Afghanistan, General Stanley McChrystal, and his aides, and wrote an article for *Rolling Stone* magazine that quoted the general and his aides disparaging the president and various American diplomats. His apparent objective was to liberate the president from a general and a strategy that was headed nowhere. "What they told me, I realized, revealed the attitudes behind one of the most brazen assaults on civilian control of the military that the Pentagon generals had ever attempted." McChyrstal was fired, although Obama had to deny it had anything to do with Hastings's article.[11]

Hastings won the George Polk Award for investigative journalism, but mainstream journalists more often than not saw him as an interloper, an unwelcome presence whose main objective was to draw attention to himself by being rude to his hosts. CNN ran a piece entitled, " 'Runaway General,' or Runaway Reporter?" CBS News' Lara Logan said, "Michael Hastings has never served his country the way McChrystal has." No one challenged the authenticity of his article, however. The Pentagon's inspector general, who looked into the matter, issued a weasel-worded report that said "not all of the events at issue occurred as reported in the article," though it concluded that this meant only that no one remembered certain things described in the article.[12]

Even before the Snowden revelations, however, Hastings had cast aside his notion of saving Obama from the Pentagon generals. On May 25, 2013, he said on MSNBC that the president had bought into George Bush's neoconservative worldview. It was the day after Obama went to the National Defense University to defend the use of drones under specific circumstances. "If you compare this speech to the speech he gave in Cairo, in 2009, or his Nobel Prize speech, you see almost a total rejection of the civil rights tradition that President Obama supposedly came out of . . . and just an embrace of total militarism."

Then came the article on the NSA's demand that Verizon turn over its records to the government. "For most bigwig Democrats in Washington, D.C., the last 48 hours has delivered news of the worst kind—a flood of new information that has washed away any lingering doubts about where President Obama and his party stand on civil liberties, full stop." That was the first sentence of his long harangue directed at the White House on BuzzFeed. Hastings reached back to find Senator Carl Levin's attack on Bush for hiding an unauthorized program of wiretapping and avoiding using the law Congress had provided for the use of warrants even where there was a supposed emergency. Urgent action on such requests could be obtained from the courts, so there was no need, Levin had said at that time, for doing something illegal and dangerous to constitutional precedents.

"Now," wrote Hastings, "we're about to see if the Obama administration's version of the national security state will begin to eat itself. Unsurprisingly, the White House has dug in, calling their North Korea–esque tools 'essential' to stop terrorism, and loathe to give up the political edge they've seized for Democrats on national security issues. . . ."

The government, he said, sought to ruin reputations where it could not prosecute, as in the case of Glenn Greenwald.

That's not to mention former NSA official Thomas Drake (the Feds tried to destroys his life because he blew the whistle); Fox News reporter James Rosen (named a "co-conspirator" by Holder's DOJ); John Kiriakou, formerly in the CIA, who raised concerns about the agency's torture program, is also in prison for leaking "harmful" (read: embarrassing) classified info; and of course Wikileaks (under U.S. financial embargo); WikiLeaks founder Julian Assange (locked up in Ecuador's London embassy) and, of course, Bradley Manning, the young, idealistic soldier who provided the public with perhaps the most critical trove of government documents ever released.

The attitude the Obama administration has toward Manning is revealing. What do they think of him? "Fuck Bradley Manning."

Screw Manning? Lol, screw us.[13]

Little wonder Hastings engendered such strong feelings. Comparing Obama to North Korean leaders is a sure way to get liberals angry. It was not surprising that many of Hastings's best press notices came in places like the *American Spectator*, a traditionally rightist journal. Of course, the neocon right had little use for his opinions, but none of that slowed him down.

Early on the morning of June 18, 2013, Hastings was killed in a one-car accident in Los Angeles, when his new Mercedes C250 jumped a median and crashed into a tree. He had been driving at very high speeds approaching the crash site. Witnesses saw three explosions and the engine thrown thirty feet from the car; it took several days to identify the driver as Hastings. At once conspiracy theories grew up around the death of the young iconoclast. The scene was soon covered with tiny American flags, and notes praising Hastings's writings were tacked to a tree. Conspiracy theories exploded all over the Web. These were mostly based on unsupported allegations that quickly evaporated. But there were some things that stood out. Hastings feared the FBI was closely watching him, and he contacted various people about his concerns. He was supposed to be writing another exposé article for *Rolling Stone*, on CIA director John Brennan.

But the most dramatic comments came from Richard Clarke, the former antiterrorism expert in the Clinton and Bush White House who had opposed the Iraq War in his last days in office. He told the *Huffington Post* that what was known about the accident was "consistent with a car cyber attack." And, "There is reason to believe that intelligence agencies for major powers" know how to seize control of a car from a remote location. "You can do some really highly destructive things now, through hacking a car, and it's not that hard." You could, for example, cause acceleration when the driver did not want it, or throw on the brakes, or cause an airbag to launch. "So if there were a cyber attack on the car—and I'm not saying there was," he added, "I think whoever did it would probably get away with it."[14]

He insisted that he was not a "conspiracy guy" and that he had spent most of his life knocking such theories. "But my rule has always been you don't knock down a conspiracy theory until you can prove it [wrong]. And in the case of Michael Hastings, what evidence is available publicly is consistent with a car cyber attack. And the problem with that is you can't prove it."

A few months later, Richard Clarke served on a committee created by President Obama to examine potential reforms to NSA programs, reforms that would strike a new balance between civil rights and security. Its report, authored by Clarke and others sympathetic to the president, refuted claims Obama had made standing next to Angela Merkel that the program had prevented fifty terrorist attacks. The report concluded that perhaps only one such attack had been prevented.

James Risen's Story

New York Times reporter James Risen's long-running fight to protect his sources began when he and Eric Lichtblau attempted to
publish a story on warrantless wiretapping in October 2004. At
that time President Bush was denying the existence of a warrantless wiretap program. The paper's editor, Bill Keller, hesitated to
publish the story without consulting the White House. Keller had
been named editor in 2003. He came in just as the Bush war on
Saddam Hussein had been sold to the public as the only way to
prevent the tyrant from using his weapons of mass destruction.
The WMD had never been found—because they did not exist.
The *Times* bore some responsibility for the war fever as its chief
reporter on WMD, Judith Miller, passed on to the paper Cheney-
esque accounts of Hussein's capabilities.

In May 2004, Keller wrote an editorial in effect apologizing for
the *Times*'s lack of rigor in challenging the White House's prewar
claims and for not following up when new evidence showed that
the stories were planted by anti-Hussein campaigners like Ahmad
Chalabi, who still had hopes of becoming the top man in Iraq.
To his credit, Keller admitted that it was not only Judith Miller
but editors at several levels who failed to be skeptical about government claims. "We consider the story of Iraq's weapons, and
of the pattern of misinformation, to be unfinished business. And
we fully intend to continue aggressive reporting aimed at setting
the record straight." Several years later he would add, "The whole
Judy Miller WMD experience was . . . one of the low points of the
last eight years."[15]

When Keller visited the White House with the Risen-Lichtblau
story documenting the NSA's activities, however, the president's
men told him that he would have blood on his hands if he published it. Inside the administration, as well as in Congress, there
were profound disagreements about whether the wiretapping was
legal. As Risen and Lichtblau wrote, the NSA was operating its
program on the basis of classified opinions from the Department

of Justice Office of Legal Counsel that said the 2001 Authorization to Use Military Force (AUMF) gave the president all the power he needed to initiate the program. But the orders were known only to a few. When one senior official learned about the operation, he recalled, "My first reaction was, 'We're doing what?' " Then he decided that there were sufficient safeguards. But the supervising judge of the normally complaisant FISA Court, Colleen Kollar-Kotelly, disagreed. Because the government was trying to cover up the existence of the NSA program, she said, there was a danger that the information obtained would not stand scrutiny. And as a former senior Bush administration figure said, "Some officials wanted nothing to do with the program, apparently fearful of participating in an illegal operation." If John Kerry were elected, he added, there might be criminal investigations. All these questions had led Bush to suspend the program for a time in order to revamp it.[16]

It remains very hard to understand why Keller yielded to White House pressure not to publish this article, especially after his "fool me once" experience and his confession that the paper had fallen prey to a "pattern of misinformation" from the same sources. Risen and Lichtblau certainly did not understand why the editor insisted that the story was not ready to publish until there was other input. The information in back of the story had come from Thomas Tamm, a Justice Department attorney, who had leaked it to Lichtblau. Tamm said in an interview with National Public Radio, "Some very experienced high-level lawyers believed that what the government was doing was illegal." It ought to have been clear to Keller that the White House's main objection had to do with embarrassment in the middle of the presidential campaign. Risen and Lichtblau kept pushing to have it printed. Finally, Risen warned Keller that he had signed a book contract and the story would be in there—along with a lot of other exposés. "He had a gun to their head," said Lichtblau. "They are really being forced to reconsider," because "the paper is going to look pretty bad." If a reporter published the story in a book instead of the paper, it would have been "catastrophic for the *New York Times*." [17]

The discussion in the editorial offices turned into a real row, recalled Risen. "That led to this massive game of chicken between me, my book, . . . and the *New York Times* over the next few months." It was finally published on December 16, 2005. The next year Risen's *State of War: The Secret History of the CIA and the Bush Administration* was published with more on the wiretapping—but even more important with a whole section on Operation Merlin, a scheme devised by the CIA to set the Iranians off on a wrong path in developing atomic bombs by giving them flawed diagrams. However, the Russian nuclear engineer chosen as a conduit—code-named Merlin—either noticed the problem and tipped off the Iranians to preserve his credibility and his life (according to Risen) or followed the CIA's instructions by telling the Iranians that the plans were incomplete and demanding more money for the rest (according to CIA internal memos released after the project was revealed). In any case, the ploy backfired, accelerating the Iranian nuclear program instead of delaying it, and helping them design a bomb more advanced than your basic Hiroshima.

The Risen and Snowden stories were entangled in various ways—and would continue to be as events played out in the media and the courtroom. Ewen MacAskill, a *Guardian* reporter who traveled to Hong Kong with Greenwald and Poitras in the first interviews with Snowden, told National Public Radio that the *Times*'s treatment of the wiretapping story was the reason Snowden had contacted Poitras and then Greenwald and Barton Gellman of the *Washington Post*. He did not trust the *New York Times*. Risen believes, moreover, that the FBI investigations of his e-mails began right after the publication of this story: "I was told by a reliable source that Vice President Dick Cheney pressured the Justice Department to personally target me because he was unhappy with my reporting and wanted to see me in jail."

Meanwhile, he had won a Pulitzer Prize for the story, his second Pulitzer since 9/11.[18]

Risen was subpoenaed after *State of War* was published to appear as a witness against Jeffrey Sterling, a former CIA analyst whom the Department of Justice accused of leaking the Merlin story. In *State of War*, Risen relates how the CIA used a Russian expatriate to carry plans for a nuclear weapon to Vienna to sell to Iranian officials. He was to show up in the Austrian capital posing as a "greedy" scientist who felt misused and neglected after the Cold War, eager to sell the plans. His CIA handlers told him that they believed the Iranians already had this information and that this plot was meant merely to confirm American intelligence sources. The plan, however, was straight out of a John le Carré novel, as the Russian was being used to plant misinformation. What the Merlin wizards had not counted on was that the Russian scientist sent on this mission would tell the Iranians in indirect fashion that the plan had flaws—and that he could help them resolve any problems![19]

Of course, that was the one thing that the Iranians should not have been told, because the plan was otherwise genuine, in the sense of being accurate. Why he did this remains somewhat of a question, but if he thought his handlers had been truthful with him, that he was not conveying new information, then he may have believed that maintaining his credibility with the Iranians would make him useful to his new bosses for other missions. The CIA had launched this dangerous scheme in the wake of a mistaken message sent to its assets in Iran that a double agent had turned over to Iranian officials. This intercepted message enabled them to "roll up" the entire CIA network in Iran.

It's important to note that Risen had no intention of sabotaging American policy. In *State of War*, he expresses concern about Iranian ties to terrorism, and his research into Merlin convinced him that the CIA's desperate efforts to play catch-up had led to a risk of *increased* damage to American security.

Nevertheless, his writing about failures and divisions within the intelligence community infuriated the Bush administration. Even so, the subpoena was eventually dropped, but then it was renewed by the Obama administration in 2010 when it formally charged Sterling with the crime of providing classified information to a journalist. Risen's contacts with Jeffrey Sterling went back to 2002, when the *Times* reporter wrote a story about Sterling's complaints that he was being discriminated against because of racial bias. All these contacts were among those listed in the indictment filings by the Department of Justice—indicating how far government had reached into personal records. "In hindsight, it was the first clear evidence the Justice Department was digging into the phone and e-mail records of both government officials and journalists while investigating leaks."[20]

When the government renewed the subpoena, Risen filed a motion asking the court to quash it on the ground that it violated the First Amendment's free press guarantee. He included an affidavit summarizing what he had written in *State of War*— "explosive revelations about a series of illegal or potentially illegal actions taken by President Bush," the warrantless wiretapping, the pressure on the CIA to use torture on prisoners around the world, ignoring information that Iraq did not have weapons of mass destruction, and punishing professionals who said the war was not going well.[21]

A federal judge, Leonie Brinkema, gave an opinion favorable to Risen's First Amendment claims. Attorney General Holder then filed a brief that rejected any notion of a reporter's constitutional privilege to protect sources in criminal proceedings. The brief dismissed the idea that such reporting could be in the public interest. And in what *New Yorker* writer Steve Coll called "a low point in First Amendment litigation," the brief asserted that a reporter who hears classified information during an interview with a government official was a witness to a crime under the Espionage Act of 1917— and was no more free not to testify than a witness to a murder.[22]

Justice Department lawyer Robert A. Parker asserted that there was no reporter's privilege in such a case and that the public's interest in a free press was not an issue of balance. "I don't think there would be a balancing test because there's no privilege in the first place," said Parker. "The salient point is that Risen is the only eyewitness to this crime." Parker then argued that what Risen did was "analogous" to a journalist receiving drugs from a confidential source, and then refusing to testify about it.

The determination of the Obama administration to bunch together actual crimes like murder, victimless or consensual crimes like drug dealing, and public-interest crimes like whistleblowing or leaking, then to push everything under the Espionage Act— that was a completely new development. The attitude displayed by DOJ lawyers was perhaps even more indicative of the direction the administration was headed, putting reporter's privilege in quotes whenever the brief addressed arguments by Risen or his attorneys.[23]

Along with this stratagem, the government denied that Sterling could be considered a whistleblower. "Jeffrey Sterling is not a whistle-blower," contended one former Department spokesperson. "He was fired for cause. He went to court [to sue] and the case was thrown out. No waste, fraud, or abuse was involved." The government argument in the Sterling case and others is that there can be no whistleblowing on any government activity that is defined by the government as pertaining to national security; thus whistleblowing can apply only to waste, fraud, or abuse in nonsecret programs, leaving a vast area of unmentionable federal actions. In effect, no reporter can legally reveal anything that officials have hidden, and "our" spies answer only to themselves.

Speaking to the National Press Club, Risen said, "It's a fairly basic constitutional issue for the press, whether or not there is a reporter's privilege. It's something a lot of people outside the press don't really understand, don't really care about. I think the basic issue is whether you can have a democracy without aggressive investigative reporting and I don't believe you can. So that's why I'm fighting it."[24]

When the appellate court handed down its decision, Risen lost. He promptly vowed to go to jail rather than break the confidentiality of his source. He even suggested in a bit of black humor that perhaps now his job of investigative journalism would be easier because sources would have even greater reason to trust him. But the court's decision invited even more serious restrictions on leakers. There was no First Amendment testimonial privilege, it said, "absolute or qualified," that protected a reporter from being compelled to testify "about criminal conduct that the reporter personally witnessed *or participated in.*"[25]

After the Supreme Court refused to take up the case for further review, Risen awaited a final decision by the administration over whether it would actually threaten jail time. Meanwhile, Attorney General Holder issued new guidelines to offer greater protections for reporters, and the administration backed proposed legislation that would give judges greater powers to quash such subpoenas. As with all past efforts to rein in the intelligence chiefs and their allies, Risen noted, the problem with such legislation was it carved out "a huge loophole" for national security reporting. "But that is the area where most leak investigations occur, and so the shield law would not accomplish much. In fact, it might have the unintended consequence of giving the government the power to determine what journalism deserves protection under the shield law, and what does not, thus creating a de facto Official Secrets Act."[26]

A shield law could actually make matters worse by setting out whole areas in which it did not apply. Given the experience of the Risen case and another one that actually spurred the administration to *get* someone, it seems fairly evident that that would be the most likely outcome of a shield law.

The Press as Co-conspirator: The Jim Rosen Case

The Justice Department took the same stance in another leaker case, the matter of Stephen Jin-Woo Kim, who was charged with criminal spying under the Espionage Act. Kim, a State

Department contractor, had handed over a classified document that suggested North Korea would probably test a nuclear weapon in response to a UN resolution condemning previous tests. He was indicted in August 2010 under the Espionage Act for giving the report to Fox News's chief Washington correspondent, James Rosen. The Justice Department named Rosen "at the very least, either as an aider, abettor and/or co-conspirator."[27]

The Kim-Rosen case had several precedent-setting aspects. No reporter had ever been charged as a co-conspirator in such a case, certainly not one in which the drastic penalties of the Espionage Act came into play. Second, Rosen's treatment more than suggested that if WikiLeaks founder Julian Assange was, as he expected to be, extradited from England to Sweden and then to the United States to face co-conspirator charges like those against Rosen, the whole WikiLeaks operation could be shut down. Kim's indictment was about one not very important speculative document. Next to Assange's or Snowden's mass revelations, it was nothing. Except it really was, for while it remained in a back corner as the front-page headlines featured Assange and Snowden, the implications were tremendous for future reporters.

Dana Milbank broke details of the story in the *Washington Post* on May 21, 2013, arguing that it was part of the administration's broad snooping into phone records, but even more serious. "The Rosen affair is as flagrant an assault on civil liberties as anything done by George W. Bush's administration, and it uses technology to silence critics in a way Richard Nixon could only have dreamed of." The revelations established the fact that the government had subpoenaed the e-mails of various news organizations going back several years—without informing the organizations. It could thus read the messages that had passed back and forth without any of the writers knowing that they were being read. Attorney General Eric Holder had signed off on the warrant to search Rosen's e-mails and continued to maintain that it was fully justified. Milbank reported that the reporter had been shadowed going in and out of the State Department. A foreign-policy hawk, Rosen was definitely a conservative, and he was on the lookout for any items that would discredit the Obama administration's supposedly "soft" policies. "Let's break some news," Rosen encouraged Kim in one of the e-mails, "and expose muddle-headed policy when we see it, or force the administration's hand to go in the right direction, if possible."[28]

That was unusually blunt, but no doubt reporters say similar things (whether they mean them or not) to induce reluctant sources to provide information. Kim told investigators that Rosen was a very convincing and persistent person. The charge against Rosen in the subpoena was that he had used flattery and other methods to cajole Kim into talking. Not surprisingly when confronted with his "options" under the Espionage Act, Kim readily agreed with prosecutors. "It is possible I succumbed to flattery," he admitted. When reporters took up the Rosen case with White House press secretary Jay Carney, they got the usual nonresponse. The president believed there must be a balance between a free press and leaks that "can endanger the lives of men and women in uniform and other Americans serving overseas."[29]

Carney added, however, that the president did not think "journalists should be prosecuted for doing their jobs." Holder also expressed the same view: journalists should not be prosecuted for *doing their jobs*. The warrant that the administration sought in the Rosen case had named him as a "co-conspirator." The administration's loophole strategy came a bit undone when House Republicans called Holder out on his testimony to the Judiciary Committee that the Justice Department was not moving to prosecute journalists. He had said on that earlier occasion, "With regard to the potential prosecution of the press for the disclosure of material: that is not something I've ever been involved in, heard of, or would think would be wise policy." Then the Rosen story broke, and the committee now wanted to know how he squared that testimony with language in the warrant that named Rosen a co-conspirator. Erik Wemple wrote in the *Washington Post* that "Holder didn't appear to break a sweat" in his answering letter.

There was a difference, the attorney general said, between an actual prosecution and what went down in the Rosen case. Under
the law, the DOJ head said, the government was required to show
that there was evidence "that the reporter had committed or was
committing a criminal offense to which the needed materials related." It was an investigative step, "and at no time during the matter have prosecutors sought approval from me to bring criminal
charges against the reporter."[30]

But there was much more to the Rosen case. To begin with,
the Privacy Protection Act of 1980 banned the government from
newsroom searches for the purposes of obtaining "documentary
materials relating to a criminal investigation" except when there
was probable cause to believe the person possessing such materials had committed a crime. In order to do such a search, therefore, it became necessary to tar Rosen. But there is still more here
that concerned the rights of journalists and all citizens. Holder's
claim about the requirements of the law could suggest that it be
amended so that in national security cases, warrantless searches,
as in the early Bush days, should be made legal—to avoid future
cumbersome and confusing distinctions between "investigation"
and "prosecution."

The attorney general's explanations, moreover, had been forced
out of the administration. Its lawyers had argued for keeping the
search warrant secret, on the remarkable grounds that some investigations have lasted for "many years." "E-mail evidence derived
from those compelled disclosures," argued U.S. Attorney Ronald
C. Machen Jr., "frequently forms the core of the Government's
evidence supporting criminal charges."[31] James Risen told an interviewer that the president was not as liberal "as people thought
he was," but even more to the point, he does not like the press.
And Democrats had not been willing to speak up against the president on this issue. It only demonstrated that government is not
willing to give up its powers once it has them, and besides, it has
proved easy to "scare people on national security issues."[32]

Machen finally concluded a plea agreement with Kim that

called for him to be imprisoned for thirteen months, far less jail time than federal guidelines recommended. The length of the term was not so important, obviously, as the conviction. A big bonus was that the State Department employee did not claim to be a whistleblower. Despite its attempt to brush off the whistleblower defense in other cases, the administration had had a hard time with backlash against its attitude that conscience doesn't count in national security cases. Getting Kim to deny that he was a whistleblower meant it had gone two for two: he admitted he had been flattered into committing an illegal act, and denying he was a whistleblower helped quiet public uneasiness. These considerations no doubt figured in the government's sentence recommendations. Machen's statement on the outcome of the case reads, "Stephen Kim admits that he wasn't a whistleblower. He admits his actions could put America at risk. . . . As this prosecution demonstrates, we will not waver in our commitment to pursuing and holding accountable government officials who blatantly disregard their obligations to protect our nation's most highly guarded secrets." [33]

Faced with the alternative of a fifteen-year sentence, Kim opted to cooperate with federal agents by admitting that he wasn't a whistleblower and that his actions could put Americans at risk—despite the absence of any evidence that a speculative government report on how North Korea would react to a UN resolution would harm anyone. When asked what specific damage Kim's revelations had caused, government prosecutors dodged the question, saying that he had betrayed a trust and put "our nation's security at risk," by indirectly alerting North Korea to what U.S. intelligence officials "knew or did not know about its military capabilities and preparedness." [34]

Kim's lawyer, Abbe Lowell, made it clear that he thought his client was being made an example of for other purposes and that national security was not the real issue, however. "Lower-level employees like Mr. Kim are prosecuted because they are easier targets or often lack the resources or political connections to fight back.

High-level employees leak classified information to forward their agenda or to make an administration look good with impunity."[35]

After the Kim case brought to light the search of Rosen's e-mails, the Obama administration decided it was time to make some cosmetic adjustments. New guidelines were put in place to stop the FBI from searching reporters' e-mails unless that person is the target of a criminal investigation, or (always the *or*) unless informing news organizations of an e-mail search would "risk grave harm to national security, or present an imminent risk of death or serious bodily harm." A search warrant for a reporter's records could not be obtained unless the reporter is "the target of the leak investigation and not because he obtained classified information while reporting." Exactly how that was a gain for the First Amendment was pretty unclear, however, because presumably if, like Rosen, the reporter initiated the contact and was not a passive recipient of information, he could be targeted. The result could be to put such prosecutions on a firmer footing by allowing the government to cite "extraordinary" circumstances.[36]

"The Justice Department does not target whistleblowers," a DOJ statement issued to respond to critics declared.

Should any federal employee wish to blow the whistle or report government wrongdoing, there are well-established mechanisms for doing so with the Offices of Inspector General of their respective agencies. With regard to classified information, there is a particular statute providing lawful mechanisms for reporting such matters. We always encourage federal employees to do so. However, we cannot sanction or condone federal employees who knowingly and willfully disclose classified information to the media or others not entitled to receive such information. An individual in authorized possession of classified information has no authority or right to unilaterally determine that classified information should be made public or disclosed to those not entitled to it. *The leaker is not the owner of such information and only the owner can declassify such information* [italics added].[37]

With this declaration, the Department of Justice endorsed a doctrine of "ownership" of a document within the federal government that has delayed publication of documents in the Department of State's Foreign Relations series, on the grounds that the final say over declassification rests with the originating agency. The novel idea that a specific government agency "owns" a classified document as a person might own ten acres of prime real estate has yet to be squared with any serious concept of open government. The doctrine is a big gift to the intelligence community. It is also another means of cracking down on whistleblowers. In the end, the Rosen/Kim case, despite the intense backlash and the superficial contriteness of the Department of Justice in setting new ground rules, left the intelligence community and its allies in the congressional oversight committees farther ahead in the game. The Kim case made only a fleeting impression in the 24/7 news parade, a fast-disappearing note on the ever-flowing ribbon at the bottom of CNN—but its effects have been long range and form a bastion for classifiers in the war on leakers.

Manning and Assange: The WikiLeaks Factor

In terms of government transparency, the megaload of documents that Specialist Bradley E. Manning sent to Julian Assange, founder of WikiLeaks, was far and away more dramatic than anything James Risen or James Rosen published on the basis of government sources. Moreover, as it pursued the case against Manning for violating the Espionage Act, the government acted as if the exposed documents were still a secret and issued a bizarre notice that all government employees were not to read or cite these documents. In other words, no one in an official position was supposed to read the stories and documents in the *New York Times* and other media outlets. At the highest level in the State

Department, only Secretary of State Hillary Clinton was permitted to read and comment on their contents—or so it would seem. One reason such a ban was imposed, of course, was to keep up the idea that the owner of a document was the originating agency, and no one else could declassify it. This pro forma pantomime only suggested how tangled in knots the government could get in response to leakers, for everyone else in the world could use the documents in discussing American foreign policy, or comment at length about their meaning.

The number of documents Manning dispatched to Julian Assange included more than 250,000 State Department cables, 500,000 U.S. Army incident reports, dossiers on terrorist suspects detained at Guantánamo Bay, and videos of two air strikes that killed civilians in Iraq and Afghanistan.[38] Meanwhile, American officials had tried to have it both ways when the WikiLeaks documents started appearing in the newspapers. Secretary of State Hillary Clinton had something of a rough go in trying to explain why, if the documents were so threatening, respectable newspapers were reprinting them day after day? In a press conference on November 29, 2010, Clinton condemned Manning's disclosures as "risking lives," the same language against all leakers. "Let's be clear: This disclosure is not just an attack on America's foreign policy interests," Clinton told journalists. "It is an attack on the international community—the alliances and partnerships, the conversations and negotiations that safeguard global security and advance economic prosperity." Later in the news conference, however, she quipped that one foreign leader had shrugged off the revelations, telling her, "You should see what we say about you."[39]

Assange promptly challenged the State Department to offer some proof that the documents put anyone's life at risk and received a tart reply from the department's legal adviser Harold Koh. There would be no "negotiations" about the release of any documents he had obtained illegally and what they meant to national security. In other words, lawyerly obfuscation. Vice President Joe Biden even called Assange a terrorist, using language that indicated that the U.S. government would certainly indict the flamboyant purveyor of documents that were, as Clinton pretty much admitted in her statement about what a foreign leader had told her, embarrassing rather than life threatening. To be sure, there is little question but that Julian Assange loved the headlines his actions brought. He has a powerful ego, perhaps as powerful as men who run for high office and then see themselves as above the law. And he made many enemies among former supporters.

The most incriminating item Manning revealed was the videotape showing an Apache helicopter firing on unarmed men trying to rescue a wounded Reuters reporter in Baghdad. At least twelve civilians are shown being methodically machine-gunned to death. "Throughout the massacre, the army radio transmissions are heard, a combination of grimly sterile orders to 'engage' the victims and a string of mocking exchanges among the soldiers, belittling the victims and celebrating the slaughter."[40] In the days after it appeared in April 2010, it became the most watched video online. The notoriety forced the Pentagon to "investigate," but it concluded to no one's surprise that the army helicopter had been following standard rules of war throughout the engagement. The Apache's crew had been pursuing armed insurgents for some time during that day and could not tell from their sightings, concluded the investigators, if the men they shot were armed or not. Besides, the report said, enemy fighters often carried cameras; it was simply a tragedy of the sort that happens in warfare.

Manning was apprehended in July 2010, after Adrian Lamo, a hacker he had trusted, informed the authorities. Daniel Ellsberg called Manning a hero.[41] Ellsberg then reflected on the period when he was a strong supporter of American policy in Vietnam. "I was no Chelsea Manning in 1964 or Edward Snowden, nor was anybody else, who could have acted as they did later and say, 'Here are the documents. Here is the evidence that we are planning a wider war right after the election.' " Manning and Snowden were too late to prevent what took place. The problem was not that they were leakers, Ellsberg contended, but that there was no one out in front of the drive for war. "The lack of a Manning or a Snowden . . . was crucial to getting us into Iraq based on lies."[42]

In the wake of the WikiLeaks exposé, the government on October 7, 2011, launched an unprecedented effort to see that such a thing never happened again. It became known as the Insider Threat program, and it commanded government workers to observe and report unusual behavior among their colleagues. The premise, which some psychologists disputed, was that it would be possible to predict who would become a leaker. The Insider Threat "documents" were themselves leaked to reporters for McClatchy DC, who wrote that federal employees and contract employees were being asked to pay special attention to the "lifestyles, attitudes and behaviors—like financial troubles, odd working hours or unexplained travel—of co-workers as a way to predict whether they might do 'harm to the United States.' "[43]

The Insider Threat program mandated that the nearly 5 million federal workers and contractors with security clearances undergo training in order to be able to recognize suspicious behavior. Immediate questions arose about the effectiveness of the program. Potential leakers in that group—if one can call 5 million a group—would presumably receive the training and be made more aware of how to avoid looking suspicious. It also presumed that one analyst could readily recognize the suspicious actions of a colleague. How was one to know if the colleague was reading a document she shouldn't be? Some of those who worked most closely with the administration in developing test profiles of potential leakers admitted the weaknesses. "We have not found any silver bullets," admitted a behavioral psychologist for the Mitre Corporation, a nonprofit company working for the Department of Defense and intelligence agencies. "We don't have actually any really good profiles or pictures of a bad guy, a good guy gone bad or even the bad guy walking in to do bad things from the very beginning."[44]

The Insider Threat program was imagined as a deterrent to future Mannings and Snowdens, but it was based on a predictive scheme that made government officials and workers at all levels spies on one another—with all the pitfalls and temptations that would involve. It was an invitation to tattletales eager to gain favor with a supervisor. Would it really work the way it was supposed to?

James Risen has not revealed the source of his story on Operation Merlin, and his behavior must make other sources more likely to trust him. The harder the government pursued him, the less it gained as deterrent and the more it stirred up its critics. Still under threat of going to jail for refusing to name his source, Risen interviewed Snowden in Moscow in an encrypted online exchange. The former government computer analyst, who had once targeted Chinese operations and taught his colleagues about Chinese cybercounterintelligence, denied that he had given any documents to either the Chinese or Russians. He said there was a zero-percent chance they had received any documents. He had given them all to journalists, who had filtered what they published. This was the first time he had said this, he told Risen, because he was concerned that the journalists would suffer greater scrutiny. Snowden had decided to reveal the existence of the NSA programs because he was concerned about the scope of the whole program, not any specific surveillance operation. He had become a whistleblower because "programs that are implemented in secret, out of public oversight, lack that legitimacy, and that's a problem. It also represents a dangerous normalization of 'governing in the dark,' where decisions with enormous public impact occur without any public input."[45]

In an interview with Lesley Stahl, Risen elaborated on this point. His story that the *Times* delayed for over a year until he declared that it would be published in his book, which the NSA then attempted to prevent being published, didn't reveal to anybody that the United States was listening to terrorist phone calls. "Everybody knew that. The terrorists have known that forever. What we were revealing was that the U.S. government was violating its own laws." Former NSA head Michael Hayden appeared in the same interview and startled Stahl by saying that he was "conflicted" by the Risen article on warrantless wiretapping. He did not retreat from the position that it had done damage. "I think, 'America will suffer because of that story.' But then I have to think about, so how do I redress that? And if the method of redressing that actually harms the broad freedom of the press, that's still wrong. The government needs to be strong enough to keep me safe, but I don't want it so strong that it threatens my liberties."

Hayden seemed to get to the heart of the matter—but not quite. The underlying issue, still unspoken, involved the careers of men like Hayden himself, who have run the intelligence agencies the way they've been run at least since the Bay of Pigs—"in the dark"—men whose influence extends to misleading the president and Congress. It's the enormous power of the spymasters, not the Snowdens or Mannings who occasionally expose them, that raises the most profound questions about the role of secrets in our democracy.

5

Prosecutions and Principles

When I chose to disclose classified information in 2010, I did so out of a love for my country and a sense of duty to others. I'm now serving a sentence of 35 years in prison for these unauthorized disclosures. I understand that my actions violated the law.
—Chelsea Manning, June 14, 2014

Though the outcome of my efforts has been demonstrably positive, my government continues to treat dissent as defection, and seeks to criminalize political speech with felony charges that provide no defense. However, speaking the truth is not a crime. I am confident that with the support of the international community, the government of the United States will abandon this harmful behavior.
—Edward Snowden to Chancellor Angela Merkel, European Parliament president Norbert Lamment, and German attorney general Harald Range, October 31, 2013

As the number of prosecutions of people charged with violations of the Espionage Act grew, it was perhaps inevitable they would form a bond. Although Chelsea Manning's trial and sentence and Edward Snowden's flight to Russia drew the most attention, there were other cases that became part of what some called a modern form of civil disobedience against the surveillance state.

James Risen, for example, happily used the Elijah Parish Lovejoy Journalism Award ceremony at Colby College to elaborate on the connections between the actions of Lovejoy, a martyred abolitionist editor, and those of post-9/11 leakers. "He was a disruptive force; that's the language we would use today." Long before the abolitionist cause became an almost irresistible force in American politics, Lovejoy had taken his stand with a newspaper in the 1830s at the center of the slave controversy, Saint Louis, Missouri. He published articles opposed to slavery three decades before the Civil War. "By doing so, he was committing the dangerous sin of challenging the conventional wisdom of his day." [1]

Risen's speech was a direct challenge to the prosecutions of leakers, citing the Intelligence Identities Protection Act and the Espionage Act as equivalents of the nineteenth-century laws protecting slavery. In his short tenure as director, David Petraeus celebrated the prosecution and sentencing of former CIA officer John Kiriakou to thirty months in prison for revealing to a news reporter the identity of a retired covert operative who had been involved in waterboarding. The prosecution had been under the Intelligence Identities Protection Act of 1982. "The case yielded the first successful prosecution in 27 years," Petraeus told CIA employees, "and it marks an important victory for our agency, for our intelligence community, and for the country." [2]

Kiriakou's conviction and sentencing stood in stark contrast to what had happened nearly a decade earlier when a high-level aide to Vice President Dick Cheney outed a *current* covert operative, Valerie Plame, in a newspaper article by Robert Novak. Her outing was a counterstrike by Bush officials who were angered that her husband, Joseph Wilson, had written a *New York Times* op-ed piece that detailed how the administration had used false information about the supposed transfer of yellowcake uranium from Niger to Iraq to build momentum for the Iraq War. Lewis "Scooter" Libby was convicted of perjury and obstruction of justice but not of violating the Intelligence Identities Protection Act. He was fined $250,000 and sentenced to thirty months in prison, later commuted to nonprison service by President Bush. Libby's leaks were politically motivated to protect the Bush administration's duplicity in selling the war; Kiriakou blew the whistle on the waterboarders, who carried out their crimes with presidential approval. "Which matters more," asked Steve Coll, a *New Yorker* staff writer and later dean of the Columbia School of Journalism, "Kiriakou's motives or his reliability, or the fact that, however inelegantly, he helped to reveal that a sitting president had ordered international crimes? Does the emphasis on the messenger obscure the message?"[3]

Manning and Thoreau

Does Coll's point about the Kiriakou case apply also to those who have taken it upon themselves to reveal government secrets en masse to challenge ongoing policies? Where does one draw the line? Chelsea Manning's actions were a direct challenge to the conduct of the Iraq War and foreign policy in general, framed around the mid-nineteenth-century idea of civil disobedience.

Writing from prison in Fort Leavenworth, Kansas, after serving four years of a thirty-five-year sentence for releasing hundreds of thousands of documents to WikiLeaks, Manning explained the process by which she became disenchanted with American policy. The turning point for her was the 2010 Iraq election, portrayed in a flood of American press stories as proving that the U.S. military had "succeeded in creating a stable and democratic Iraq." Those stationed in Iraq, she wrote, knew that the reality was much more complicated. Military and diplomatic reports detailed "a brutal crackdown against political dissidents" by Iraqi authorities, including torture and assassination. Having received orders to investigate a number of individuals who had been arrested on suspicion of printing "anti-Iraq literature," Manning learned that they instead were publishing a scholarly critique of the Maliki administration. After forwarding this finding to the officer in command in eastern Baghdad, Manning was told to give that case up and assist the federal police in locating more "anti-Iraq" print shops. Manning wrote, "I was shocked by our military's complicity in the corruption of that election. Yet these deeply troubling details flew under the American media's radar."[4]

More shocks were to come as Manning realized that there were no more than a dozen vetted reporters embedded with American forces. Worse, the reporters were given favorability ratings that determined whether they should be included on the "yes list." Upon being approved, reporters had to sign a ground-rules statement that permitted authorities to terminate a reporter's embed without appeal. One of those who'd had his access pulled was Michael Hastings, following his critical article about General McChrystal in *Rolling Stone*. A Pentagon spokesman said, "Embeds are a privilege, not a right."[5] The system was rigged, making it all but impossible for the public to hold its military and political leaders accountable. That was the situation Manning wished to challenge by sending WikiLeaks secret documents that ranged from combat reports in Iraq to American diplomacy in a number of countries. Like Edward Snowden's actions, this was not an impetuous gesture by a naive young soldier who didn't understand the big picture.

Turned in by a hacker "friend," Manning was arrested in May 2010, brought back to the United States, and put in a cell on a marine base in Quantico, under "suicide watch" rules that critics said were used as pretrial punishment, which is unlawful even in the military. Manning was kept in a six-by-eight-foot cell twenty-three hours a day and allowed twenty minutes of "recreation" a day but was not permitted to exercise and was forced to wear a suicide smock instead of clothes. After finally being examined by army psychiatrists, Manning was removed from the potential suicide list—but the prisoner's treatment remained the same. Asked why that was so by defense attorney David E. Coombs, the brig commander replied that, even though regulations say such a prisoner "shall" be moved to a less restrictive cell, he did not move Manning into the general prison population because "*shall* does not mean immediately or right now" (emphasis added).[6]

Even though it is less bodily painful than other methods, long-term solitary confinement is considered a form of torture. For example, the highly respected author of *Being Mortal*, the doctor and medical writer Atul Gawande, pointed to numerous studies about what long-term solitary confinement does to an individual. Confinement for periods exceeding a week produces a constellation of symptoms that include anxiety, confusion, hallucinations, and violent self-destructive behavior. Manning was held in solitary for months before trial, illegal pretrial punishment that in Europe would be a violation of the European Convention on Human Rights.[7]

Questions about Manning's treatment came up at a White House press conference in March 2011. The president responded by saying that he had "actually asked the Pentagon whether or not the terms of confinement were appropriate and are meeting our basic standards. They assure me that they are." He added, "I can't go into details about some of their concerns, but some of this has to do with Private Manning's safety as well." About this same time, however, P.J. Crowley, the State Department's spokesman, was forced to resign after calling the Pentagon's treatment of Manning "ridiculous, counterproductive and stupid."[8]

Moreover, the judge at Manning's court-martial, Colonel Denise Lind, ruled that, yes, the pretrial treatment had been illegal. Manning's confinement was "more rigorous than necessary," she said, and conditions "became excessive in relation to legitimate government interests." As a result, before the trial began, she reduced any sentence given by 112 days, the time he spent in Quantico before being transferred to the next prison—scarcely more than a nod toward admitting government obligations to respect human rights.[9]

Meanwhile, President Obama's other pretrial statements were equally tendentious. A few weeks after the Crowley firing, he addressed a $5,000-a-ticket fund-raising dinner in San Francisco. After the speech he was approached by a Manning supporter, Logan Price, who wanted to know why he hadn't mentioned the concerns of the protesters who had come to defend the leaker.

Obama defended draconian measures first by saying, "So people can have philosophical views [about Manning] but I can't conduct diplomacy on an open source [basis]. . . . That's not how the world works. . . ." Then he pretended to be in the same boat as Manning. "And if you're in the military . . . I have to abide by certain rules of classified information. If I were to release material I weren't allowed to, I'd be breaking the law."

Price responded that Manning had released evidence of war crimes. Obama replied, "What he did was he *dumped—*"

Wasn't that what Daniel Ellsberg did? asked Price.

"No, it wasn't the same thing. Ellsberg's material wasn't classified in the same way."

The president would have been better off if he had said that Ellsberg's leak was of historical documents, while Manning actually leaked *less* highly classified but more contemporary files. The White House PR crew immediately swooped in to say that the president was not prejudging Manning's case. He was only making a "general statement that did not go specifically to the charges against Manning." Instead, "The president was emphasizing that, in general, the unauthorized release of classified information is not a lawful act," but "he was not expressing a view as to the guilt or innocence of Pfc. Manning specifically."[10]

Parsing presidential "off the cuffs" is always a challenge. Meanwhile, Manning's trial was delayed; a verdict did not come until July 2013. In the meantime, Edward Snowden had met with reporters in Hong Kong.

Catching Snowden on the Run

A few days after Snowden's arrival in Russia, President Obama told a press conference in Senegal, "I'm not going to be scrambling jets to get a twenty-nine-year-old hacker." That line got all the attention in the press, but Obama's longer answers to questions about Snowden were not nearly so dismissive.

One came in response to a pointed question: "How frustrated or angry are you, sir, that China's defiance and Russia's indifference have vastly complicated the pursuit of Mr. Snowden and turned it into what some people regard as kind of an international game of cat and mouse that's almost farcical?" Obama replied:

> I have not called President Xi personally or President Putin personally. And the reason is because, number one, I shouldn't have to. This is something that routinely is dealt with between law enforcement officials in various countries. And this is not exceptional from a legal perspective.
>
> We've got a whole lot of business that we do with China and Russia. And I'm not going to have one case of a suspect who we're trying to extradite suddenly being elevated to the point where I've got to start doing wheeling and dealing and trading on a whole host of other issues simply to get a guy extradited, so that he can face the Justice system here in the United States. . . .

He was sure, he said, that the Snowden story would make quite a movie, but he was interested in making sure that everyone understood that the purpose of the NSA programs was to protect America, not to be a Big Brother snooping over everyone's shoulder. He did not deny, however, that efforts were being made to convince countries not to grant asylum. He continued:

OBAMA: And my continued expectation is that Russia or other countries that have talked about potentially providing Mr. Snowden asylum recognize that they are part of an international community, and that they should be abiding by international law. And we'll continue to press them as hard as we can to make sure that they do so.

QUESTION: Do you believe that all the damage that he can do has been done by Mr. Snowden? Is that what you're saying, Mr. President?

OBAMA: What I'm saying is that he has those documents. He has released some of them. Not all of them have been released. The damage that's been done essentially goes to the fact of some of these programs. And we don't yet know what other documents he may try to dribble out there. . . . And we are trying to declassify as much as possible, so that the American people and our international partners feel confidence about how we operate in this regard.

Despite what the president claimed in Senegal, the *Washington Post* reported that his aides held daily White House meetings searching for ways to nab Snowden. When the newspaper asked about these meetings, the busy National Security Council spokesperson Caitlin Hayden "clarified" the president's remarks. His comments, it appeared, referred only to the prospect of using military assets. "The president made clear he wouldn't," said Hayden. "Not because we weren't working hard to get Snowden back to the U.S.," but because it was a law enforcement matter.[11]

White House aide Lisa Monaco chaired these daily sessions. "The best play for us is him landing in a third country," Monaco told the members of this special committee, which included senior officials from the FBI, CIA, State Department, and other agencies. In case that happened, the United States had indeed scrambled a CIA-operated Gulfstream business jet with the tail number N977GA and sent it to Denmark to be ready in case Snowden made that misstep. Denmark had been a fully cooperating country in the Bush "rendition era," and Gulfstream N977GA was the plane of choice for such missions. The plane was tracked over Scotland on June 25, 2014—*just two days before Obama told reporters that he would not be scrambling jets to nab Snowden.* The trackers belonged to an Internet aircraft-tracking network. "We knew the reputation of this aircraft and what it had done in the past," a member of the group told a British paper.[12] The White House special committee met every day for weeks, according to the *Washington Post*, but always came up against the reality that unless the government took the final step of naming him an "agent of a foreign power," he could not be a target for a special operation overseas.

The desire to nab Snowden resulted in a notorious episode when Bolivian president Evo Morales visited him in Moscow and signaled publicly that he would consider giving the leaker asylum in his country. "Why not?" he asked during his visit. "Bolivia is there to welcome personalities who denounce—I don't know if it's espionage or control." Washington took the "threat" seriously and immediately enlisted its NATO compradors France, Spain, Italy, and Portugal to intercept the Bolivian president's flight home.[13] "We have been in touch with a range of countries that had a chance of having Snowden land or travel through their country," said a State Department official. Of course, explained Caitlin Hayden, "The United States did not request any country to force down President Morales's plane. . . . What we did do . . . was communicate via diplomatic and law enforcement channels with countries through which Mr. Snowden might transit." How those countries might then respond to the American message was apparently a matter of free choice.[14]

Having been denied permission to transit western Europe, Morales's flight made a sudden U-turn as it crossed Austria and landed in Vienna. Austrian authorities boarded the plane and searched the cabin—with Morales's permission, officials said—but there was no sign of Snowden. Austria claimed that the plane had been making a refueling stop, but a *Washington Post* article said Austrian officials had been "skeptical of the plan from the outset" but apparently were arm-twisted into detaining the plane. "We would have looked foolish if Snowden had been on that plane sitting there grinning," said a senior Austrian official. "There would have been nothing we could have done."[15]

The Bolivian president had no good reason to help in the search for Snowden, for the United States had turned down his request to extradite former Bolivian president Gonzalo Sánchez de Lozada, accused of genocide and crimes against humanity. The U.S. government had already filed an extradition request in case Snowden was on the plane, but Bolivian officials called the United States' extradition request "strange and illegal," because Morales had not even spoken with Snowden in Moscow, nor had Snowden requested asylum. It was all theoretical. But the Bolivian president, the first from among the nation's indigenous people, made his "humiliation" into a great show when he returned home. It gave him a great opportunity to declare that he had both defied and been a victim of the "Great Colossus of the North."

Morales had no sooner landed in La Paz than the Organization of American States (OAS) passed a resolution condemning "actions that violate the basic rules and principles of international law such as the inviolability of Heads of State," and called upon the European governments involved—France, Italy, Portugal, and Spain—to explain their actions and apologize. It was a sad lesson for Obama, who, during his press conference in Senegal, had called upon Russia to abide by the requirements of international law despite the absence of an extradition treaty with the United States. "My continued expectation," he'd said then, "is that Russia or other countries that have talked about potentially providing Mr. Snowden asylum recognize that they are part of an international community, and that they should be abiding by international law. And we'll continue to press them as hard as we can to make sure that they do so." [16]

Despite Washington's pressure, all members except Canada and the United States voted for the OAS resolution. When Snowden was nominated for a European human rights award, the former NSA head Michael Hayden quipped at a panel on cybersecurity hosted by the *Washington Post*, "I must admit in my darker moment over the past several months, I'd also thought of nominating Mr. Snowden, but it was for a different list." The audience laughed. Representative Mike Rogers, who had declared that Snowden was under Russian control, was there and chimed in, "I can help you with that list." The list they were talking about, of course, was the "kill list" decided upon in the Oval Office on Tuesdays. [17]

Getting rid of Snowden by a drone strike was a fantasy, a bit of black humor, but the panic Snowden had caused had become a genuine menace to the conduct of foreign relations, marring the self-image of the United States as an exceptional nation—or rather, *the* exceptional nation. David Pozen, writing on the influential centrist-conservative website *Lawfare*, put Washington's predicament accurately in an essay titled "What Happens When We Actually Catch Edward Snowden?" It was important to ask this question, Pozen wrote, because the denouement to this drama might well be unpleasant not just for the fugitive, but for his captors as well.

Snowden faced prison time in the United States; no court has ever allowed a classified-information leaker to go scot-free. But the Obama administration, Pozen wrote, had taken "leak enforcement to a new level," with unpredictable results. Polls suggested that many Americans agreed with Snowden that his leaks had revealed an unconstitutional and undemocratic system of surveillance. Then there was the public clamor sure to accompany Snowden's trial, with high-powered lawyers, journalists galore, and pickets outside. It was inevitable that a trial would drag on for months; all that time, the focus would remain on NSA spying, not the crime of exposing it. "It could be a focal point for domestic and international outrage. From the executive branch's institutional perspective, the greatest danger posed by the Snowden case is not to any particular program. It is to the credibility of the secrecy system, and at one remove the ideal of our government as a force for good."

The Assange Factor

Meanwhile, in London, WikiLeaks founder Julian Assange had entered the Ecuadoran embassy in July 2012 seeking asylum. The British were determined to extradite him to Sweden to face charges of sexual assault. From Sweden, the United States would be able to have him extradited to face trial in America. Indeed,

Assange maintained, a grand jury in Virginia was already meeting on his case. There Assange remained, with police guarding the exits 24/7, prepared to nab him the second he tried to leave. His living quarters were certainly better than Manning's, but he was cramped in more ways than one, although he continued to monitor new WikiLeaks releases of documents. Inside the embassy, Assange sleeps on an inflatable mattress, has a lamp that mimics natural light, and jogs on a treadmill given to him by a film director. When he first took refuge there, the British Foreign Office threatened to go in after him, but pulled back in deference to the general international rule against host countries attacking foreign embassies. For the first two months, Ecuadoran diplomats slept in the embassy, where there had been no bedrooms, just in case something untoward did happen. And indeed, Ecuador's intelligence service discovered a microphone hidden in the ambassador's office, leading the foreign minister to complain of a "loss of ethics at the international level in relations between governments."[18]

Assange would play a key role in securing Snowden's escape from Hong Kong, providing the funds for his air flight and sending a top assistant, Sarah Harrison, to accompany him on his journey. Harrison also became Snowden's amanuensis in Russia, arranging his news conferences and sitting beside him as he spoke to various groups. Harrison has since left Moscow and taken up residence in Berlin, because she fears that if she attempts to return to England she will be arrested. She noted that "Britain has a Terrorism Act, which has within it a portion called Schedule 7, which is quite unique . . . it gives officials the ability to detain people at the border as they go in or out or even transit through the country. This allows them to question people on no more than a hunch, giving them no right to silence, no right to a lawyer."[19]

Assange took one step too far when he tried to push Ecuador into giving Snowden asylum. A WikiLeaks statement when Snowden left Hong Kong, stewarded by Sarah Harrison, asserted that he was not headed for Moscow—at least on a permanent basis. "He is bound for the Republic of Ecuador via a safe route for the purposes of asylum," and "is being escorted by diplomats and legal advisors from WikiLeaks. Mr. Snowden requested that WikiLeaks use its legal expertise and experience to secure his safety. Once Mr. Snowden arrives in Ecuador his request will be formally processed." President Rafael Correa then went on television to say that such statements were unauthorized—though understandable, given fears for Snowden's welfare. The embassy felt that Assange could be perceived as usurping the role of the country's diplomats, that he was running things and conducting business on Ecuador's behalf. Assange duly apologized to Ecuador's foreign minister.[20]

Outside the embassy, a block away from an entrance to Harrod's, two Metropolitan Police vans remain parked. As of mid-2015, the cost to British taxpayers for this twenty-four-hour surveillance is £11 million and counting.

Assange's hideout became a popular site for leakers to gather. Among the pilgrims to WikiLeaks' temporary head office has been Daniel Ellsberg, who commented that "we are exiles and émigrés." In December 2012, Thomas Drake—the former NSA senior official who had been charged with violating the Espionage Act—met with Assange and returned the next month for a potluck dinner with other supporters. Laura Poitras, the filmmaker and later go-between for Snowden and Glenn Greenwald, interviewed Assange several times while making her short documentary *The Program*, which featured another former NSA veteran, William Binney, who was also the target of an FBI investigation for an alleged leak of secrets to a reporter.[21]

Poitras's video of Ellsberg and Binney meeting supposedly changed Edward Snowden's life forever. After seeing the film, he contacted her, asking for her encryption key and suggesting that they might find a secure channel to communicate—the beginning of the most famous leak of all time. However their experiences persuaded Snowden to act, they also left him with no doubt about what he was risking when he went to Hong Kong to meet with Poitras and Greenwald.

The Thomas Drake Affair

In March 2010, a DOJ prosecutor named William Welch told a preliminary hearing that a former NSA computer expert and supervisor, Thomas Drake, had endangered the lives of U.S. service personnel. "This is not an issue of benign documents," Welch solemnly announced. He would explain why the crime was so serious. The NSA collects "intelligence for the soldier in the field. So when individuals go out and harm that ability, our intelligence goes dark and our soldier in the field gets harmed." The assistant attorney general who supervised the Department of Justice's criminal division told the *New Yorker's* Jane Mayer, "You don't get to break the law and disclose classified information just because you want to."[22]

What Drake had done, according to the DOJ, was to sneak documents out of NSA headquarters in 2007, then leak these documents to Siobhan Gorman of the *Baltimore Sun*. A former air force officer and a Republican, Drake had gone to work for the NSA on September 11, 2001. He had been in the air force as a cryptolinguist, flying in an RC-135 in the latter years of the Cold War. "We called ourselves the 'vacuum-cleaner of the sky' because our capability to gather information was enormous at the time. But it was always outward-facing: we could not collect on US targets because that was against the law." After the attacks on 9/11, the day he went to work at the Fort Meade headquarters of the National Security Agency, everything changed—and stayed changed when Barack Obama came into office. "To the US government today, . . ." according to Drake, "we are all foreigners."[23]

In the wake of 9/11, Drake began full-time work on a project called Thin Thread. The team that developed Thin Thread believed it addressed a key problem that had contributed to the intelligence failures leading to the attacks on the World Trade Center and the Pentagon. That problem was data overload. The proposed solution was a way to process collected data and eliminate useless information on the spot instead of sending it all back to headquarters for analysis. It also operated on the basis of an "anonymizing feature," ensuring that all American communications would be encrypted and citizens' privacy protected until a warrant was issued. A key player in the Thin Thread project was William Binney, who perfected the feature.

A brilliant analyst whose work went back to the Vietnam War, Binney said Thin Thread was ready to go operational in 2000. Prototypes had been deployed in Washington State and Germany. "That's why we proposed early deployment in January 2001." Various midlevel intelligence officers witnessed demonstrations, but, Binney complained, NSA head Michael Hayden never showed up at any of them. "Not once." On August 21, 2001, at 4:30 p.m., noted one of the Thin Thread team, they were notified that it would not become operational.[24]

At the same time, another data-tracking program, Trailblazer, was being developed outside government labs by private contractors and was already proving to be a very expensive sinkhole without any practical results. Nevertheless, Hayden shepherded and defended Trailblazer from development to failure. When it was shown off to congressional representatives and intelligence leaders, said Drake, there were big TV screens and fancy computers stacked high in a large building leased to one of the contractors, Northrop Grumman. "But that's all it was: show and tell, a dog and pony show." Trailblazer was "an industrial-age model so inappropriate for the digital age. . . . Here we were going in the completely opposite direction." When it was finally canceled in 2006, Trailblazer had cost the government $1.6 billion with no results. Hayden admitted that Trailblazer had overreached. "We tried a moonshot and it failed."[25]

When their favored solution came up short, NSA officials reworked Thin Thread, stripping it of privacy controls. "When you remove that, you can target anyone," Binney said. Drake heard about the arrangements being made with telecom and credit-card companies to supply the government with metadata including individual identifiers. The transformation of the NSA was so radical, he later told Jane Mayer of the *New Yorker*, that "it wasn't just that the brakes came off after 9/11—we were in a whole different vehicle." [26]

Binney left the agency in 2003, fed up with the corruption, but also with the changes in Thin Thread. The United States, he told an investigative reporter later, had created a police state with few parallels in history. "It's better than anything that the KGB, the Stasi, or the Gestapo and SS ever had." Drake had stayed on for a while, protesting both Trailblazer's costs and the changes in Thin Thread, in what became a bitter bureaucratic battle on top of everything else. Told by his immediate superior to talk to the agency's general counsel, Drake said he did, and the top lawyer, Vito Potenza, told him, "Don't worry about it. We're the executive agent for the White House. It's all been scrubbed. It's legal." When he pressed further, Potenza told him, "It's none of your business." [27]

In 2005, however, the Pentagon's Office of the Inspector General carried out an audit that confirmed what the critics had been saying: Trailblazer was a waste of resources and a garden of fraud. The agency had even "modified or suppressed" studies that put Thin Thread in a positive light. The OIG also noted that the atmosphere in the NSA under Michael Hayden had made those who came forward afraid of retaliation. "Many people we interviewed asked not to be identified for fear of management reprisal." [28]

Drake's persistence had annoyed a lot of people, especially those who believed in the White House desire to collect it all and keep it all secret. Drake didn't back off but continued to pepper colleagues with e-mails denouncing the way he believed the NSA had transformed itself into a freewheeling semiautonomous detective agency with the capacity of peering into private lives. A former NSA consultant recalled Drake's increasing frustration in "alarmist memos and e-mails," including one that declared, "The place is almost completely corrupted." Still he stayed on. In his quest to rescue Thin Thread, Drake approached a series of internal watchdogs and "developed a close relationship with . . . Diane S. Roark, who tracked the security agency for the House Intelligence Committee." She had long had doubts about Trailblazer and had fought to keep Thin Thread alive. It was her idea, said people who knew Mrs. Roark, that Drake contact Siobhan Gorman of the *Baltimore Sun*.[29]

And there began the story of how Drake's determination led to his prosecution. Drake sent Gorman a series of encrypted e-mails signed only, "The Shadow Knows." He did this half in jest, he told Jane Mayer, but he warned the journalist not to reveal his identity. He also demanded that she not use any tips he sent her as the sole source for a story and said he would not supply any classified material. He did admit, however, that he had copied some words from classified documents and put them in the e-mail. Perhaps concerned a bit about the Deep Throat comparison, Drake abandoned his cover, showed up at the newspaper, and introduced himself to a surprised Gorman.[30]

Then came a crucial fusion of suspicions by eager government security agents. The leaker who had spoken with James Risen about the warrantless wiretaps remained unknown at this time, but it was easy for NSA officials to believe that whoever it was also had connections to Trailblazer critics. The idea of a conspiracy on the inside came naturally to those whose jobs involve both finding other people's conspiracies and creating their own when ordered to do so. Diane Roark, who had left Washington in 2003, was called in by the FBI and signed an affidavit that she was not the source for the *Times* story on wiretapping or for Risen's *State of War*. The search for Risen's source eventually led to Jeffrey Sterling, the alleged Operation Merlin whistleblower, and the trial that developed into an ambiguous victory for the Obama administration's use of the Espionage Act against leakers. On July 26, 2007, federal agents raided Roark's house and the homes of Binney and another former NSA specialist. As it happened, they were all connected at this time in a venture to pursue commercial projects based on Thin Thread—a plan that had received clearance from NSA—but their inability to get much interest indicated to them that they had been blackballed for their role in uncovering Trailblazer's sorry history. Now the government was doing more than harassing. Binney was in the shower, and he recalls, "They went right upstairs into the bathroom and held guns on me and my wife, right between the eyes." They confiscated computer equipment and documents, including a copy of the Inspector General's report on Trailblazer. Binney professed innocence of any charges, and was told, "We think you're lying. You need to implicate someone."[31]

Binney suggested that his interrogators look elsewhere for criminal conspirators: they should focus on Bush and Hayden for allowing warrantless surveillance. Roark, like Binney and Drake, had always been a law-and-order person. Drake expected that he was next, but no one came for a while. Then on the morning of November 28, 2007, he saw armed agents streaming across his lawn. After they advised him that he could remain silent, Drake decided that this was yet another opportunity to blow the whistle. When he talked about Trailblazer, sitting across from agents at his kitchen table, they told him they were not interested in cost overruns of a defunct project, or in warrantless wiretapping. They wanted to know about the *Times* story and his connections to James Risen. Drake denied he was their man but did confirm his many contacts with Gorman, in fact several hundred e-mails.[32]

The "dialogue" continued for several months, until April 2008, when he was told by a DOJ prosecutor, "You're screwed, Mr. Drake. We have enough evidence to put you away for most of the rest of your natural life." The haul from Drake's computer and home office netted a few low-level classified documents, some pertaining to dates of meetings and others that he had kept because the Pentagon inspector general had suggested that witnesses keep copies of documents they had used in preparation for the hearings. These documents all pertained to the internal debates over

Trailblazer; it was not the evidence that the Bush men had hoped to find, showing that he had leaked the warrantless-wiretap story to James Risen. When the meager nature of what had been found seemed not to merit an indictment, the government shifted its position. The Bush administration declined to pursue the matter, but Attorney General Holder's Department of Justice resurrected the Drake case and pushed ahead with charges. Now he was charged under a separate section of the Espionage Act for illegal retention of documents, and for collecting data from unwitting colleagues to give to Ms. Gorman.

The case soon collapsed. Most of the documents found in Drake's home, admitted a DOJ lawyer, were not even low-level classified. Other officials had been talking publicly about the same questions. Drake finally pleaded guilty to a misdemeanor for improper use of a government computer, and received a sentence of two hundred hours of public service, which he performed by collecting oral histories of veterans. Drake's government career was finished, however, and his security clearance was stripped. When the judge handed down the sentence, he said it was "unconscionable" that Drake and his family had endured "four years of hell" before the government dismissed the ten-count felony indictment.[33] Nonetheless, the judge vastly underestimated the damage done to Drake's career, his future livelihood, and his family. He now works in a retail Apple store in Bethesda, Maryland.

In 2008, the unknown leaker who told James Risen about the Bush warrantless wiretapping finally revealed himself. The source was a colleague of DOJ spokesperson Matthew Miller, a Justice Department lawyer named Thomas Tamm. But Eric Holder decided not to prosecute that case, explaining there had to be a balance "between what our national-security interests are and what might be gained by prosecuting a particular individual." Tamm stated that the prosecution of Drake should never have proceeded at all because he never revealed anything to the *Baltimore Sun* of the same order of sensitivity as the wiretapping info: "The program he talked to the *Baltimore Sun* about was a failure and wasted billions of dollars. It's embarrassing to the N.S.A. but it's not giving aid and comfort to the enemy."[34]

The experience has made Drake a dedicated opponent of the surveillance state. He is as tireless in supporting fellow whistle-blowers as he had been in pursuing fraud in Trailblazer "advertisements." In public appearances, noted the social critic Jacob Silverman, Drake speaks "with a humorless fervor, like a preacher in a Western." He told an audience on Long Island, "I've lived the surveillance state already. This is not something that's coming. I've already lived it."

It is of little comfort to Drake that his old antagonist at the NSA Michael Hayden agrees that the prosecution under the Espionage Act was overreach. "He should have been fired for unauthorized meetings with the press. Prosecutorial overreach was so great that it collapsed under its own weight."[35]

Kiriakou's Punishment

Thomas Drake escaped prison time, but the CIA officer who led the team that located and captured senior Al Qaeda operative Abu Zubaydah in Pakistan in 2002 was later given a thirty-month sentence for giving freelance journalist Matthew Cole and *Times* reporter Scott Shane the names of two CIA agents who could provide information about the Bush torture program. The *Times* never printed the names. Nevertheless, the government achieved a plea deal that put John Kiriakou in jail for thirty months.

Threatened with a much longer prison sentence under the Espionage Act, Kiriakou pleaded guilty to violating the Intelligence Identities Protection Act. It was one of several high-five moments for Ronald Machen and the Department of Justice. Unlike Stephen Kim, however, Kiriakou did not go quietly into the federal prison at Loretto, Pennsylvania, on February 28, 2013, and he did far more damage to the surveillance state after being imprisoned, with a series of Letters from Loretto that appeared on the website FireDogLake.com.[36]

Kiriakou maintains that his "crime" was revealing details about the Bush torture program to a reporter, thus confirming that the United States was indeed using such methods in an effort to obtain information about the perpetrators of 9/11 and about future plots. He was arrested in early 2012 and charged with three counts of espionage and one count of violating the Intelligence Identities Protection Act for giving the name of a former CIA colleague to a reporter. President Obama and Attorney General Eric Holder had admitted that waterboarding went on and that it was torture. But the new administration had quickly declined to go any deeper into the matter, much less to consider possible prosecutions of those in the CIA who carried out or approved the "enhanced interrogations," let alone the ex-president. The name Kiriakou supplied to Scott Shane was of a retired agent, not one still undercover. Even so, Kiriakou's willingness to talk about what had happened was infuriating to people who were enjoying Obama's gift of immunity.

Critics questioned the president's insistence that it was time to look ahead, not to remonstrate about the past or carry out investigations that could inhibit CIA agents from following illegal orders out of fear of prosecution. In 2010 this policy was heavily underlined by the Department of Justice's refusal to prosecute Jose Rodriguez Jr., a former clandestine officer who had approved the destruction of ninety-two video recordings of the waterboarding of two prisoners out of concern that the tapes could harm the CIA. Rodriguez had ordered their destruction in the Thailand prison where they had been kept, even though doing so disobeyed instructions given him by CIA lawyers and the White House. DOJ spokesman Matthew Miller felt that the decision was the right one. A team of prosecutors and FBI agents "conducted an exhaustive investigation into the matter," he explained, and decided against prosecution. Obama's new CIA director, Leon Panetta, welcomed the announcement with relief. "We will continue, of course, to cooperate with the Department of Justice on any other aspects of the former program that it reviews." Apparently Panetta did not even dare to use the word *torture*, lest it harm "morale" in the agency. Lest there be any doubts about his feelings about the legal question, he said, "We are pleased that the decision was not made to charge any Agency officers for the destruction of the tapes."[37]

Kiriakou, ironically, felt the same way—initially. After he left the agency, his first appearance on ABC News in 2007 was in defense of waterboarding as effective almost immediately in bringing Zubaydah to confess. He was not present in the room at the time, however, and only later learned that it had been applied over eighty times—and that it had not produced the evidence claimed.[38]

As his views evolved under such revelations, he continued to be asked about waterboarding. He still thought it wrong to second-guess the CIA's actions in 2002, but he now began to think that it was essential to have a national debate over whether we should be waterboarding in the future. "Some human rights activists even suspected—wrongly, as it turned out—that the intelligence agency was orchestrating his public comments." But the CIA began sending referral slips to the Department of Justice, heads-ups that Kiriakou was discussing classified information—the already exposed torture program, not the revealing of an agent's identity. John Rizzo, then a top CIA lawyer, told Scott Shane of the *Times*, "It was fairly brazen—a former agency officer talking on camera. . . . He started being quoted all over the place."[39]

Rizzo insisted that there had not been a campaign against Kiriakou, but Scott Shane's reporting and his interviews with Kiriakou make it plain that the CIA had been gunning for the former officer for a long time before the charge was made that he passed on a name of an interrogator. They believed that was something that could stick, whereas all the other stuff about torture—the main reason for going after Kiriakou after he changed his mind and started expressing doubts—had only bounced around the offices of the Department of Justice. Kiriakou even admits that he was wrong to discuss any names, even though one man, Deuce Martinez, who had worked with him to catch Abu

Zubaydah, had never posed as a diplomat or businessman. He did work now with Mitchell Jessen and Associates, the CIA contractor founded by two psychologists that helped devise the interrogation program that became the subject of deep, soul-searching investigations by the American Psychological Association, resulting in the resignations of several top APA officials for ethics violations. The FBI called in Kiriakou in 2012 to "help us with a case." After an hour's conversation about various and sundry things, including the Pittsburgh Steelers, it became clear that he was the target of the investigation. The FBI had Shane's e-mail exchanges, which ultimately became part of the indictment. It is not too much to say that there was a whole lot of straw grasping, despite what Matthew Miller wrote arguing that the indictment had "nothing to do with the disclosure of information about waterboarding or other torture tactics during the last administration, but with the identities of career intelligence officers."

It is true that Kiriakou gave out the name of a man who had a supervisory role in the rendition program to a freelancer, Matthew Cole, who exchanged e-mails with a human rights advocate, John Sifton, who worked with the John Adams Project, a group of lawyers who worked with other lawyers for detainees at Guantánamo Bay. Officials were alarmed that the lawyers wanted names in order "to call the C.I.A. officers as witnesses in future military trials, perhaps to substantiate accounts of torture or harsh treatment." The name Kiriakou supplied to Cole did not become public until four years later, when it appeared on a whistleblowing website. Shane commented that "the source was not clear."

Former Department of Justice spokesperson Matthew Miller insists it is clear-cut: "The same principles that applied in the Libby case—that the identities of covert officials are sacrosanct and revealing them endangers their lives—apply today." Against that view, Kiriakou wrote, "At the CIA, employees are trained to believe that nearly every moral issue is a shade of grey. Some issues are black-and-white—and torture is one of them." Instead of calling the CIA torturers to proper account, all efforts are focused on neutralizing the whistleblower as part of a plan to force him "into personal ruin, to weaken him to the point where he will plead guilty to just about anything to make the case go away."[40]

Kiriakou also noted, "When it comes time for trial, the espionage charges invariably are either dropped or thrown out." Having the subject plead guilty is enough. The length of the sentence, thirty months, also seems inadequate against the dramatic wording of the original indictments. But again, the guilty plea is enough, along with what accompanies it in terms of legal costs— Kiriakou incurred a debt of over $500,000 before accepting the deal—and the social and personal costs. Even Bruce Reidel, a retired veteran of the CIA who led President Obama's review of the Afghan situation in 2009 and then turned down an offer to be considered for CIA director, questioned Kiriakou's conviction: "To me, the irony of this whole thing is, very simply, that he's going to be the only C.I.A. officer to go to jail over torture," even though he denounced it. "It's deeply ironic under the Democratic president who ended torture."[41]

As usual, the rule seemed to be that lower-level officers should not only not be seen but also not heard, while the top floor can write memoirs. Kiriakou defended himself in an article in *The Guardian* citing such discrepancies. "When former Defense Secretary and CIA Director Leon Panetta boastfully revealed the identity of the Seal Team member who killed Osama bin Laden in a speech to an audience that included uncleared individuals, the Pentagon and the CIA simply called the disclosure 'inadvertent.'" There was no espionage charge for Panetta. "But there was a $3m book deal."[42]

Appointment in Berlin

Berlin had been the epicenter of espionage in the Cold War. Now it is again. In John le Carré's famous 1963 novel, *The Spy Who Came In from the Cold*, a secret agent sent to East Germany discovers he has been deceived by his masters in London as part of a deadly gambit to protect a valuable asset for British intelligence in the East German Secret Service. Moral ambiguities about the way intelligence services operate dominate the narrative. In the final scene of the novel, the disillusioned agent, Alec Leamas, chooses death after the shooting of his lover by East German guards at the Berlin Wall. In an almost Shakespearean ending, Leamas refuses calls to leap to safety over the Berlin Wall, where his superiors wait to welcome him back to the Free World. "Jump, Alec! Jump, man."

John le Carré's real name is David John Moore Cornwell, and *The Spy Who Came in from the Cold* was followed by a series of bestselling novels about the Circus (his name for the elite stratum of British spies) and its world-weary ringmaster George Smiley, the man who had sent Leamas on his false mission. Smiley's bouts with conscience never rise to remorse, but they express complicated emotions just short of disgust with the whole business. Cornwell wrote the novel after serving as an undercover agent in the British embassy in Bonn, Germany. Like Edward Snowden, he had joined the service out of patriotic motives, and like him he had access to secrets, particularly about the tunnel built under Berlin to listen in on Red Army plans. Codenamed Stopwatch by the British and Gold by the Americans, it cost $6.7 million, an enormous sum at the time. The story of the tunnel was almost the same as le Carré's plot. The KGB had learned about the plans for the tunnel in 1955, before it was even constructed, but concealed the information from the Soviet military in order to protect a mole, George Blake, inside MI6.

Over the span of eleven months until April 1956, the Gold wiretappers recorded nearly half a million phone calls. Then the Russians called a press conference and bused fifty thousand East German citizens to witness the uncovering of the "treachery of the West." Arrested in 1961, Blake claimed he didn't know how many operatives he had betrayed to the Russians—because there were so many. In a final twist to the story, he escaped from prison five years later and somehow found a way to get to Moscow. A segment of the tunnel is a prize exhibit at the Allied Museum in the former American sector of Berlin.[43]

Two months before the Snowden revelations, in April 2013, John le Carré wrote an introduction for the fiftieth-anniversary edition of *The Spy Who Came in from the Cold*, explaining how it originated in his disillusionment at age thirty. The introduction appeared first in *The Guardian*.

> The merit of *The Spy Who Came in from the Cold*, then—or its offence, depending where you stood—was not that it was authentic, but that it was credible. The bad dream turned out to be one that a lot of people in the world were sharing, since it asked the same old question that we are asking ourselves 50 years later: how far can we go in the rightful defence of our western values, without abandoning them along the way? My fictional chief of the British Service—I called him Control—had no doubt of the answer:
>
> "I mean, you can't be less ruthless than the opposition simply because your government's policy is benevolent, can you now?"[44]

Snowden's letter to Angela Merkel went along the same lines. "I look forward to speaking with you in your country when the situation is resolved," he wrote from Russia, "and thank you for your efforts in upholding the international laws that protect us all." It was a very clever maneuver to enlist Merkel in his cause, and it produced headlines and consternation among German politicians.

The timing was no accident. A few days earlier, *Der Spiegel* had reported that, using equipment installed on the rooftop of the American embassy, the NSA and CIA had been routinely intercepting and storing nearly all communications made by cellphone, satellite phone, landline, and wireless network in the government district of Berlin (not to mention eighty other cities), including Chancellor Merkel's personal cellphone, a story based on evidence from the Snowden documents. Merkel then "placed a strongly worded phone call" to President Obama about the matter and later told a European Union summit in Brussels, "Spying between friends, that's just not done. Now trust has to be rebuilt." Previously she had half joked that one expected the Russians or the Chinese to listen in on German officials, but not the Americans.

After the first Snowden revelations but before the cellphone scandal, a German delegation had gone to Washington to seek an agreement like the one among the "Five Eyes," which supposedly prohibits spying on top officials of the Anglo partners who share intelligence gathered by data and telephony monitoring—the United States, Great Britain, Canada, Australia, and New Zealand. The German mission was not successful, but Interior Minister Hans-Peter Friedrich put the best face he could on the discussions. Conversations had been open and constructive, he said, and the "US side was able to understand and relate to the concern on the German side."[45]

Despite such anodyne comments, the Germans left Washington feeling they had been let down badly. Later reports described their reaction when they heard what would be expected of them if they joined the Five Eyes: they "blanched when they heard what kind of responsibilities they would have for intelligence collection and cyberoperations around the world if they ever joined that elite club." Chancellor Merkel began talking about creating a "Germany only" segment of the Internet "to keep German emails and web searches from going across American-owned wires and networks."[46]

Merkel had grown up in East Germany, where the hated Stasi had engaged in domestic wiretapping and eavesdropping on a huge scale, using a network of perhaps as many as 2 million full- and part-time spies in a population of less than 17 million. The 2007 German film *The Lives of Others* reminded everyone of what it felt like in those days. It won the Academy Award that year as Best Foreign Film. For Germans, however, it had happened "here" twice, first under the Nazis and then the Communists.

How could Merkel not be horrified by the Snowden documentary evidence of NSA spying on allies, even before the revelations about her own cellphone? During the recent election campaign in Germany, her coordinator of secret services, Ronald Pofalla, had announced that there would be a review of German-U.S. intelligence cooperation, but he hastened to assure Germans that "there have not been millions of violations of fundamental rights in Germany."

Then came the revelations about Merkel's cellphone. In a poll, 62 percent supported the chancellor's strong protest to Obama but another 25 percent thought she had been too mild. "In a gesture of displeasure usually reserved for rogue states," the *Der Spiegel* staff wrote, "German Foreign Minister Guido Westerwelle summoned the new US ambassador, John Emerson, for a meeting at the Foreign Ministry."[47]

In the aftermath, with crowds of people outside carrying posters depicting President Obama in headphones above the words STASI 2.0, the lower house of the German parliament, the Bundestag, created a commission to investigate the NSA and its operations from the newly built American embassy on Pariser Platz, with its roof terrace, "which offers a breathtaking view of the Reichstag and Tiergarten Park. Even the Chancellery can be glimpsed. This is the political heart of the republic, where billion-euro budgets are negotiated, laws are formulated and soldiers are sent to war. It's an ideal location for diplomats—and for spies."[48]

The idea of bringing Snowden to Germany to testify before the committee was nixed, in part, because of fear of offending Washington in the worst possible way by granting him temporary asylum for such a visit. But there were two prominent whistleblowers eager to testify, former NSA employees William Binney and Thomas Drake. Both men had been threatened with prosecution under the 1917 Espionage Act, and both had a great deal to say about the ultimate aims of the American code-breaking agency. Binney compared the surveillance by the NSA with that by dictatorships. "They really want to have information about everything.

This is really a totalitarian approach. The goal is control of the people." Drake said the NSA's "monitoring regime has grown into a system that is strangling the world."[49]

Suddenly the whole history of wiretapping going back to the Vietnam War and earlier again became headline stories. From his exile in Russia, the "rogue contractor" was having an immense impact on American foreign policy. While American officials talked about the "incalculable damage" he had done to the ability of the intelligence services to protect the nation from terrorist attacks, by far the greater damage the nation suffered was to its ability to persuade other nations that what it did was in the interests of all equally in the Great War on Terror. The facts simply did not support such a view, so distrust eroded support at home as well—and no end was in sight.

The leader on the American side of the failed talks with German officials about a no-spying agreement was Lisa Monaco, a former Department of Justice prosecutor, chief counsel to Robert Mueller when he headed the FBI, principal deputy to Attorney General Eric Holder, and most recently moderator in the White House discussions about apprehending Snowden. President Obama had named her to be his assistant for homeland security and counterterrorism on January 25, 2013, replacing John Brennan, who had been the president's closest adviser on drone warfare and who now headed the CIA. It was well recognized that the documents in his possession had long passed to other persons, but the goal now was to remove him from the international spotlight. It was the same reasoning as using the Espionage Act for its deterrent value whether prosecutions succeeded or not.

On the other side, Thomas Drake has taken up Snowden's cause as a universal affirmation of the individual's sovereignty. The surveillance state has inverted the traditional relationship between citizens and their government, maintained Drake a month after Snowden's revelations. In a surveillance state, "we're all suspicious" by definition. What Snowden had revealed "is still the tip of the iceberg," he wrote. "They have this extraordinary system, in effect, a 24/7 panopticon on a vast scale that is gazing at you with an all-seeing eye." Therefore not only was Snowden morally justified in his actions in revealing some of the workings of the surveillance state, but also, having witnessed what happened to other whistleblowers, Drake believes Snowden was justified in seeking asylum. "He went preemptively overseas because that at least delays the prying hand of the US government."[50]

The prying hand of the *U.S.* government is not the only component of the surveillance state, of course. The NSA's British partners were doing their part as well. Laura Poitras, who had been Snowden's first contact, had moved her seat of operations to Berlin. Her computers had been retained and searched so many times when she reentered the United States from abroad that Poitras finally decided that that was the only way to sustain her work and protect her sources. One of her visitors in Berlin was David Miranda, Glenn Greenwald's partner. On a flight back to Brazil, where the two lived together, Miranda was detained at Heathrow Airport for nine hours by officers who wanted to question him under schedule 7 of the 2000 Terrorism Act. That law allows persons to be detained for up to nine hours before being released or charged. Only one in two thousand people being detained had been kept more than six hours, the usual period being under an hour. Miranda was kept the full nine hours and his laptop, mobile phone, camera, and memory sticks were all confiscated, along with DVDs and games consoles. In response to the uproar over Miranda's detention, the British Home Office replied that the police and government had an obligation to protect the public, "and our national security. If the police believe that an individual is in possession of highly sensitive stolen information that would help terrorism, then they should act and the law provides them with a framework to do that." The Home Office could not resist lecturing its critics in schoolmarmly fashion: "Those who oppose this sort of action need to think about what they are condoning."[51]

Alan Rusbridger, editor of *The Guardian*, retorted that the action was clearly a reprisal for its publication of Greenwald's articles citing Snowden documents. It quickly became apparent that Washington had received a heads-up on the intended detention of Miranda, but White House spokesman Josh Earnest claimed that the administration had not asked the British to detain him. It was "a law enforcement action" taken by the British government. Asked to substantiate his claim, Earnest would not elaborate on any "classified" conversations between the two governments. The Brazilian government immediately expressed "grave concern" over a detention that was "without justification . . . since it involves an individual against whom there are no charges that can legitimate the use of that legislation."[52]

The Miranda detention stirred deep emotions and formed unusual alliances. CNN legal analyst Jeffrey Toobin, asked if he thought the British had a right to detain him, replied, "I sure do." Toobin, usually classified as a liberal, had been sharply critical of Snowden and Greenwald from the beginning. He described Greenwald's partner as a "drug mule," saying, "I don't want to be unkind, but he was a mule. He was given something, he didn't know what it was, from one person to pass to another at the other end of an airport. Our prisons are full of drug mules."[53]

Greenwald based his defiant response on the right of people to know what their leaders are doing. "If the U.K. and U.S. governments believe that tactics like this are going to deter or intimidate us in any way from continuing to report aggressively on what these documents reveal, they are beyond deluded. If anything, it will have only the opposite effect: to embolden us even further." Increasingly, the language on both sides of the debate over whether Snowden was a hero or a traitor signaled an eagerness to engage in gotcha moments. If the United States couldn't get Snowden back, it and its Five Eyes allies would work together to stop the leaks at alternate outlets or at least harass the leakers and their families and friends. Toobin had denied that Miranda was a journalist with any right to First Amendment protections. He later added that "the word journalism is not magical immunity sauce that you can put on anything and eliminate any sort of liability."

Despite Toobin's views, the David Miranda case became the turning point for critiques of British antiterrorism laws. The courts had dismissed Miranda's suit against the Home Office and Metropolitan Police Service, but in July 2014 the United Kingdom's independent reviewer of terrorism legislation, David Anderson, who had been appointed by the Home Secretary, issued a scathing report that said the Miranda case suggested that the legislation was overly broad "and some would say alarming, " and the definition of terrorism was edging into dangerous territory. Meanwhile, Miranda's suit had been renewed with an appeal from the court's earlier decision. It was not about the right to stop suspected terrorists, it was argued, but rather the question of using the antiterrorist law to intimidate journalists. If the border authorities had wished only to seize the documents, said Miranda's partner, Glenn Greenwald, he would have been held for only a few minutes. Instead he was held for the maximum, nine hours. The colossus of U.S.-U.K. counterterrorism powers, he said in an interview with *Newsweek*, has enjoyed mission creep since 9/11. "These powers now go well beyond the scope of terrorist surveillance—they are monitoring economic conferences, climate change conferences, our allies, our enemies, even corporations."[54]

Greenwald proved these points a few weeks after Miranda's detention when he reported that Canadian intelligence had spied on Brazil's Ministry of Energy and Mines. As a result of this new revelation, Brazilian president Dilma Rousseff postponed an official visit to Washington. Addressing the UN General Assembly, she said that the state-run Petrobras corporation was "no threat to the security of any country. Rather, it represents one of the greatest assets of the world's oil and the heritage of the Brazilian people."[55]

On October 12, 2013, the *New York Times* reported on an interview with the NSA director General Keith Alexander. Alexander defended the surveillance efforts, and argued that the agency could not have been more transparent about its methods before the Snowden revelations because that would have been in violation of privacy requirements for individuals and companies. He hoped that the explanation would turn the argument around against the leakers as violators of individual rights. But he did agree the agency had stumbled in its response to Snowden's actions. The chief problem, he said, was not the programs themselves but public misunderstanding of what the agency collects. "The way we've explained it to the American people has gotten them so riled up that nobody told them the facts of the program and the controls that go around it."[56] Less than two weeks after Alexander's friendly chat with *Times* reporters, Snowden's revelation that Chancellor Angela Merkel's personal mobile phone had been tapped set off a firestorm of complaints and questions. The White House was quick to say that she was not being tapped at present and would not be in the future. The president said that he was now initiating a review of the way U.S. intelligence operates "outside the country." He wanted to make sure that what "they're able to do doesn't necessarily mean what they should be doing."[57]

Heightened scrutiny of government behavior as the result of the Snowden revelations was, at the least, becoming deeply embarrassing. And it did not get any better when, at the same time, the White House suggested that the president had not been fully informed about individual wiretaps on foreign leaders. Director of National Intelligence James Clapper tried a twofold defense. First he asserted in testimony that the United States spied on foreign leaders and other officials to see "if what they're saying gels with what's actually going on," and how the policies of other countries "impact us across a whole range of issues." He added that National Security Council officials were aware of spying on friendly governments but hesitated to say how high up the information went. Senator Dianne Feinstein, normally a devoted defender of NSA activities, called for a complete review of American intelligence policy—something more than Obama had said he would do about the way intelligence was collected. She was more concerned, however, about the White House's ambiguous statements about what the president knew. If the president was not aware of the bug on Merkel's phone, which had been in place since 2002, then it was indeed a "big problem" for the president, because it went to his credibility as commander in chief.[58]

It was certainly no comfort to the White House to have to debate on those terms. The president's advisers were perplexed about what line to take and shimmied back and forth on what Obama knew about the tap on Merkel. A senior official said that "the vast majority of intelligence that made it into Mr. Obama's daily intelligence briefings focused on potential threats, from Al Qaeda plots to Iran's nuclear program." He explained, "These are front-burner, first-tier issues. . . . He's not getting many briefings on intelligence about Germany." Besides, according to another administration official, the president "did not generally rely on intelligence reports to prepare for meetings with Ms. Merkel." Why should he? "He knows her well, he speaks with her regularly and our governments work together every day on a wide range of issues."[59] Despite such throwaway lines, that position was an unstable perch for anonymous White House aides. "Is it really better for us to think," asked a *Times* editorial, "that things have gone so far with the post-9/11 idea that any spying that can be done should be done and that nobody thought to inform President Obama about tapping the phone of one of the most important American allies?"[60]

Obama had called the German chancellor when the reports came out to deny that he was wiretapping her, but American officials were afraid to release any documents that would confirm what he said. Instead the incident confirmed the uncertainty that reigned about the NSA's reach and intentions. A German reporter wrote, "The problem was always that the documents were vague and complicated and left a lot of room for interpretation. . . . The US government, unsurprisingly, refused to help." That raised suspicions about what the NSA *was* doing.

Unfortunately for the White House, Director James Clapper then testified that the NSA had kept senior officials in the National Security Council fully aware of all the spying it did on allies, though he would not venture to say precisely what the president knew about individual wiretaps.[61] Maybe the president knew the specifics, and maybe he didn't. The Merkel phone taps caused uproar in Germany that would continue to bedevil the administration. Refuting claims that the NSA programs were under tight controls, the issue had become much bigger than listening in on Angela Merkel. As the confusion at the White House demonstrated, Obama's credibility as the leader of the "exceptional" nation had suddenly become a matter of great controversy. "What I can't do," Jay Carney had said on behalf of President Obama, "and won't do is answer every allegation that appears in print about intelligence activities that have been engaged in, or may or may not have been engaged in by the United States, because the path that leads us down is not one that we can travel."

That answer could have been lifted from the pages of *The Spy Who Came In from the Cold*. Obama had announced a review. The question now was: what would change?

6

A Time of Testing Limits

As my Administration previously informed Congress, I will interpret those sections consistent with my authority to direct the heads of executive departments to supervise, control and correct employees' communications with the Congress in cases where such communications would be unlawful or would reveal information that is properly privileged or otherwise confidential.
—President Barack Obama, signing statement on National Defense Authorization Act of 2013, January 3, 2013

The prime reason for secrecy is that you don't want the targets to know what you are doing. But often in democracies, another reason is that you don't want your citizens to know what their government is doing on their behalf to keep them secure, as long as it's within their country's law.
—Walter Pincus, in the *Washington Post*, December 25, 2013

It's self-evident. If the president of the United States calls a review of everything to do with intelligence, and that information only came into the public domain through newspapers, then it is self-evident, is it not, that newspapers had done something which oversight failed to do.
—Alan Rusbridger, statement to Parliament, December 5, 2013

The swirling arguments around Edward Snowden's release to journalists of the NSA's most carefully guarded secrets all came together in December 2013. Almost from the moment the articles appeared in *The Guardian* and the *Washington Post*, he became an international sensation. Awards from various countries and organizations piled up outside the door of his Moscow apartment.

The journalists who wrote the stories and the newspapers that printed them received Pulitzer Prizes. Then came the revolt of the tech companies whose integrity had been compromised by their more or less coerced cooperation with the U.S. government in granting access to personal data. Obama was confronted by a phalanx of the biggest Internet outfits demanding new limits on surveillance because the NSA was doing great damage to their business abroad and at home. At the same time, a federal judge, Richard Leon, said the world the NSA had made was an almost Orwellian place, or at least one where the Constitution was considered only a technicality.

Two months after the initial revelations, in August 2013, President Barack Obama had appointed a small committee of intelligence and legal experts to review the NSA's programs, to see, as he said, if there was another way to skin the cat. Although naturally the members would back away from the implications of their own report in public statements, the report bluntly called into question the central premise of the agency's arguments—that the programs were essential to protect the nation from terrorist attacks.

The Snowden affair unfolded against a background of foreign policy crises all over the globe. Policy makers still feared another 9/11, but there was already good evidence of an emerging "Iraq syndrome," or war weariness, that divided the nation not along traditional political lines, but in new ways that saw alliances arise outside the mainstream of party politics. The rise of ISIS shattered illusions that somehow things would turn out for the better in Iraq, where the United States had spent a trillion dollars. No matter where one looked, Washington faced a discouraging aftermath to its hopes of exporting American values to the Middle East from Afghanistan to Yemen. *Foreign Policy* magazine reported, for example, that aid to Afghanistan had far surpassed the Marshall Plan, which saved Europe from communism after World War II. "The Marshall Plan has now been knocked off its pedestal as America's most expensive nation-building project. Afghanistan now reigns supreme, having gobbled up $104 billion in American aid. And, unlike in Europe, that money hasn't bought the kind of world-class infrastructure that became the cornerstones of numerous flourishing economies. Instead, the funds have mainly bought empty buildings, malfunctioning power plants, and a corrupt government that will be wholly dependent on Western—read: American—aid well into the future."[1]

The flip side of that failure was a rationale for ever better information about what was going on everywhere: a panopticon in which spies can see the dark corners. Ironically, the intelligence services became so powerful in the first place not because of their successes but because of anger at their failures, such as Pearl Harbor, the Bay of Pigs, 9/11, and the politically skewed evidence of weapons of mass destruction that preceded the 2003 war with Iraq—this last arguably not just the worst policy fiasco in American history but a tragedy of immense consequences yet to be fully understood as the United States still struggles with the aftershocks. These failures also presented whistleblowers in a better light to much of the public, as the search for answers to foreign policy reverses disabused people of faith in the mystique of spycraft.

The Afghanistan war against the Taliban had been "over" several times since 2001, for example, but inside the country nothing was ever settled, and while American casualties were nowhere near those of Vietnam, frustration levels were nearly as high. The reach of that conflict into American civil liberties, moreover, was perhaps an even more momentous development than outspending the Marshall Plan. War fatigue and distrust thus fueled a rising controversy over the way the NSA and other agencies had taken the antiterrorism laws to what the always provocative counterterror chief in the Clinton and Bush White Houses, Richard Clarke, called "the breaking point," and to what State Department pariah Peter Van Buren called a "post-Constitutional" society. To top it off, this furor came at a time when American internal politics were caught in a vise of discontent and disenchantment in the middle of Barack Obama's second term.

President Obama was now ensnared in a historical quandary

that went back to World War II and the origins of the national security state. It began in 1945, when early expectations of perfect security after Hiroshima had quickly evaporated. Instead, the bomb had made Americans feel *less* secure. To manage that contradiction, Congress and President Harry Truman had created the Central Intelligence Agency, the beginning of a path that led to the imperial presidency. The search for a winning weapon and perfect security had shifted from Oak Ridge and Los Alamos to Langley and Fort Meade.

Intelligence became an all-consuming addiction that supported the president when he needed reassurance but also depleted scarce resources for other needs important to the health of a democratic society. Such tensions proved to be a powerful constraint on President Obama as he wrestled with the competing claims of his constituents in the federal government and the critics who assailed him from left and right. Perhaps it was worse for him than any of his predecessors because he had promised before his first election not only to end the wars in Iraq and Afghanistan, but also to end the mind-set that had led to those quagmires. "I will offer a clear contrast as somebody who never supported this war, thought it was a bad idea," he said in a 2008 campaign debate with Hillary Clinton. And then he delivered the most dramatic statement of his political career, which sent hopes soaring among critics—not just of the war but of the assumptions behind exceptionalist American policy. "I don't want to just end the war, but I want to end the mindset that got us into war in the first place."

The Snowden Effect

Only a few days after the first *Guardian* article in June 2013 revealing the NSA programs, Richard Clarke wrote a stunning article in the *New York Daily News* warning about the dark implications of the "vacuum cleaner approach to telephone records." Although acknowledging that Obama inherited the program from Bush, he wrote, "I am troubled by the precedent of stretching a law on domestic surveillance almost to the breaking point. On issues so fundamental to our civil liberties, elected leaders should not be so needlessly secretive." Moreover, he pointed out, the vacuuming is about power, not safety. "The argument that this sweeping search must be kept secret from the terrorists is laughable. Terrorists already assume this sort of thing is being done. Only law-abiding American citizens were blissfully ignorant of what their government was doing."[2]

Obama would never be so blunt, at least not in public, but he appointed Clarke to the small review group, which reported in December with forty-six recommendations for changes, starting with the metadata phone collections. Clarke struck another blow at the rationale for the NSA program when the group made its report. The program's defenders had argued that it had prevented more than fifty terrorist attacks—an assertion that the president also made during a visit to Berlin. But, said Clarke, "I reviewed each case. . . . The 215 program did not influence the outcome of any of those cases. . . . All claims of stopping terrorism were bullshit."[3]

Clarke had no use for Edward Snowden, however. He spoke bluntly about the whistleblower, calling for him to be prosecuted and put away for a long time and saying he had aided the enemies of the country. "What Mr. Snowden did is treason, was high crimes, and there is nothing in what we say that justifies what he did," Clarke told television reporters after the review group's report became public. "Whether or not this panel would have been created anyway, I don't know, but I don't think anything that I've learned justifies the treasonous acts of Mr. Snowden."[4]

Clarke himself thus reproduced the confusions evoked by Snowden's actions. It has taken almost two years to sort out the differences between rhetoric and reason, and even now the hemming and hawing by defenders of the NSA programs continues to cloud congressional debates. The "safe" official line has become that, while public debate and change are necessary, Snowden has committed crimes and must face justice in an American courtroom, even though there would be no possibility of debate and change without those crimes. Of course the fate of Chelsea Manning had just been decided at court-martial—a thirty-five-year sentence—showing Snowden what he could expect from American justice. The effort to divide the Snowden question into two parts was complicated by the administration's previous unwillingness to move against newspapers that printed WikiLeaks documents that Manning had sent to Julian Assange. The prevailing precedent, of course, was the Pentagon Papers, which had embroiled the Nixon administration in a losing battle. It looked like a lose-lose proposition.

The case also raised a perplexing question that would continue to be debated as events unfolded. Who was really to blame if leaks actually produced serious harm to individuals or the nation? *New York Times* editor Jill Abramson raised that question when she spoke about an effort the British embassy made to retrieve documents *The Guardian* had sent to New York. In London government agents had pulverized the hard drives where the documents were being stored. It made no difference that copies had already been sent to various places overseas, said one of the officials, who added that it was possible for someone to listen to conversations in *The Guardian* offices by aiming a laser beam at plastic coffee cups. The non sequitur (or threat?) apparently had become the last refuge of British intelligence.[5]

Or so it seemed to Abramson. She said it was hard to conceive of such a thing—the raid and destruction of hard drives—happening in the United States. "I can't imagine that. The only equivalent I can think of is years ago when the New York Times was enjoined by a lower court from publishing the Pentagon Papers, but the supreme court came in and overruled that decision. Prior restraint is pretty much unthinkable to me in this country."[6]

The British embassy made just the one contact, she added, then gave up. No CIA agents armed with pulverizing tools showed up demanding access to *Times* computers. There had been occasions when the Obama administration had asked the paper to consider withholding certain information, Abramson said, and the paper always gives "sober consideration to the requests," but "our default position is usually to weigh on the side of informing the public." There was a war on terror being waged in both countries, and the public had a right to have information about it. "That's critical. The Guardian as well as the New York Times are providing a very valuable service, allowing people to decide for themselves whether the intelligence agencies are being too intrusive in their data collection." [7]

People to decide for themselves? That was really the point where government agents on both sides of the Atlantic wanted to draw the line on any reforms. It was all well and good, American officials and some well-known pundits argued, to talk about the people's right to know more about the NSA programs, but to let them decide for themselves what could be released? In what previous war was that ever allowed? Weren't Abramson and others claiming the right to decide on behalf of the people where the line should be, based on the Snowden documents? Why should she and her colleagues be allowed to assign themselves such a role at the risk of another 9/11 or worse? Yet Abramson could also point to the president's agreement—forced as it was by the Snowden revelations—that there needed to be a public debate. "I think it's not only healthy but vital to have that."

In the midst of this debate over press rights in the United Kingdom and the United States, Obama's predicament was well illustrated by comments the new American ambassador to London made shortly after he arrived. He was asked almost immediately by a BBC commentator to respond to actions taken against *The Guardian*. He declined the opportunity to criticize the newspaper, saying he wanted to focus instead on the importance of the debate about trade-offs between security and privacy. President Obama, said Matthew Barzun, was clear that his response to the leaks should not have "a chilling effect on the press." At the very moment that Barzun was making his comments on the BBC, however, the U.S. intelligence community knew of the planned strike on *The Guardian* to retrieve or destroy Snowden-supplied documents.

When *The Guardian* told its readers what had happened in its offices, complete with dramatic photographs, the White House gave something of a tut-tut answer to questions about American complicity, suggesting that such a thing could never happen here. "It's very difficult to imagine a scenario in which that would be appropriate," White House spokesman Josh Earnest told reporters. But internal NSA e-mails obtained under the Freedom of Information Act showed that American intelligence officials knew about and applauded the action beforehand. In an e-mail from the deputy director to General Keith Alexander entitled "Guardian data being destroyed," the writer told his boss, "Good news, at least on this front." Asked to explain, DNI James Clapper's office replied that, yes, it did know in advance but took no action because the destruction of those hard drives "cut down on the repositories of the raw documents and reduced the risk they would be more widely disseminated in bulk."[8]

There is scarcely any other way to read these exchanges but to conclude either that the agency wished it could disregard the White House statement and demand return of the documents from the *Times* or that it believed *The Guardian* headquarters was an unsafe location. Much of the e-mail to General Alexander had been blacked out. Perhaps it contained some words about that novel threat of laser spying. Given those choices, the White House demurred again, saying that it was not known "how high up in the administration that information was shared." Of course, that presented, also again, a further question as to whether the intelligence agencies were ignoring the president in their day-to-day decisions.

Retired general Michael Hayden, who has headed both the CIA and NSA, made it his goal in public debates to prove that "Jimmy Madison"—often cited by NSA critics as a reminder of the Fourth Amendment's origins as a shield against unwarranted government searches—would have approved of the NSA programs because they met his test. The president, both branches of Congress, and the federal courts had approved them. "You have all three co-equal, competing branches of government going check, check, check," he said. A lot of the problem nowadays was young people, he added. "The cultural shift is that a lot of people in your generation," he told a group in Aspen, Colorado, "say that what I just described to you no longer constitutes the consent of the governed. . . . That's a very different formula for representative democracy. What we're seeing in Snowden . . . is a really big deal in how we decide as a people to create consent of the governed."[9]

Much as it did in the Vietnam War era, the alleged generation gap provided a convenient "father knows best" explanation for the dissent that had developed as the revelations continued to mount up in the years before Edward Snowden's appearance on the scene. As before, however, it failed to acknowledge the cross-generational cultural *and* political divide that made any "reform" a question mark. More and more the issue *does* involve the consent of the governed—and, to use Hayden's phrase in a different way, how consent is "created." It is of some interest, then, that one of Snowden's harshest critics, Senator Dianne Feinstein, who became chair of the Senate Select Committee on Intelligence after the 2006 election, commented about the Bush administration's efforts to keep its NSA authorizations secret, "It's such an affront to the balance of powers and it's what this administration has been doing, which is gathering executive power and dismissing the Congress." In other words, Hayden should read his "Jimmy" Madison again.[10]

When Snowden was granted temporary asylum in Russia, it became almost an obligatory pilgrimage for other leakers to visit him to offer support and to receive words of encouragement for future leakers. General Hayden minced no words about Snowden, however, putting him in the same category as Kim Philby, the infamous mole high in MI6 who successfully fled to Moscow in 1963 and betrayed British spies to the Soviet Union. Hayden was asked about Snowden on *Face the Nation* and replied, "I used to say he was a defector, you know, and there's a history of defection. Actually, there's a history of defection to Moscow, and that he seems to be part of that stream. I'm now kind of drifting in the direction of perhaps more harsh language"—such as "traitor."

Based on what? he was asked by the moderator. "Well, in the past two weeks, in open letters to the German and Brazilian government, he has offered to reveal more American secrets to those governments in return for something. And in return was for asylum. I think there's an English word that describes selling American secrets to another government, and I do think it is treason." [11]

Hayden then turned to American double agents working for foreign governments, Robert Hanssen and Aldrich Ames, and as serious as their crimes had been, he said, "You could argue whether that was a cup of water that was leaked or a bucket of water that was leaked. What Snowden is revealing . . . is the plumbing. . . . It will take years, if not decades, for us to return to the position that we had prior to his disclosures."

It was an incredible comparison. Aldrich Ames had been responsible for the disappearance of dozens of CIA sources in the Soviet Union in the 1970s and had received more than $4.6 million from his Russian contacts. Hanssen sold secrets to the Russians over a twenty-year period, including the identities of the largest number of U.S. spies outed by a single person, in return for $1.4 million and precious jewels. Snowden showed the whole world it was being spied on and in return got little more than trouble.

But the intelligence community was not in a relenting mood. Hayden's successor, General Keith Alexander, and his "senior leadership team at the National Security Agency," were quick to assert that the president's call for reform seemed more like repudiation of an established and necessary relationship. Thus, wrote Shane Harris in *Foreign Policy*, prior to the Snowden revelations, the administration had relied on the intelligence agencies to carry out its most important foreign policy objectives, from killing Osama bin Laden to undermining Syria's Bashar al-Assad. "The

White House's embrace of the dark world of spycraft has been near-absolute. A rift between America's intelligence and political leaders could be more than fodder for Beltway cocktail parties. If left unchecked, it could start to erode the trusted relationships that have been at the heart of how the U.S. government handles global threats since 9/11." [12]

A former lawyer in the agency, its onetime general counsel Stewart Baker, thought Obama had pulled his punches when dealing with the NSA's critics. "The President is uncomfortable defending this [the programs]. Maybe he spends too much time reading blogs on the left. That's fatal in cases like this. You have to make the case because nobody else will." [13]

Such language about "blogs on the left" became hard to sustain when libertarian critics joined the protesters in demanding an end to the mass surveillance programs. The results from Snowden's revelations would indeed be more than a cup or bucket of water. They washed away old certainties to reveal an emerging, if still inchoate, set of political alliances.

The Oracle

The mounting frustration Baker and others felt was fueled partly by the intelligence community's feeling that Obama did not have its back, despite his repeated statements that Snowden was no hero and must return home to face trial on the government's charges. But the agents and administrators were perhaps even more angered by the number of awards and prizes the fugitive received and the way his statements were treated as uncontested truths. It did seem a bit over the top at times, as reports of visits to Snowden in Moscow contained every detail of his demeanor—how he smiled, his graciousness, and, of course, his intelligent responses about almost everything. Everything but where he lived, adding to the Snowden mystique. His statements that he would gladly go to Guantánamo to serve time, or to a U.S. prison if he could return home—"as long as it served the right purpose"—seemed to be a martyrdom wish. But there were always escape routes in his offers. "I care more about the country than what happens to me. But we can't allow the law to become a political weapon or agree to scare people away from standing up for their rights, no matter how good the deal. I'm not going to be part of that." [14]

The first award he received, in July 2013, was the Whistle-blower Prize from Transparency International Germany, for exposing at great risk to himself the large-scale surveillance of European citizens by Western secret services. The chair of Transparency Germany, Edda Müller, even asserted that Great Britain, as Washington's partner in this behavior, "must explain very clearly in Brussels"—where the European Union parliament meets—"its position on the basic rights of EU citizens." That was unlikely to happen, but even broaching the idea of enforcing international laws protecting privacy showed how charged the atmosphere had become in only a few weeks since the first publication of Snowden's revelations. It also continued a progression that had developed in recent years of escalating "lawfare," or the effort to force individual countries to accept the norms of behavior adopted by international bodies. The best example was the effort of the United Nations to write rules for drone warfare.[15]

A better-known and especially galling prize followed—the Sam Adams Award for truth telling, given by the Sam Adams Associates for Integrity in Intelligence. The organization was made up of former senior national security officials and others who had each taken a solemn oath "to support and defend the Constitution of the United States against all enemies, foreign and domestic." Samuel A. Adams was the CIA official who challenged the Pentagon's official count of enemy forces in the Vietnam War as giving a false impression that the war was being won. A previous winner of the prize, Thomas Drake, called what Snowden did "an amazingly brave act of civil disobedience." Drake traveled to Moscow to present the award along with other past winners, including former FBI agent Coleen Rowley, who had told her superiors and Congress that officials at FBI headquarters inexplicably had failed to act on information sent from an FBI field office before 9/11 that might have prevented the tragedy. Her memos to the director, Robert Mueller, and her testimony to Congress had led to changes in the agency's approach to information from field offices. After leaving the FBI, Rowley became a frequent commentator on national security affairs for various online publications.

Snowden was among those shortlisted for the European Union's top human rights prize, the Andrei Sakharov Award in honor of the famous dissident Soviet physicist, father of the Russian atomic bomb, and counterpart to J. Robert Oppenheimer—who dared to challenge the Kremlin's nuclear and foreign policies. Sakharov was arrested in 1980, force-fed in hospitals, sent to Gorky in internal exile, and forbidden to travel to Moscow until 1986, when Mikhail Gorbachev began the attempt to liberate the Soviet Union from its Stalinist past. Snowden did not win. The prize went to Malala Yousafzai, a Pakistani teenager shot by the Taliban for attempting to go to school, as her story better fit a human rights definition of courage in the face of tyranny, but the nomination itself demonstrated the wide range of Snowden's appeal. That he was now in exile in Russia added to the narrative of a protest against state force.

Snowden was also nominated to be *Time* magazine's Person of the Year but lost to Pope Francis. He was named rector of Glasgow University, an honorific position that he accepted via a video hookup from Moscow. In accepting, he said, "I'm disappointed and I must apologize for being unable to attend in person, but unfortunately I've discovered that I'm barred from entering the United Kingdom on the grounds that my presence is considered detrimental to the public good."

The speeches and interviews Snowden gave became instant headlines. Meanwhile, prizes were handed out to the Snowden collaborators who wrote the stories that appeared in *The Guardian* and the *Washington Post*. The George Polk Award for national security reporting went to Glenn Greenwald and Laura Poitras, and the Pulitzer Prize for 2014 went to the two newspapers. In addition, the 2014 Academy Award for best documentary film went to *Citizenfour*, Poitras's account of Snowden's actions and the subsequent events in his life as an international phenomenon. Two Norwegian parliamentarians nominated Snowden for the Nobel Peace Prize for 2014. The last American nominated was Barack Obama, who won the 2009 prize and delivered a speech that cited another winner, Martin Luther King Jr., but came down firmly for the thought of Reinhold Niebuhr, a Christian "realist" who was a strong advocate of using American power while understanding the sin of self-justification. The Norwegians said in their nomination letter, "The public debate and changes in policy that have followed in the wake of Snowden's whistleblowing have contributed to a more stable and peaceful world order." [16]

The Empire Strikes Back

The group that traveled to Moscow to congratulate the Adams Prize winner included Ray McGovern, a former CIA analyst who had become a persistent critic of American foreign policy, and Jesselyn Radack, another former Adams Prize winner. A graduate of Brown University and Yale Law School, Radack had begun a career in government in the attorney general's Honors Program working as a Department of Justice ethics adviser. Her life changed dramatically when she exposed the tactics used to extract a confession from John Walker Lindh, the "American Taliban." Lindh was the first prisoner taken in the original Afghan War in December 2001. The FBI interrogated him without telling him that his father had secured a lawyer for him. Radack had sent memos to her boss in the Department of Justice explaining that Lindh's confession could not be used in a criminal case, but those e-mails later disappeared from documents the court ordered the government to turn over at the demand of Lindh's lawyers. [17]

The Lindh case was particularly important to the Bush

administration because he was a substitute for Osama bin Laden, who had escaped into Pakistan after the invasion of Afghanistan. Despite the evidence that he was at most a very minor figure, his successful prosecution was something of a trophy for the Department of Justice in the battle against terrorism. That he was an American citizen made the catch all the more useful as providing an example of the insidiousness of the enemy in subverting our own citizens and by extension proving the need for surveillance. Whether or not that motive factored into the severity of the punishment government lawyers proposed for Lindh, the DOJ did not want Radack's memos to become public for other reasons. They exposed the nascent torture program that became a major scandal with the revelations about Abu Ghraib and waterboarding at rendition sites. When she attempted to bring them to her superior's attention, she was told to back off—and later was given a poor efficiency report, below even mediocre. Finally, she disclosed the e-mails to *Newsweek* "in accordance with the Whistleblower Protection Act." The government then withdrew its most serious charges against Lindh, but even so the deal struck with Lindh's lawyers led to a twenty-year sentence.

For blowing the whistle, Radack was the subject of an investigation by the Justice Department that continued for months but produced no charges. But that was hardly the end of it. Like the treatment given to Thomas Drake and others, the DOJ pursued Radack by other means, placing her on a no-fly list supposedly reserved for suspects somehow connected to terrorism, and attempting to have her disbarred in Maryland and the District of Columbia. It succeeded in having her fired from a job she had obtained with a law firm after leaving the government. In her case, the vendetta backfired, as Radack has become perhaps the most effective and famous lawyer for Drake, John Kiriakou, and others. As the principal figure in the Government Accountability Project, she is constantly in demand as a speaker, and she is the author of *Traitor: The Whistleblower and the "American Taliban"* (2012), wherein she tells the whole story of how the government finagled the Lindh case.

The Lindh documents were a potential source of great embarrassment to both Bush and Obama. Even though it was no longer politically profitable to harass Radack in such obvious ways, politicians and the media still demonized Lindh.

> The case was constantly in the news, and every journalist in print, radio, and television seemed to be reading off the Justice Department's script as the government released a steady stream of false, misleading, and inflammatory propaganda to the media. Bush, Cheney, Rumsfeld, Powell, and Senators Hillary Clinton and John McCain made prejudicial statements that Lindh was an Al Qaeda fighter, had fired his weapon, had attended a terrorist training camp, and had foreknowledge of 9/11—even though the government, from the first day of Lindh's capture, possessed facts to the contrary. The media acted largely as a stenographer, rather than doing any independent investigation.[18]

As late as 2012, Radack's interviewer points out, the triumph of the Lindh case was cited by Eric Holder as an important accomplishment by the Department of Justice in battling terrorism. "Holder is too smart not to 'know,' or to remember, the trophy photos of Lindh—naked, blindfolded, tied-up, and bound to a board with duct tape—that circulated worldwide," says Radack. "That was our first glimpse of American-sponsored torture, and we didn't even flinch."[19]

Tech Man of the Year

Perhaps Snowden's influence was best gauged by the tech companies concerned about how the NSA programs were affecting their business around the world. In late October 2013, he sent a statement to a protest rally staged by the Stop Watching Us coalition in Washington, D.C. Snowden's revelations had brought the coalition into being—an amazing collection of interest groups spread across the ideological horizon. Among them were the American Civil Liberties Union, the Mozilla Foundation, the Electronic Frontier Foundation, the Green Party, the Libertarian Party, the social news website Reddit, the Council on American-Islamic Relations, Demand Progress, and Students for Liberty. It is hard to imagine any other issue that would bring together such a rally and protest—to be held on the Patriot Act's birthday.

From Moscow Snowden sent a statement that sounded like a party keynote speaker's call to the faithful to battle the forces of evil.

In the last four months, we've learned a lot about our government. We've learned that the U.S. intelligence community secretly built a system of pervasive surveillance. Today, no telephone in America makes a call without leaving a record with the NSA. Today, no Internet transaction enters or leaves America without passing through the NSA's hands. Our representatives in Congress tell us this not surveillance. They're wrong.

Now it's time for the government to learn from us. On Saturday, the ACLU, EFF, and the rest of the StopWatching.Us coalition are going to D.C. Join us in sending the message. Stop Watching Us.[20]

The coalition released a video to go with Snowden's statement. It featured actor John Cusack, filmmaker Oliver Stone, Representative John Conyers, and Snowden's most famous predecessor, Daniel Ellsberg, who was now back in the public's attention with his appeals for action against the government surveillance programs. Starting in July 2014, six-foot billboards began appearing along public thoroughfares near the State Department, the Defense Intelligence Agency, the Department of Justice, the FBI, and the White House. There were thirteen of the posters, which pictured a solemn-looking Ellsberg staring ahead like a weary prophet whose voice had not been heard. He implores government workers, "Don't do what I did. Don't wait until a new war has started, don't wait until thousands more have died, before you tell the truth with documents that reveal lies or crimes or internal projections of costs and dangers. You might save a war's worth of lives."

Ellsberg was a member of the advisory board of ExposeFacts, which was encouraging more whistleblowers to disclose "information that citizens need to make truly informed decisions in a democracy." ExposeFacts offered a SecureDrop submission system that would protect the identity of whistleblowers, foil hackers, and stymie government prosecutors. Ellsberg also founded the Freedom of the Press Foundation, with the stated goal of encouraging more whistleblowers. Edward Snowden was named a member of the board. "He is no more traitor than I am," Ellsberg declared.

The only possible link—a tenuous one—to interference with actual warmaking had to do with exposure of American cyberwar capability. The United States and Israel had infected Iranian computers with the Stuxnet worm to mess up Tehran's nuclear production by destroying centrifuges used to enrich fissile material. David Sanger, a *New York Times* reporter, revealed the Stuxnet operation in July 2012. Up until that time, the Pentagon had been adamant that American cyberwar planning was only defensive in nature and called all other talk and rumors pure fantasy. All at once, those who had been unwilling to talk about U.S. cyberwar capability suddenly worried about the supposedly weak American position in the cyber arms race! "We have to catch up" became the cry and the justification. A former FBI cyberintelligence director who now works in the private sector said, "There's no way that we are going to win the cybersecurity effort on defense. We have to go on offense." While offense was still defined as pursuing the "perpetrators back into their own networks," the goal was nothing less than establishing "cyber superiority," another update on the old quests for land, sea, air, and atomic supremacy. And what was Stuxnet but a preemptive first strike? [21]

As in many other instances, the original Bush program had been speeded up by President Obama. Unlike the investigations of other leaks, however, there were accusations that the Stuxnet leak was a deliberate White House effort to influence the presidential campaign, to show how tough Obama was in order to win swing states. Senator John McCain called for a special prosecutor. "There is no legitimate reason," he said, for the information to be out in public. It only "harms our national security and the men and women sworn to protect it." The reason for the leaks about that program and the kill list of targets for American drones, he claimed, was to make the president look strong on national security issues. [22]

McCain had inadvertently hit on a key point. The ability to plant stories by anonymous sources has always been a presidential perk. Nevertheless, perhaps because of pressure from the intelligence agencies, a free-ranging DOJ investigation centered on the man Republicans called Obama's favorite general, U.S. Marine general James "Hoss" Cartwright, the former vice chair of the Joint Chiefs. The general had been a longtime skeptic of Pentagon claims about progress in the Middle Eastern wars, making him less than cozy with the intelligence community. Eventually, Cartwright would be stripped of his security clearance. He denied all the accusations, but the investigation continued. If Cartwright was the culprit, Obama's vigorous pursuit of other leakers with the Espionage Act did become a much heavier political burden. "This was a man with whom the president shared a great many secrets. For now at least, that sharing is over." [23]

Despite the growth of the cyberwarrior brigades, the uneasiness about this latest NSA cyberwar effort added to concerns about mass surveillance. Agency advertisements for computer scientists who specialized in "vulnerability discovery"—the hottest new job listed on its career pages—showed the direction things were going. But not everyone was ready for the ride. "Offense is the biggest growth sector in the cyber industry right now," said Jeffrey Carr, an analyst and author of *Inside Cyber Warfare*. Older warnings, dating back to the Eisenhower years, about the growth of the military industrial complex were now updated to include cyberwarfare interest groups. Former NSA analyst William Binney, who had become a vocal critic, saw it all as empire building. He was not referring to offensive cyberwar specifically, but to the "influence and power the intelligence community has over the government." It gets whatever it wants. "Look at what they've built! Have you ever looked around all the buildings they've built up because of 9/11?"[24]

Stuxnet had shown what future warfare might be like. For the first time, said enthusiasts, a preemptive attack could take down enemy computers and actually destroy physical weapons—with no civilian casualties! That was perhaps the ultimate dream (or fantasy) of American technology, certainly far better than a "clean" atomic bomb without radiation effects. "Used preemptively, it could keep a conflict from evolving in a more lethal direction." But the integration of a nation's economy and its well-being by the computer-operated systems that permeate everything, including schools, water treatment plants, hospitals, and airports, belies the notion of cyberwarfare as victimless. In the twenty-first century, a cyberwar attack could be as deadly as a hydrogen bomb.[25]

At the same time that the Ellsberg posters were urging whistleblowers not to wait, Washington metrobuses featured banners with Snowden's picture staring out at pedestrians, paid for by a new organization, the Partnership for Civil Justice Fund. Beginning in a hand-lettered constitutional font and then switching to huge black letters on a white background, the banners read "We the People oppose the Surveillance State, and say, THANK YOU, EDWARD SNOWDEN!" At the bottom, viewers were urged to take action at ThankYouEdSnowden.org.

There could be no doubt that the government's effort to

degrade Snowden's appeal by labeling him a fugitive had failed. He kept on making headlines, not only with specific revelations of documents, but with a series of exposés that embarrassed not only the government but also the tech companies that had cooperated with the NSA. At year's end, Channel 4 in Great Britain carried a Christmas message "alternate" to the queen's traditional message to the nation. Snowden was not the first alternate speaker to be given this opportunity, but his international standing was obviously a compelling attraction for the managers of Channel 4. He began his two-minute message with a reference to George Orwell's *1984*. The technology described in that classic dystopian surveillance state was nothing compared to what is available to states today, he said, adding, "A child born today will grow up with no conception of privacy at all. They'll never know what it means to have a private moment to themselves, an unrecorded, unanalyzed thought. The conversation occurring today will determine the amount of trust we can place both in the technology that surrounds us and the government that regulates it." [26]

Six months later, Snowden gave an interview to his favorite newspaper, *The Guardian*, in which he claimed that NSA watchers enjoyed fringe benefits—such as sharing spy photos of people who are naked and/or making love. One could hardly imagine a more effective, attention-grabbing, and believable subject than the tried-and-true sex scandal. "You've got young enlisted guys," Snowden said, suddenly thrust into positions of extraordinary responsibility, "where they now have access to all of your private records." A picture pops up on their screen—and, well, the temptation is too great not to tell Bill, who sends it on to George, who sends it on to Tom. . . . Because the auditing system is so weak, nobody ever knows. He had personally witnessed numerous instances of such violations of citizens' rights to privacy, he said, so many, in fact, that it was "routine enough, depending on the company you keep." In response, agency spokespersons insisted that such behavior would not be tolerated but did not deny that it might have happened. Analysts refer to this spy porn as loveint—a play on surveillance lingo like humint (human intelligence) and sigint (signals intelligence).[27]

Intelligence analyst and historian James Bamford traveled to Moscow in 2015 and revealed from his conversations with Snowden and other information how this purloined loveint can be used against anyone who challenges the system, either domestically or by giving other countries information about the sexual behavior of dissidents. For instance, Bamford said, "One document from the NSA director, for example, indicates that the agency was spying on visits to porn sites by people, making no distinction between foreigners and 'U.S. persons,' U.S. citizens or permanent residents. He then recommended using that information to secretly discredit them, whom he labeled as 'radicalizers.' But because this was revealed by the Huffington Post, an online publication viewed as progressive, and was never reported by mainstream papers such as the *New York Times* or the *Washington Post*, the revelation never received the attention it deserved."[28]

The Revolt of the Tech Companies

The adulation and awards Snowden received were angst-producing phenomena for the White House, but more serious was the response of tech companies, who had once been big supporters of Barack Obama. Tech companies had pumped $7.8 million into his campaign in 2012. Now they were worried about losing much bigger sums to foreign competitors after the documents revealed that the government had established a secret back door into undisclosed interception points to copy entire data flows from the fiber-optic cables between data processing centers. The trouble had actually started even earlier, when Snowden's revelations first appeared in *The Guardian* on June 5, 2013. Among the first revelations were details about PRISM, short for either Planning Tool for Resource Integration, Synchronization, and Management or Personal Record Information System Methodology. The program—a court approved mandate that required Google, Yahoo, and other major Internet companies to allow NSA collection of metadata under provisions of the Patriot Act. The original mandate had excluded mass collection of information of American citizens inside the country without a warrant. But that restriction had little meaning because of American membership in Five Eyes. The distinction between local and foreign had all but disappeared.

The first to complain were the Chinese, with whom American tech companies had a thriving and growing business. Of course, this was not the China of the old weak imperial dynasties, ripe for pillage in the Opium Wars, but a very modern country (at least in some respects) that engaged in industrial spying to gain advantages over American companies. In addition, the Pentagon's Defense Science Board had evidence that China had secured access to detailed designs of military weapons and aircraft. President Obama and his aides had planned to address this complaint during a summit conference in California with President Xi scheduled to begin two days later, on June 7, 2013. Instead, he found himself on the defensive. The tables had been turned, explained an American China expert, Cheng Li of the Brookings Institution.[29] As soon as President Xi returned home, American tech companies in China experienced a loss of consumer confidence. Sales fell off precipitously. IBM's China revenue declined by 22 percent, causing an overall profit decline for the company of 4 percent. Chinese tech firms moved in to take the business after Snowden's revelations.

Then came the news that, in addition to PRISM, the NSA had a backdoor program called Muscular, by which it entered into the tech companies internal networks without anyone knowing. In one month, the agency gathered and processed more than 180 million new records. "The Muscular project [operated jointly with NSA's British counterpart, GCHQ]," wrote the *Washington Post* reporters who had been the beneficiaries of Snowden's document release, "appears to be an unusually aggressive use of NSA tradecraft against flagship American companies. The agency is built for high-tech spying, with a wide range of digital tools, but it has not been known to use them routinely against U.S. companies."[30]

An NSA slide presentation of the way Muscular works was revealed by Snowden. One slide showed a sketch of where the Google cloud data resided and where it was intercepted. The artist had added a "smiley face, a cheeky celebration of victory over Google security." As the shock of revelation wore off, a Google executive declared that the company was racing to encrypt the links between its data centers. "It's an arms race," said Google vice president for security Eric Grosse. "We see these government agencies as among the most skilled players in the game." The White House did not comment, but NSA defenders like John Schindler, a former chief analyst and now teacher at the Naval War College, had no qualms in saying it was obvious why the agency would prefer to avoid restrictions where it could. "Look," he told the *Washington Post*, "NSA has platoons of lawyers and their entire job is figuring out how to stay within the law and maximize collection by exploiting every loophole."

Aside from the legion of NSA lawyers squinting through magnifying glasses, looking for tiny loopholes, the home headquarters in Fort Meade, Maryland, was more like the Spring of Amymone in Greek legend, near the deep cave where resided the multiheaded water monster Hydra, symbolizing in myth not so much establishment power as native revolts against the invading Greeks. Cut off one head, and two new ones sprang forth from the stump—kind of like both the NSA programs *and* their opponents. In addition to the provisions of the Patriot Act, for example, the president could exercise less well known authority under Executive Order 12333, issued by President Ronald Reagan in 1981. That order—which has been used by every president since—contains no exceptions for American citizens if the data are gathered outside the United States. Even as Obama began to consider reforms to the way the NSA gathered metadata and the operation of the FISA Court in camera with no advocate for those subject to surveillance, he was extremely protective of EO 12333.

A State Department official, John Napier Tye, learned just *how* protective when he wrote a speech for his boss about how anyone who disagreed with executive policies and practices could use the democratic process to seek changes under the Whistleblower Protection Act. Tye's original draft read, "If U.S. citizens disagree with congressional and executive branch determinations about the proper scope of signals intelligence activities, they have the opportunity to change the policy through our democratic process." Tye was instructed by White House counsel to take out of the talk references to "executive branch determinations" and refer only generally to laws. If he talked about executive branch determination, some investigative reporter might indeed pursue a story about one-two-triple-three, as it was known. Tye's op-ed stressed that he was not revealing any secret information, only talking about instructions he had received. It was a neat ploy that apparently saved him from a federal investigation.[31]

The term *arms race* was now being used differently, to describe tech companies' efforts to protect their interests against the NSA's Muscular cyberoffensive. Companies even began competing to show users how well their data were protected from prying eyes, said a report in the *New York Times*, "with billions of dollars of revenue in the balance." More than half of Americans surveyed in a national poll now said that surveillance had intruded on their personal privacy rights. "We want to ensure that governments use legal process rather than technological brute force to obtain customer data," said Microsoft general counsel Bradford Smith, giving an apt description of the backdoor program. Microsoft planned to open transparency centers where foreign governments could inspect the company's code so as to assure them that it does not plant back doors for "spy agencies in its products."[32]

Avoiding a showdown with the intelligence community had been Obama's highest priority, certainly higher than having an open debate over the future role of the NSA and other agencies, even though he well understood that playing the crisis card was the favored technique of the intelligence and military to distract attention from embarrassing questions. He had learned from the furor he encountered over closing Guantánamo, for example, that the intel community feared most the tales that would be told by former inmates about the enhanced interrogation techniques practiced on them by CIA questioners. On the other hand, Obama had failed to anticipate the mounting opposition he now faced from the tech companies, pushback that threatened to force him to go well beyond anodyne recommendations. On December 9, 2013, eight tech companies placed a full-page ad in the *Times* and *Washington Post* that said, "We understand that governments have a duty to protect their citizens. But this summer's revelations highlighted the urgent need to reform government surveillance practices worldwide." Here was the strongest demonstration yet of what Snowden's actions had wrought. "The balance in many countries has tipped too far in favor of the state and away from the rights of the individual—rights that are enshrined in our Constitution. This undermines the freedoms we all cherish." The key phrase here was "in many countries," for America's close cooperation with the other members of the Five Eyes—Australia, Canada, Great Britain, and New Zealand—would enable the U.S. intelligence services to piggyback on their resources to gather information. The situation really did resemble the ancient Greek legend of the Hydra.

While the companies were moved to act by the very real threat of the loss of billions of dollars in revenues as other countries and their users moved away from American technology, the emphasis on the Constitution and the language used in the letter suggested political opportunities of a left-right alliance against the government, one particularly dangerous to President Obama's already fading hopes that his second term, after the long fight over medical insurance, could somehow move ahead on other pressing issues such as immigration reform and climate change. It seemed now that there was no way of avoiding a serious debate over the intelligence community's near independence from Congress and even from its supposed masters in the White House.

The changes the tech companies demanded included an end to bulk collection of e-mails, online address books, and other personal information, as well as limits on how easily the NSA could obtain court orders for Internet data. These changes would definitely rebalance the scales. A week after the letter appeared, Obama met with the tech company execs in the White House. They pressed their case "loudly" in a meeting that lasted more than two hours. Administration officials unsurprisingly described the meeting as "constructive, not at all contentious." One participant even suggested the unspeakable. Why not pardon Snowden? He couldn't do that, said Obama. The former analyst was accused of leaking classified information and faced felony charges. He should be returned as soon as possible to the United States, "where he will be accorded full due process and protections." The answer was unlikely to satisfy the questioner or the tech companies. It made it seem that the Russians were responsible for not "returning" Snowden to face justice, as if he were the source of trouble instead of what he had revealed.

Company representatives made clear their dissatisfaction after the White House conference. "We urged him to move aggressively on reform." The companies were facing lawsuits from shareholders who felt that they were suffering from the association with the NSA. These were not ideological protests stirred by leftist "troublemakers." The Louisiana Sheriff's Pension and Relief Fund said in its lawsuit against IBM, for example, that the company's relationship to the NSA presented a "material risk to the company's sales" to China. Despite knowledge of the risks, IBM officials had misrepresented the situation to investors by claiming that it "expected solid improvement in the sales of its hardware division." [33]

The issue here concerned yet another NSA program, this one for placing listening devices or malware inside computers before they were delivered. These programs originated from a special division inside the NSA, the Office of Tailored Access Operations (TAO), a unit that tracks targets' orders of new computers, intercepts those shipments, and reroutes them to its own work-shops. At these "load stations," agents carefully open the packages and install malware or hardware components to provide backdoor access, allowing the TAO agents to access any information on the networks those computers are connected to. Instead of having to be on site, the listeners can conduct their eavesdropping from the comfort of a remote computer. The TAO spies have been described by the *Der Spiegel* editors as "on-call digital plumbers," an allusion to the Plumbers who carried out Nixon's burglaries. And the claim by TAO hackers that they had succeeded in getting "some of the most significant intelligence our country has ever seen" reminds one of the claims, soon to be rebutted by the president's own commission, that the NSA programs had prevented fifty-five terrorist attacks.[34]

Der Spiegel documented the truth of TAO boasts of gaining access to targets in eighty-nine countries. "TAO specialists have directly accessed the protected networks of democratically elected leaders of countries. They infiltrated networks of European telecommunications companies and gained access to and read mails sent over Blackberry's BES email servers, which until then were believed to be securely encrypted. Achieving this last goal required a 'sustained TAO operation,' one document states." The pretense by defenders of the NSA programs that these über-Orwellian outcomes are fantasies of the "crazy" left or right reveal a very blinkered outlook on what is happening and what can happen in the future. When NSA director Keith Alexander went out to hackers' conferences to recruit computer science graduates for TAO and other spots in his organization, he often wore jeans and a T-shirt—the uniform of a new kind of military.

The Courts and the Commission

During the meeting with tech executives, the president joked with the Netflix chief, asking him if he had brought advance copies of *House of Cards*, the award-winning series about a ruthless congressional leader from South Carolina who lies and murders his way into the Oval Office. Reed Hastings laughed and invited Obama to do a cameo appearance on the show, saying, "This guy's getting a lot of stuff done." The president replied, "I wish things were that ruthlessly efficient." Everyone laughed.[35]

Obama had several reasons to complain about the way things were going at this moment. The day before the contentious meeting with tech executives, Judge Richard Leon, sitting on the Federal District Court for the District of Columbia, determined that the NSA's collection of telephone metadata was indeed "Orwellian" and probably violated Fourth Amendment protections against unwarranted police searches. It was the first time a federal judge had issued such a ruling. He imposed an injunction on the further collection of such records but promptly stayed his ruling until the government had a chance to appeal. Leon had been appointed to the court by George W. Bush. The challenge had come from Larry Klayman, a compulsive litigator and professional pain in the neck, who charged that the NSA programs had violated his constitutional right to privacy and brought the suit.

Right after Snowden's original revelations, Klayman was the first out of the gate to bring legal action against the NSA. He had had an adventurous life as a lawyer representing all sorts of right-wing causes. He was also a "birther" who challenged Obama's right to be president as not a natural-born citizen. But that was only among the more recent of his causes, which go back to the Clinton years. During the 1990s, he had represented Gennifer Flowers in a suit against Hillary Clinton for defamation of character. Not successful there, he also brought eighteen lawsuits during President Clinton's terms for ethical misconduct and criminal activity. None succeeded. Two months before Judge Leon ruled in his favor on the NSA question, Klayman had urged a conservative rally in Washington, D.C., to begin a second, nonviolent, American Revolution, then wrote that President Obama should "put the Quran down . . . [and] figuratively come out with his hands up."[36]

Before Snowden, when court actions were attempted, the

standard government reply had been that the plaintiffs had no standing to bring suit because they could not prove they had been subject to surveillance. Of course they couldn't; it was secret. The unraveling of plaintiffs' catch-22 position began with the information suddenly made public that the NSA had gathered data on millions of Americans.

Even after Judge Leon's ruling, the DOJ lawyers came back to court to claim that two plaintiffs represented by the Electronic Frontier Foundation—Carolyn Jewel, who sued on behalf of all AT&T customers, and Virginia Shubert, who sued on behalf of all Americans—could not sue because they could not prove that they were being subjected to surveillance. Asking the government to provide evidence whether or not they were subject to surveillance, its lawyers argued, could cause "exceptionally grave damage" to national security by revealing collection methods. National Intelligence Director James Clapper said in a court filing that in his judgment, despite public knowledge of the programs, "the disclosure of still-classified details regarding these intelligence-gathering activities, either directly or indirectly, would seriously compromise, if not destroy, important and vital ongoing intelligence operations." Playing the crisis card no longer had the same impact, however, after Judge Leon's ruling. The plaintiff's lawyer, Cindy Cohn, quipped that such a claim had become "ridiculous at this point. . . . The government is trying to reset the clock in order to avoid an open judicial determination about whether that surveillance is legal."[37]

Klayman was only the culmination of discontent, not its instigator. Indeed, as National Security Advisor McGeorge Bundy once quipped about the 1965 raid on Pleiku in South Vietnam, the raid that launched a thousand bombing strikes and settled the question of American involvement, "Pleikus are like streetcars." There would be one along soon enough. There would be another Klayman soon enough.

The first blow against the government after Snowden had come from the FISA Court itself. In September 2013, the court

ruled that the publication of a Section 215 order to tech companies requiring them to supply the metadata meant that all the
secret rulings had to be published so that there could be an informed debate. The government had resisted making FISA Court
legal opinions public to prevent precisely that. Used to finding
every loophole possible in oversight laws for their own benefit, officials did not want independent attorneys scouring legal opinions
for flaws that would bring on more regulation or congressional
action. Little wonder that the more sections 215 and 702 of the
Patriot Act were questioned, the more the executive branch fell
back on EO 12333—a place where Congress couldn't reach even
if it someday actually did want to exercise serious oversight.

As early as 2004, Justice Department lawyers had told the FISA
Court that the reason illegal searches had been carried out was
because of the inability to get Congress to agree on legislation. It
was a remarkable, nay an astounding, claim, which implied that
Congress need not and should not be trusted with debating national security matters. "Seeking legislation," government lawyers
claimed, "would inevitably compromise the secrecy of the collection program the government wishes to undertake." Attorney
General Alberto Gonzales made no mention of what NSA was
doing when he briefed the Senate Intelligence Committee the
next year, in 2005. As a result, Judge Reggie Walton shut down
the program in 2009 because of unauthorized dragnet searches
over the past five years. It was reinstated the very next year and
in fact expanded under a new ruling by Judge John Bates—even
though he noted the record of unauthorized acquisitions and the
total failure of NSA oversight. All these maneuvers remained secret until a Freedom of Information Act suit by the Electronic
Privacy Information Center forced DNI James Clapper to release
the relevant documents in August 2014.[38]

As he released documents that revealed the persistent failure
of oversight to catch the illegal collections, Clapper tried to make
it appear that the NSA had corrected itself, saying, "As previously
stated, this internet communications metadata bulk collection

program has been discontinued." But the agency had already launched a new program to permit its analysts to do their searches under EO 12333! As fast as one defense unraveled, then, the government was busy trying to re-ravel the yarn into a tighter ball protecting its ever expanding ambitions to collect data. The effort to subject the government's legal reasoning to public scrutiny had achieved a victory in a ruling in September 2013 by Judge Dennis Saylor IV that the American Civil Liberties Union had the right to seek disclosure of the FISA Court's interpretation of Section 215 of the Patriot Act—as a result of the Snowden revelations about how Verizon had been compelled to provide its telephony records to the government under the "business records provision" of Section 215. What was of special interest here, wrote Spencer Ackerman, was that this interpretation permitted the collection *prior* to any specific ongoing terrorism investigation "and the records collected involve[d] millions of Americans who are not under suspicion of wrongdoing." [39]

All this exposition is complicated, but it helps to explain Judge Leon's sixty-eight-page ruling on December 16, 2013, which excoriated the NSA program as an almost Orwellian reshaping of American political life that would have left James Madison "aghast" at what was being done to the Constitution in the name of national security. The ruling contained several arguments that undermined the government's ultimate fallback position—that it couldn't be sued because plaintiffs lacked legal standing because they couldn't prove they'd been spied on. But he wasn't finished. The Obama administration maintained that the 1979 Supreme Court decision *Smith v. Maryland* trumped all other court findings and proved that the program was constitutional. In that case, the Supreme Court had ruled that government surveillance of an uninformed suspect, including a search of phone records, was legal: the subject had no expectation of privacy because the calls were all reported on phone company records for billing purposes.

Leon attacked that argument head-on. He pointed out that the government's ability to search telephone records had changed by orders of magnitude since 1979, before the first commercial sale of cellphones. These multitask instruments were different in almost every way from those that figured in *Smith v. Maryland.* In Leon's words, "The notion that the Government could collect similar data on hundreds of millions of people and retain that data for a five-year period, updating it with new data every day in perpetuity, was at best, in 1979, the stuff of science fiction."[40]

Thus he asked, "When do present-day circumstances . . . become so thoroughly unlike those considered by the Supreme Court thirty-four years ago that a precedent like *Smith* simply does not apply? The answer, unfortunately for the Government, is now." As soon as the ruling was announced, Glenn Greenwald received a statement from Snowden in Moscow: "I acted on my belief that the N.S.A.'s mass surveillance programs would not withstand a constitutional challenge, and that the American public deserved a chance to see these issues determined by open courts. Today, a secret program authorized by a secret court was, when exposed to the light of day, found to violate Americans' rights. It is the first of many."[41]

David Rivkin, a former White House lawyer in the George H.W. Bush administration, believed Leon had overstepped badly into areas beyond his competence. "*Smith v. Maryland* is the law of the land," he maintained. "It is not for a District Court judge to question the continuing validity of a Supreme Court precedent that is exactly on point." Yet this was not so certain. Leon had pointed to a 2012 Supreme Court decision that held it was unconstitutional for the police to use a GPS tracking device to monitor a suspect's public movements without a warrant. Five of the nine justices, moreover, separately questioned whether *Smith v. Maryland* was still valid in an era of modern technology systems and capabilities. The judicial debate continued when, eleven days after Leon's bombshell ruling, Judge William Pauley, the presiding judge for the Southern District of New York, rejected a suit similar to Klayman's brought by the American Civil Liberties Union, ruling that the *Smith* decision remained valid despite advances in technology. But the real basis for his decision was his obiter dictum that the terror threat after 9/11 warranted giving the state "exceptional deference."

Writers for *Forbes* magazine described the situation as a Fourth Amendment Quartet, a tug-of-war among Snowden, Judge Leon, President Obama, and the NSA. That was not a bad way of thinking about the tensions that swept through the government after Leon's ruling. And it was likely to last a long time as the appeals process played out. In another sense, the tug-of-war was over the question of which side was being naive, national security hawks or civil libertarians. The *Forbes* writers, Jens F. Laurson and George Pieler, argued that Judge Leon had the better of the argument. To say that the government could have access to one's phone data without a warrant when there is a *specific crime-related cause to do so*—the basis of the *Smith* decision—was a far cry from saying the government can maintain a comprehensive record of *all* phone calls just in case some terror-related communication might pop up in the future. "What the NSA does now is not just a fishing expedition, it's a massive net over every and all fish current and future."[47]

Judge Leon's ruling and the demands of the tech companies at their White House meeting with the president forced Obama to release the report of the special commission weeks earlier than he had wished to do. In August, he had charged the commission with recommending changes in the data-gathering programs that would give the nation greater confidence in what the NSA had done in the years since 9/11. Ostensibly, that meant greater confidence in what it had done to protect not only homeland security but also the privacy of American citizens. Under that rubric, however, the president could mean real changes or merely cosmetic alterations to make the programs appear more acceptable to critics. At a press conference the day after the report was released, on December 20, 2013, the president said, "In light of the disclosures that have taken place, it is clear that whatever benefits the configuration of this particular program may have may be outweighed by the concerns people have on its potential abuse. *And if that's the case, there may be another way of skinning the cat"* (emphasis added).

The commission consisted of five members: Richard Clarke, Michael Morrell, Geoffrey Stone, Cass Sunstein, and Peter Swire. After five months of investigation and deliberation, the task force produced a three-hundred-page report with forty-six specific recommendations. All members of the commission were quick to point out that their report did not in any way recommend "unilateral disarmament" in the intelligence wars. It was significant, however, that advance copies had not been provided to the interested three-letter agencies, perhaps explaining why the White House felt uneasy about releasing it to the public ahead of schedule. As had been the case since 2009, Obama hated being put in such a position. The three-letter agencies all had a bite that was worse than their bark.

There was no way, however, to cushion the public or the intelligence agencies from this flat-out statement in the report: "Our review suggests that the information contributed to terrorist investigations by the use of section 215 telephony metadata was not essential to preventing attacks, and could readily have been obtained in a timely manner using conventional section 215 orders." The report also included the sort of line that any administration hates to hear: "Although we might be safer if the government had access to a massive storehouse of information about every detail of our lives, the impact of such a program on the quality of life and on individual freedom would simply be too great."

President Obama promised to take the report with him on vacation in Hawaii over Christmas and to give his formal response sometime in the new year. But before he left the White House, he had already decided against splitting Cyber Command from the NSA. It would, said officials, be too much for Cyber Command, given its newness—it became operational only in 2010—and the fact that it was charged with carrying out defensive and offensive operations that relied on the NSA. Of course, that meant the NSA would continue to be directed by a general or an admiral.

Even so, said a *New York Times* editorial, these were "Bad Times for Big Brother," a week that had seen Judge Leon's ruling, the presidential review panel report, and yet another release of documents by Snowden. The editorial expressed no surprise that surveillance had grown in the Obama years. No matter the occupant, it said the Oval Office would always test and often transgress the limits of its power. What was surprising was the *Times* comment, "Over the long run, the nation cannot bank on presidential self-restraint or timely and favorable court rulings to stop the invasion of privacy on a mass scale."[43]

The *Times* had never seemed so anxious for Congress to step in and amend the laws to halt government collection and analysis of bulk data. Indeed, it argued, the future now shaped up as a battle between the executive and the intelligence community on one side, and the president's panel and Congress on the other. There were bills in the works to make the necessary changes with provisions that matched recommendations in the panel report, especially one authored by a persistent skeptic, Democratic senator Patrick Leahy, and by Republican representative James Sensenbrenner, one of the original authors of the Patriot Act, where it all began.

Whether such a bill could ever become law was of course very much a question. The opposition was already mounting its considerable counterattack. The chair of the review panel, Michael Morell, a former deputy director of the CIA, all but renounced the central findings of the panel in a *Washington Post* op-ed, entitled "Correcting the Record on the NSA Recommendations." In this remarkable article, he began by saying that the big danger of such a long report was that readers got to choose what they thought was the bottom line. Commentators had used words like *sweeping* to characterize the recommendations, asserting they would roll back the capabilities of the intelligence community. Not true. The recommendation had been to shift custody of the metadata so that the government would no longer hold it itself and would need a court order to search it. Many commentators had said that the program had not been "essential to preventing attacks," but that was not the same thing as saying the program is not important to national security—"which is why we did not recommend its elimination."[44]

Not satisfied that he had corrected the record, Morell resuscitated the argument that the program would have prevented 9/11. "Had the program been in place more than a decade ago, it would likely have prevented 9/11. And it has the potential to prevent the next 9/11. It needs to be successful only once to be invaluable." Unfortunately for his argument, four days before Morell made this assertion Lawrence Wright, a highly respected author and expert on Al Qaeda, anticipated such a claim and effectively refuted his comment by citing what actually happened after the NSA tracked calls by one of the planners of the attack. The information was not passed on to the FBI. All the information about Al Qaeda figures in America was kept back in isolation. The FBI was told, "This is not a matter for the F.B.I." The reason, apparently, was that the CIA hoped to turn the Al Qaeda operatives into its own agents. "Edward Snowden broke the law, and the Obama Administration has demanded that he be brought to justice," wrote Wright. "No one has died because of his revelations. The C.I.A.'s obstruction of justice in the [USS] Cole investigation arguably also was a crime. Its failure to share information from the Al Qaeda switchboard opened the door to the biggest terrorist attack in history. As long as we're talking about accountability, why shouldn't we demand it of the C.I.A.?"[45] Then came the top blogger at *Lawfare*, the formidable Benjamin Wittes, predicting an unending and debilitating debate. He foresaw nothing but trouble from the panel report. "To put the matter bluntly, there is no way the administration will embrace a bunch of these recommendations. And from this day forward, any time the White House and the intelligence community resist these calls for change, the cry will go out that Obama, in doing so, is ignoring the recommendations of his own review panel."[46]

He was right on both counts.

7

A House Divided Against Itself

Our system of government is built on the premise that our liberty cannot depend on the good intentions of those in power. It depends on the law to constrain those in power.
—President Barack Obama, speech at the Department of Justice, January 17, 2014

In a speech that was otherwise reasonably balanced and appropriate in tone and substance, the one striking omission was a clear statement by President Obama about the damage to our national security caused by Snowden's disclosures and a similarly emphatic statement that those who take it upon themselves to disclose our nation's intelligence, diplomatic, and military secrets (like Snowden or Bradley Manning) should be condemned, not lauded. A forceful statement by the President would help to prevent future damaging disclosures by self-appointed whistleblowers.
—John Bellinger, former legal adviser to the National Security Council, January 19, 2014

I think what we are going to see in the speech . . . is all of the language in the speech kind of fading left about transformation and transparency and checks and balances, but, frankly, I think the substance of the speech is going to be holding his ground. I don't know that American intelligence agencies are going to be doing a whole lot of things different in a week, a month, or a year from what they are doing right now.
—General Michael Hayden, former CIA and NSA director, January 17, 2014

After President Obama's January 17, 2014, speech, the national debate over leakers and government spying on Americans only intensified. In the media, the debate reached red-hot temperatures among reviewers of Glenn Greenwald's book about the Snowden revelations (and his role in promoting the leaks), *No Place to Hide*. Meanwhile, Congress continued to debate a Freedom Act introduced in the House by Patriot Act co-author and Wisconsin Republican representative James Sensenbrenner and in the Senate by Vermont Democrat Patrick Leahy, who vowed to make reform a key part of his legacy. Sensenbrenner's comment to a reporter when his bill was introduced raised the central issue: "I can say that if Congress knew what the NSA had in mind in the future immediately after 9/11, the Patriot Act never would have passed, and I never would have supported it."[1]

In response the White House, as usual, tried to focus on the messenger instead of the message, but there was really no way to shift the spotlight—until events outside the United States intervened. The beheadings of Americans captured by the jihadist group ISIS produced a new sense of fear about future terrorist attacks on the homeland originating from bases in the Middle East. Someone had to keep track of potential or possible homeland terrorists who get their skills and assignments from abroad, it was argued, and the National Security Agency was the only agency that could do it. Not surprisingly, given this development, the remarkable bipartisan backing for the Freedom Act disappeared faster than ice melting in the Arctic Ocean.

The debate didn't end there, of course, neither in Congress nor in the media. The intertwining of Snowden's revelations with the question of how to fight terrorism caused a great deal of soul-searching on all sides. The point of connection chosen by the Obama administration was the Espionage Act, which linked Snowden to a list of leakers whom the government wished to punish in order to stop the flow of classified information to the public. The point of connection for Snowden's supporters, and by extension to other leakers, was the Constitution's First and Fourth amendments. In short, it was a confused battlefield with front lines constantly shifting from one question to another, from leakers themselves to press responsibility in a democracy. Moreover, the espionage industrial complex had grown unchecked for more than half a century, so there was no way to separate the Snowden revelations from earlier programs authorized long before 9/11.

Senator Leahy promised "not to give up the fight." As events unfolded, the Freedom bill's difficulties in gaining passage did not exactly please the White House, either, because it had been watered down in negotiations with congressional leaders, and without some new legal basis for metadata programs there were sure to be new debates when the Patriot Act expired. More than anything else, the White House feared an endless distracting debate. In a press conference on August 9, 2013, the president, with a straight face, claimed that Snowden had actually *impeded* reform.

> There's no doubt that Mr. Snowden's leaks triggered a much more rapid and passionate response than would have been the case if I had simply appointed this review board to go through [the programs] and I had sat down with Congress and we had worked this thing through. It would have been less exciting. It would not have generated as much press. I actually think we would have gotten to the same place, and we would have done so without putting at risk our national security and some very vital ways that we are able to get intelligence that we need to secure the country.

Obama had tried to head off debate then, and he later tried to regain control with his January 2014 speech, but his biggest challenge came now from the expert panel he himself had appointed to recommend reforms.

The Dust Won't Settle

Several days before the president's speech, in fact, Geoffrey Stone, a distinguished Chicago lawyer and a member of the panel, expressed disappointment at the president's lack of contact with the group after its report in early December 2013. There had been no contacts to speak of, he said in a discussion at the National Press Club. Instead, the president had spent a month meeting with officials in the espionage agencies and in the congressional committees charged with oversight, "largely on one side of the picture. And instead of our report being truly understood as a middle ground, based upon taking into account all of those perspectives on both sides of the spectrum, I think the White House got moved by thinking of our report as a liberal report." Intelligence officials—like Michael Morrell, a member of the panel—were "pushing [Obama] and the White House generally more to what we can call the right." He did not know what concrete proposals would emerge in the speech, "But it's all in the details."[2]

Stone's concerns were well justified. Obama began his speech by asserting a prominent role for "surveillance" in the successful fight for independence from Great Britain. His remarks only deepened the controversy over the terms of debate. "At the dawn of our Republic, a small, secret surveillance committee born out of the 'The Sons of Liberty' was established in Boston. The group's members included Paul Revere, and at night they would patrol the streets, reporting back any signs that the British were preparing raids against America's early Patriots."

America's success in the world, he continued, owed much to its spies, from the time of the Sons of Liberty to the post-9/11 era. True, the agencies had overreached during the Vietnam War, but those abuses had already been dealt with by Congress with additional oversight laws "to ensure that our intelligence capabilities could not be misused against our citizens."

The post-9/11 world had brought home in the most brutal fashion new dangers, he went on, "where a bomb could be built in a basement, and our electric grid could be shut down by operators an ocean away. We were shaken by the signs we had missed leading up to the attacks—how the hijackers had made phone calls to known extremists, and traveled to suspicious places." Later in the speech, he returned to this subject, referring to a "gap" that might have prevented 9/11, as the NSA saw the call made by one of the hijackers to a safe house in Yemen but could not see that it was coming from someone in the United States.

The argument that the NSA program would have prevented 9/11 had been ably refuted several times over, but that fact seemed not to matter to the president in fashioning this speech. These comments were a preemptive strike against future leakers as well as a justification for indictments of Snowden and others under the Espionage Act. We had failed to detect the plotters because the NSA programs were not in place before the attacks, he still insisted, and therefore must guard against those who would reveal the nation's intelligence gathering methods. But there were some concessions to the authors of the Freedom bill being debated in Congress. We must recognize there were potential risks of government overreach, he said, which he linked to the use of "enhanced interrogation techniques that contradicted our values." The connection he sought to make between permitting eavesdropping and deploring torture was odd, and once again he insisted, as in his comments about Vietnam-era violations of civil liberties, that the worst excesses of Torturegate had already been curbed by the time he took office; hence his decision not to pursue the waterboarding tapes or other supposed "relics" of the Bush years. The slate had been wiped clean. Yet he promised eternal vigilance—to prevent torture, stating, "To say that our intelligence community follows the law, and is staffed by patriots, is not to suggest that I, or others in my Administration, feel complacent about the potential impact of these programs." Earlier in the speech, he had been less apologetic about secret universal espionage.

Intelligence agencies cannot function without secrecy, which makes their work less subject to public debate. Yet there is an inevitable bias not only within the intelligence community, but among all of us who are responsible for national security, to collect more information about the world, not less. So in the absence of institutional requirements for regular debate—and oversight that is public, as well as private or classified—the danger of government overreach becomes more acute. And this is particularly true when surveillance technology and our reliance on digital information is evolving much faster than our laws.

He had advocated reforms in a speech at the National Defense University in May 2013, he said, by asserting that the nation needed "a more robust public discussion about the balance between security and liberty." But whatever he planned as a follow-up—and there were few details—had been overtaken by events. "What I did not know at the time is that within weeks of my speech, an avalanche of unauthorized disclosures would spark controversies at home and abroad that have continued to this day."

Before Snowden, then, he had already been headed in the right direction, and now he would propose the reforms needed to complete the process, reforms that would not leave the nation in peril. First, he would issue a new presidential directive to strengthen executive branch oversight of intelligence activities, so as to provide a better review of "sensitive targets." He promised that his "senior national security team" would regularly scrutinize the hundreds of separate espionage operations being run at any one time by the seventeen known U.S. government agencies that constitute what is so blandly called the intelligence community.

In addition, Obama promised greater transparency regarding FISA Court opinions, i.e., more than none. However, instead of adopting the panel's recommendations for a public defender type of figure in the court to challenge the government's requests for surveillance, he called upon Congress to establish "a panel of advocates from outside government to provide an independent voice in significant cases."

Leaving it up to Congress to help him fix things distributed responsibility and let him claim that the debate would make the nation stronger. The speech ended with an unusual twist on the theme of American exceptionalism.

> And I also know that in this time of change, the United States of America will have to lead. It may seem sometimes that America is being held to a different standard, and the readiness of some to assume the worst motives by our government can be frustrating. No one expects China to have an open debate about their surveillance programs, or Russia to take the privacy concerns of citizens into account. But let us remember that we are held to a different standard precisely because we have been at the forefront in defending personal privacy and human dignity.

Like many other speeches, this one was essentially a plea—Trust me. I'm not Dubya.

But how did that reverse exceptionalist standard apply specifically to Edward Snowden, without whom there'd be no debate? On that subject, he left no room for interpretation, nor would there ever be any, even after Congress finally passed the Freedom Act in 2015, a law that owed everything to Snowden's efforts. He had already called upon the former computer analyst to come home and face the charges against him in the courtroom, including two under the 1917 Espionage Act that could put him in prison for a very long time. If convicted, he could face a sentence like Chelsea Manning's—thirty-five years. Yet Obama now asked Congress to come up with legislation to address the threat that long-term government possession of metadata poses to citizens' expectations of privacy as guaranteed in the Fourth Amendment. There was no contradiction here, the president insisted, because he had ordered a review of the NSA programs before Snowden blew open the door to the agency's well-guarded secrets and Director of National Intelligence James Clapper had had to admit that he had lied to Congress about them.

If the president tried to place himself above the arena of debate, other members of the commission were not buying it. It was precisely on this point that Geoffrey Stone and former White House terror chief Richard Clarke voiced dissatisfaction with the immediate aftermath of their report. Despite what Obama implied in the speech about how the "gap" in intelligence gathering—rather than intelligence sharing—was crucial to understanding the dangers facing America, Stone told NBC News, that he was "absolutely" surprised when he discovered the agency's lack of evidence that the bulk collection of telephone records had thwarted any terrorist attacks. "It was, 'Huh, hello? What are we doing here?' The results were very thin." One question the White House wanted answered was whether it had actually stopped "any [terror attacks] that might have been really big."

"We found none," said Stone.[3]

Clarke, who had headed the White House counterterrorism office for Clinton and Bush until after 9/11, was even blunter. "I reviewed each case," he said in a panel discussion of claims by the NSA and President Obama that fifty-five possible terrorist incidents had been stopped by the metadata program. "All claims of stopping terrorism were bullshit."

Former CIA director Michael Hayden, who appeared alongside Clarke on this panel, confined himself to a grumpy demurral: "There are a range of views on that." That only made Clarke push harder for a response: "We don't have a surveillance state. But the technology is there. . . . A future president may decide to turn the surveillance state on. And in the future, once you give up your civil liberties, you may never get them back." Hayden had no answer.

On another occasion, Clarke talked about how difficult it was to write laws to prevent abuse. "If you're not specific, an agency that bugs phones is going to bug phones. The NSA is an organization that's like a hammer, and everything looks like a nail." Despite all, he still believed that the NSA had been a force for good—so far. "It could, with another president or after another

9/11, be a force not for good. Once you give up your rights, you can never get them back. Once you turn on that police state, you can never turn it off."[4]

No one could have anticipated Clarke's most provocative assertion, however: "Even if NSA had solved every one of the [terrorist] cases based on [the phone collection], we would still have proposed the changes."[5]

Reactions from Snowden

It almost seemed as if one could not turn on a television, read a newspaper, or scan the Web without seeing Edward Snowden professing his patriotism (with mock humility, his critics would say). His Moscow residence quickly turned into a salon where he constantly entertained kindred spirits and leading lights from the media. In an interview with *Guardian* editors, he scoffed at the claim being made that he was lonely and socially unconnected. "I think there are guys who are just hoping to see me sad. And they're going to continue to be disappointed."[6]

Snowden was financially secure, *The Guardian* told readers. He had money from his "substantial savings from his career as a well-compensated contractor," but also from numerous awards and speaking fees from around the world. He also had foundation funding for a new press freedom initiative—one that would supply tools for journalists to communicate securely. He was well aware that both liberals and conservatives had marked him down as holding political views that would both explain his behavior and make him less of an accurate witness to government wrong-doing. He was neither a wacko libertarian, as some liberals wanted to label him, nor a Russian spy, as conservatives wanted to insist. About the latter accusation, he said, he could give a blanket answer. If the U.S. government had the "tiniest shred of evidence, not even that [I was an agent], but associating with the Russian government, it would be on the front page of the New York Times by lunchtime."[7]

As for the accusation that he had done untold damage to the intelligence capabilities of the West, Snowden held that that was ridiculous. First, the fact that people know their communications are being monitored does not stop them from communicating, "because the only choices are to accept the risk, or not communicate at all." That was self-evident. Suppose we are talking about terrorist cells. These cannot operate except by collective action. "So if they abstain from communicating, we've already won. If we've basically talked the terrorists out of using our modern communications networks, we have benefited in terms of security—we haven't lost."

Snowden's opponents, of course, would not grant that premise. Was the government program really "intrusive"?, they asked. Why, asked an interviewer, was NSA data collection any different, really, from what Google and others gathered? Why trust Google any more than we trust the state? "One, you don't have to. Association with Google is voluntary. But it does raise an important question. And I would say while there is a distinction— in that Google can't put you in jail, Google can't task a drone to drop a bomb on your house—we shouldn't trust them without verifying what their activities are, how they're using our data."[8]

Brian Williams, then NBC's star anchor, came to the Moscow apartment for a one-on-one interview broadcast to the biggest audience Snowden ever had. Snowden came across as reasonable and well motivated, not at all the supposedly estranged figure who had set out with "evil intent" to satisfy his personal grievances by betraying his country's trust, nor a naive Russian puppet who didn't understand what he had done.

Snowden knew what was being said about him, he told Williams, and was ready to answer any question. Why hadn't he tried to go through regular channels if he felt the NSA programs were so egregiously damaging to individual rights, and unconstitutional? He had, he said, He had sent messages to his bosses listing what he believed were violations of the laws. He had tried to go through channels before leaking documents to journalists, repeatedly raising objections inside the NSA, only to be told, "more or less, in bureaucratic language, 'You should stop asking questions.' " American officials confirmed that Snowden sent at least one e-mail to the NSA's Office of General Counsel raising policy and legal questions, but they objected in reply that one message hardly counted as a serious effort to pursue his concerns in a serious way. And there had allegedly been no more attempts to go through proper channels. The Snowden message they found, moreover, said nothing about abuse of citizens' rights. It asked whether executive orders took precedence over laws, nothing else. "We have searched for additional indications of outreach from him in those areas and to date have not discovered any engagements related to his claims."[9]

In reply to the NSA response, Snowden accused the agency of not trying very hard to find his protests, insisting that he had sent e-mails to different people and engaged in "conversations" during which he explained his concerns. He was playing on NSA's turf here, and he tried to slide around a trap he had laid himself:

Ultimately, whether my disclosures were justified does not depend on whether I raised these concerns previously. That's because the system is designed to ensure that even the most valid concerns are suppressed and ignored, not acted upon. The fact that two powerful Democratic Senators—Ron Wyden and Mark Udall—knew of mass surveillance that they believed was abusive and felt constrained [from doing] anything about it underscores how futile such internal action is—and will remain— until these processes are reformed.

Still, the fact is that I did raise such concerns both verbally and in writing, and on multiple, continuing occasions—as I have always said, and as NSA has always denied. Just as when the NSA claimed it followed German laws in Germany only weeks before it was revealed that they did not, or when NSA said they did not engage in economic espionage a few short months before it was revealed they actually did so on a regular and recurring basis, or even when NSA claimed they had "no domestic spying program" right before we learned they collected the phone records of every American they could, so too are today's claims that "this is only evidence we have of him reporting concerns" false.[10]

Keeping one's credibility by invoking the experience of other critics—who had not revealed the secrets, in fact—was not the strongest line to take. Still, he no doubt knew that protests from his level would never break the surface, and he must have assumed that when he decided to act, he would have to be the final authority on what his oath meant and to whom he owed his loyalty. His revelations, he said, were in defense of the Constitution against the illegal actions of NSA officials. Furthermore, he had not taken an oath to not disclose classified information, although he recognized he had broken laws in doing so. The point was that the penalties stipulated for such acts did not include punishment under the Espionage Act. In many ways that was the heart of the matter, because, as Amy Davidson wrote in the New Yorker, it went back to the question of character. "There are a lot of people in the government, and public, who are simply dismayed by Snowden's actions, and by everything about him, down to his glasses and haircut. The oath he swore was supposed to be humbling, and he is presumptuous."[11]

Hence what stung NSA fans the most was an NBC Twitter poll taken after the interview, which showed that 59 percent of the respondents saw him as a patriot, and 41 percent believed he was a traitor. Secretary of State John Kerry, himself a dissenter during the Vietnam War, wished people would stop comparing him to Daniel Ellsberg, the most famous leaker from that troubled time. A naval officer who had won three Purple Hearts and a Bronze and a Silver Star, Kerry had testified before Congress on April 22, 1971: "We could come back to this country, we could be quiet, we could hold our silence, we could not tell what went on in Vietnam, but we feel, because of what threatens this country, not the

Reds, but the crimes which we are committing that threaten it, that we have to speak out."

Elected to the Senate in 1984, Kerry ran for president against George W. Bush in 2004 and was attacked by a group of prowar veterans who had also served on Swift Boats, river patrol craft like the one Kerry commanded. They took out ads to accuse the senator of lying about his war service and about the war crimes he purportedly witnessed. The charges were proven false by military records, but they played an unquantifiable part in his defeat in the election.[12] Such organized smear campaigns have since become known as *swiftboating*. It was ironic, then, that Kerry's was the loudest voice to condemn Snowden as a "coward and traitor" on NBC News in the wake of the Brian Williams interview a day or so earlier.

Kerry was not interested in counting e-mail exchanges to determine the truth. "Edward Snowden is a coward, he is a traitor and he has betrayed his country." He should "man up" and return from Russia to face charges of espionage and theft. "If he cares so much about America and he believes in America, he should trust in the American system of justice. But to be hiding in Russia, an authoritarian country, and to have just admitted that he was really trying to get to Cuba, I mean, what does that tell you, really? I think he's confused. I think it's very sad." Kerry did not stop there. He went on to contrast Snowden with Ellsberg. "There are many a patriot—you can go back to the Pentagon Papers with Dan Ellsberg and others who stood and went to the court system of America and made their case. . . . And if he wants to come home tomorrow to face the music, he can do so."[13]

If Kerry had hoped to take back the high ground from Snowden with that last statement, he had completely misread history and had somehow missed "Dan's" recent activities. Snowden couldn't come back to the United States and receive a fair trial, charged Ellsberg. If he returned, as Kerry demanded he do, he'd be thrown into a cell at once with no chance of bail. He himself had been out on bail the whole time, Ellsberg went on, able to speak to rallies and go on television with Walter Cronkite. But even so, at trial he could not present his motivations as part of his defense. And much more recently, Thomas Drake's defense lawyers were barred from even uttering the words *whistleblowing* and *overclassification* just before the government's case fall apart. Ellsberg ended by saying that Kerry was a man he had once admired, but "that was a long time ago." What the secretary of state said about Snowden betraying his country "is one of the most despicable statements I have heard from a politician or anyone else who I can remember. It is very much to his discredit and I think very much the less of him." [14]

The Stakes of the Debate

The debate after Obama's speech was already entering its second or third round when Kerry and Ellsberg had this exchange. Kerry's description of a "confused" young man had become central to the arguments made by those who, while they might agree that the NSA had overstepped its authority, saw Snowden as more of an ideological threat than a danger to national security. Many of them were reluctant defenders of programs they hadn't known existed, and being duped only intensified their anger at the unduper. To these mostly liberal figures, it appeared that Snowden had declared war on their beliefs. He posed a challenge to the "elite consensus" (or EC) that had lined up behind President George W. Bush in 2003 to remove Saddam Hussein from Iraq so that it could enjoy the freedoms afforded to all members of the Wilsonian brotherhood of nations led by the United States. The EC had been strained to the breaking point when that war didn't go the way they had hoped it would. But, they consoled themselves, that was because of Bush's mistakes and the false pretenses by which support had been generated, not the fundamental assumptions— the good intentions—behind American policy that had been undone by bad management and crude mistakes like the siege of Fallujah. For many Americans, liberals and neoconservatives alike, it seems history always moves in one direction, despite all the obstacles of the moment, so why look back?

By this accounting, President Obama had been pretty successful in welding the consensus back together, even though many disagreed with his stand that it was best not to look back in anger, at least not to the point of setting off a debate over torture. What was done was done—and should stay that way. This attitude also goes a long way toward explaining the administration's use of the Espionage Act as a threat of punishment to prevent leakers from reopening the fissures so recently healed but as yet hardly strong enough to withstand a lot of pressure.[15]

Viewed from this perspective, the stakes could hardly be any higher. Certainly not everyone who went after Snowden's motives instead of his revelations wished to have him imprisoned for thirty-five years, nor did all advocates of punishment necessarily agree that the Espionage Act was the best weapon to use. Finally, there was no agreement in the establishment that all leaks were bad and all journalists equally guilty of endangering national security. Even so, Snowden's crime—and those who abetted it—had to be condemned, lest American "security" be put at risk by a loss of whatever faith remained in national institutions. In this reading, what Geoffrey Stone and Richard Clarke had said about the lack of proof that NSA programs had prevented a single terrorist attack mattered less than the potential, and still less than the need to maintain a basic faith in the government by keeping citizens blissfully ignorant. The debate thus went to questions far beyond which party controlled Congress or held the White House.

As it happened, Kerry was wrong about Snowden wanting to escape to Cuba. He had tried to get to Ecuador. But it obviously sounded better to critics to have him headed for still-Communist Cuba, a holdout from Wilsonian liberalism.

Sean Wilentz, a professor of history at Princeton University and a former contributing editor of the New Republic, seemed as offended as John Kerry in a long article for that traditionally liberal journal. The title perfectly captured the concern (and mystification) of many who felt betrayed, not by the revealers but by the apostasy of some in the liberal brethren: "Would You Feel Differently About Snowden, Greenwald, and Julian Assange If You Knew What They Really Thought?"[16]

"What's astonishing about their ascent to heroism is the breadth of their support," Wilentz began. It was to be expected that the antiwar left and libertarian right would come out for Snowden, but the New York Times? Well, perhaps that was explainable, he said, as the paper had come to rely on leakers as prize sources and was now "crusading" on Snowden's behalf. To criticize the leakers as had legal journalist Jeffrey Toobin "and a few other writers" is to invite moral condemnation for "outright complicity with Big Brother." So far, however, the adulatory treatment the leakers had received "closely mirrors their own self-presentation." But there were important "caches of evidence" that have gone largely unexamined by the media, he wrote. This evidence was housed in documents of their own on the Internet. What was especially important about these writings, Wilentz argued, was that much of it appeared before the leakers had even entertained the possibility of a global audience. "They are documents in which one can glimpse their deepest beliefs and true motives."[17]

Snowden's conversion to the view that the NSA's activities posed an "existential threat to democracy," Wilentz found, is far more complicated than he tells people. And to discover the roots of his illicit acts, one must go back to his teenage years, when, as a high school dropout enamored of computers, he first began posting on the website Ars Technica. Amid the usual postadolescent banter about sex, Snowden talked about his gun: "I have a Walther P22. It's my only gun, but I love it to death." Following this supposedly telling introduction to Snowden's political leanings, Wilentz takes us through the next few years, a time when the future dissident "vilified leakers and defended covert intelligence," lambasting the New York Times and President Obama for appointing a "politician," Leon Panetta, to head the Central Intelligence Agency and for indicating that he would seek a ban on assault weapons. Snowden even supported Representative Ron Paul's call for the United States to return to the gold standard and contributed money to his 2008 presidential campaign. *And*, perhaps worst of all, he was indifferent to the social dislocations caused by the Great Recession: "Why is 12% employment [*sic*] so terrifying?"

All these beliefs, Wilentz avers, did not really change just because he turned on the NSA in 2013. "Other evidence challenges trustworthiness." To put it differently, Wilentz believes that Snowden's actions in making off with the NSA documents were part of a pattern, not a 180-degree turn. At most, as John Kerry said, he was a confused young man; at worst, a schemer. "It's hard to see evidence of a savvy—or even consistent—mind at work." But he was smart enough, Wilentz says, to contact Glenn Greenwald, identified simply as "a blogger at *The Guardian*," who possessed the sophistication about politics that the computer nerd lacked.

Having disposed of what Snowden's revelations meant by disposing of Snowden, he turned to Glenn Greenwald. Snowden's abettor started out as a "conventional liberal" but one who liked to stir up trouble by getting into "cyber-brawls" with social conservatives on the Internet. As a lawyer, he often defended people with white-supremacist credentials, as well as members of the neo-Nazi National Alliance, the latter charged with brutal beatings of Mexican day laborers. Nothing wrong with that; indeed, many liberals see a need to defend unpopular clients. But then his career took a very different path as he went full-time onto the Web, launching his own blog and becoming a regular columnist for *Salon*, where he became famous for his slashing attacks on the Bush White House. On certain issues, however, Wilentz then says, he took a rightist hard line—immigration, for example. He defended nativist congressman Tom Tancredo from charges of racism, and wrote of the "unmanageably endless hordes of people [who] pour over the border in numbers far too large to assimilate, and who consequently have no need, motivation or ability to assimilate." True, he has now reversed his position on this issue but has blamed the rediscovery of his immigration writing on "Obama cultists" out to discredit him.

Greenwald can hardly be considered a serious thinker, in other words, or one ever suited to make decisions about American national security and the dangers leakers pose. All in all, writes Wilentz dismissively, Greenwald "has come to reside in a peculiar corner of the political forest, where the far left meets the far right." He found much to admire in Ron Paul's views on the Constitution and foreign policy, while admitting that his views on immigration and abortion bordered on the fringes. After Paul dropped out of the 2008 presidential race, Greenwald wrote articles "tepidly" supporting Obama, but he kept up contacts with the Cato Institute, a libertarian activist organization, as well as with the leftist FireDogLake.com, in an effort to forge a new political alliance. When bloggers confronted Greenwald about his association with libertarians, "the darling [Greenwald] of the netroots and MSNBC left angrily batted the claims away as distortions," and attacked his critics as "McCarthyite" purveyors of "falsehoods, fabrications, and lies."

In 2010, meanwhile, Greenwald spoke to Julian Assange for a *Salon* column, praising WiliLeaks for its vital work. "His enthusiasm for Assange's mission drew him into the world of computer hackers and security leakers—a world where it became possible not simply to criticize the national security state, but to sabotage it." Pretty strong words. Presumably Wilentz doesn't believe that the United States *has become* a national security state, but one doesn't really know what he believes about the NSA programs and the power of the intelligence community. Understanding Assange's "bizarre historical understanding and the messianic sense of mission that pervades WikiLeaks" is essential to evaluating his career. His personal history and beliefs fuel a philosophy that posits "conspiracies of operatives" who have created an authoritarian power. To destroy that apparatus, defenders of "truth, love, and self-realization" must disrupt "the authority's communication

systems and cut off its secret information flows." Stealing and leaking secrets thus became vital tactics for Assange in his personal
struggle against authoritarian evil.

The high point for WikiLeaks so far was the vast trove of classified documents supplied by Chelsea Manning, the so-called Iraq
War Logs, the biggest leak of classified material in the history of
the Department of Defense. Five major news organizations in
the United States, Great Britain, and Europe published stories
based on these DoD documents, as well as diplomatic materials
included in the Manning trove. Perhaps the publication record
would suggest to Wilentz something more like sensationalism, or
cooperation with WikiLeaks to sabotage national security, but we
do not know. In any event, Assange's trustworthiness comes into
play, as it does in regard to Snowden and Greenwald. Wilentz
points out that two Swedish women have leveled accusations of
"sexual violence" against the founder of WikiLeaks, leading to the
"weird sequence of events that landed" Assange in the Ecuadoran
embassy in London in 2012—where he still is today.

Whatever one makes of the way the accusations have been
handled by Swedish authorities, Wilentz moves on to describe
Assange's increasingly cozy relationship with Vladimir Putin and
WikiLeaks' supposed role in perpetuating the dictatorship in Be-
larus. "Without much public commentary," he writes, "Assange
has acquired something like Russian government media sponsor-
ship." Indeed, and perhaps inevitably in this account, Assange's
connections to Putin's regime "would appear to have something
to do with the next chapter in the NSA controversy—how and why
Edward Snowden came to seek asylum in Russia."

The article ends with a long recital of how valuable Snowden
is to the Putin regime, implying along the way that there was a
"plan" from the outset to exploit his actions for Russia's benefit
in its post–Cold War struggles to reassert its power and embarrass the United States. Wilentz argues that these three, Snowden,
Greenwald, and Assange, have largely set the terms of the debate
over transparency and privacy. "But the value of some of their

revelations does not mean that they deserve the prestige and influence that has been accorded them." So there apparently is no denying that the revelations have some value, but weighed against the dangers to American security they matter much less. To understand his critique, however, one must focus on the second part of the sentence. They do not deserve the "prestige and influence that has been accorded them." Here again is the argument that the most serious damage the leakers had done was to the ideological framework of the modern liberal state, not to any specific loss in tracking down a potential enemy. The leakers "and their supporters" would never grant the state "modern surveillance powers, even if they came wrapped in all sorts of rules and regulations that would constrain their abuse." They were right, he ends, to worry about potential abuses, but not to distrust democratic governments in the paranoid way their actions reflected. "Surveillance and secrecy will never be attractive features of a democratic government, but they are not inimical to it, either. This the leakers will never understand."

Wilentz had spent a great deal of time detailing what he believed were similar behavior quirks of the Big Three leakers, as well as their supposed hatred of modern society. Without the NSA to shoot at, in other words, probably they would have all found another way of attempting to undermine the state.

But was the question really the links between the Big Three or rather what had changed in the nation's political atmosphere that required constant tinkering with the balance between security and privacy? By the time of Snowden's leaks, the Obama administration had already brought or continued a series of investigations and prosecutions against revealers. As Thomas Drake put it in a panel discussion with others, "I am Exhibit No. 1. . . . I was charged with 10 felony counts. I was facing 35 years in prison. This is how far the state will go to punish you out of retaliation and reprisal and retribution. . . . I lived on the blunt end of the surveillance bubble. . . ."[18]

"The Reviews"

Another *New Republic* blast against Greenwald and his ilk came from its highly regarded longtime editor Michael Kinsley, who had recently returned to the journal after several stints with other publications and being an editor at *Vanity Fair*. The Kinsley review of Greenwald's *No Place to Hide* appeared in the *New York Times Book Review*, a traditional meeting place for intellectuals and members of the EC. It deserves special attention because it triggered a national controversy about leakers and those who aid and abet them. The review framed the debate in the way Snowden's and Greenwald's critics preferred, but in doing so it also led to a dispute within the paper.

Kinsley's starting point was David Gregory's famous question (or accusation) to Greenwald on *Meet the Press*: "To the extent that you have aided and abetted Snowden . . . why shouldn't you, Mr. Greenwald, be charged with a crime?" Greenwald had paused, noted Kinsley, before finally saying Gregory's formulation could be used to justify any baseless insinuation. Greenwald did not deny he had "aided and abetted Snowden." He had dodged the central issue. Not an accusation, the broadcaster's question was a "perfectly reasonable question that many people were asking. . . . But Greenwald seems to feel he is beyond having to defend himself. . . . In his mind, he is not a reformer but a ruthless revolutionary—Robespierre, or Trotsky. The ancien régime is corrupt through and through, and he is the man who will topple it." [19]

To Kinsley, however, it was very much a question about what to do about leakers and those who aided and abetted them. "There is no invisible hand to assure the right balance is struck"—a reference of sorts to Adam Smith's economic theories of the marketplace's supreme function as the regulator of choice, especially for diehard libertarians. "So what do we do about leaks of government information? Lock up the perpetrators or give them the Pulitzer Prize? (The Pulitzer people would chose the second option)."

It was not an easy question, Kinsley admitted, calling the

Snowden revelations an important story. But in the end, the press cannot make the final decision, especially if Glenn Greenwald represents it.

> The question is who decides. It seems clear, at least to me, that the private companies that own newspapers, and their employees, should not have the final say over the release of government secrets, and a free pass to make them public with no legal consequences. In a democracy, (which, *pace* Greenwald, we still are), that decision must ultimately be made by the government. No doubt the government will usually be overprotective of its secrets, and so the process of decision-making—whatever it turns out to be—should openly tilt in favor of publication with minimal delay. But ultimately you can't square this circle. Someone gets to decide, and that someone cannot be Glenn Greenwald.

It's interesting that the only reference to anyone other than Greenwald in this part of Kinsley's declamation is "the private companies that own newspapers, *and their employees.*" The absent names are the *Washington Post* and Barton Gellman. Snowden had not given *The Guardian* and Glenn Greenwald an exclusive, had not thrown open his computer files only to the modern Robespierre or Trotsky he saw behind the mask of a journalist that Greenwald apparently wore. True, the review was about Greenwald's book, but not talking about the articles written by Gellman, who also received the Pulitzer, suggested that Kinsley had prioritized personality over policy.[20]

Kinsley's critics, beginning with the *New York Times* public editor, Margaret Sullivan, reminded him of the role of the press in a democracy. In a column on May 27, she wrote that even though the review had not yet appeared in print, "it's already infuriated a lot of people." Sullivan wrote, "Mr. Kinsley's central argument ignores important tenets of American governance. There clearly is a special role for the press in America's democracy; the Founders explicitly intended the press to be a crucial check on the power of the federal government, and the United States courts have consistently backed up that role. It's wrong to deny that role, and editors should not have allowed such a denial to stand."

Kinsley shot back that Sullivan was "talking through her hat" when she argued that the Founders had specified a "special role" for the press. Instead, he said, the courts had repeatedly turned down opportunities to create a "journalist's privilege." Sullivan might not like that, he wrote, "Heck, I don't especially like it. But it's a fact. The First Amendment protects the right to speak. The right not to speak (e.g. to protect a source) is more problematic." With this comment, Kinsley veered off the Greenwald review track to make a point about the courts' refusal to overrule the government on a subpoena to *Times* reporter James Risen to testify about who leaked to him a CIA plan to disrupt Iran's nuclear program. Then he commented that his critics all brought up the Ellsberg/Pentagon Papers case to ask if he thought Ellsberg should have gone to jail. Like most people—except Greenwald, he said—he thought the issue was complicated. But no, he finally says, Ellsberg should not have gone to jail. "It should be an affirmative defense that any leak was—in hindsight—in the public interest."

If one looks carefully at that statement, however, what Kinsley is really saying is that Ellsberg should indeed have been brought to court, where he could have mounted an "affirmative defense" that his leak was in the public interest "in hindsight." Public interest defenses, however, had not been admitted into the court proceedings in the cases of Thomas Drake or Chelsea Manning at the time he wrote this review. They were admitted only, as in Manning's case, at the time of sentencing. Hence he meant the phrase "in hindsight" not as one would look at the case while it was being decided, but only after a criminal conviction!

As *The Atlantic*'s Conor Friedersdorf pointed out, critical reviews of Greenwald's book, such as those by Kinsley and by *New Yorker* journalist George Packer, have tended to "understate the radicalism of the international security state and to overstate the radicalism of its critics." The dire consequences predicted by one side in the debate are always in the future: if the government is not allowed free rein, there will be another 9/11 or a series of terrorist attacks likely to be much worse than 9/11. The other side insists that the oversight protections and the regulations enacted in the wake of the Vietnam War and Watergate to prevent government abuses have proven so woefully insufficient to protect individual rights that unless someone blows the whistle the Fourth Amendment will become a dead letter.[21]

The charge that Greenwald felt he was beyond having to defend himself frequently came up in articles by Snowden critics, often by Kinsley or Packer, a lapsed believer in the Iraq War who now described Snowden, and by implication Greenwald, as loners whose self-proclaimed mission was to retake the Internet after the invasion of government agencies. Snowden and Greenwald were "uncompromising Thoreauvians" in their beliefs, wrote Packer. "The scale of it—nearly two million documents, by some accounts—is a measure of the purity of his [Snowden's] conviction." Moreover, he added, "Not caring about the outcome is what Max Weber, in 'Politics as a Vocation,' called 'the ethic of ultimate ends,' in contrast with 'the ethic of responsibility.'" Henry David Thoreau appears several times in Packer's meditation on Edward Snowden's actions as a principled dissenter willing to go to jail for his refusal to pay taxes for the Mexican War—unlike the impulsive computer analyst who "fled to Russia and sought asylum."[22]

Thoreau's one-night imprisonment, all too often invoked by Snowden's critics, was for failure to pay a poll tax. Comparing that to the sentence handed out to Chelsea Manning, the one Thomas Drake faced, or the term any indictment under the Espionage Act could mean is quite simply ludicrous. Likewise, the accusation that Snowden had "fled" to Russia was yet another effort to frame the debate around personal character. In fact he had planned to seek asylum in Ecuador. Going through Moscow and Havana was the safest way to Quito, given the ability of the U.S. government to intervene with other countries to intercept and search passenger flight, which, it was later learned, was exactly what Lisa Monaco, acting for President Obama, hoped to do to get him back. While en route to Moscow, the United States revoked his passport, making him a man without a country. It was good only for a trip back to the United States. Stranded in the transit zone at Russia's Sheremetyevo Airport without proper travel papers, Snowden's chances of safe passage to Ecuador via Cuba became much more complicated. To gain the proper papers for a flight to Quito would require leaving the transit zone and visiting the foreign embassy of Ecuador, but first he would have to go through customs and into Russia proper. Gaining temporary asylum was the necessary first step, but there he remains, living in a Moscow apartment.

No doubt Putin's government is quite happy with the current situation, which allows its leader to posture as a champion of dissenters everywhere, while persecuting them in his own country—and woe be unto anyone he sees as a serious threat. Putin's advantage stems from Snowden's lack of another option, not a desire on his part to damage American defenses. But Snowden's bind is also an advantage to his former employers in the intelligence community, providing another way to paint both Snowden and Julian Assange as men without a country, whose fate depends on their willingness to admit guilt and voluntarily take the consequences for actions they believe were just.[23]

Thus for Packer, Greenwald's book reveals "a mind that has liberated itself from the basic claims of fairness," while Snowden in the year since the revelations "has drifted a long way from the Thoreauvian ideal of the majority of one. He has become an international celebrity, far more championed than reviled." Such comments reflect indignation at the prestigious prizes the "Snowden Team" has received. Critiques of Snowden and Greenwald often insinuate that money and fame are powerful motivators for the papers to publish the stories, whatever form of martyrdom Snowden might choose and never mind Greenwald's supposed mission to expose the truth.[24]

This fusillade of criticism did not prevent a continuing stream of favorable judgments from other organizations. There was the Ridenhour Prize for Truth-Telling, awarded to Snowden and filmmaker Laura Poitras, who now lives in Berlin. Named for Vietnam veteran Ron Ridenhour, who exposed the My Lai massacre, the prize had previously been awarded to Thomas Drake. A spokesperson for the committee that chose the winners, Danielle Brian, commented, "I don't think we have any illusions we can erase all of their struggles," but the award, she hoped, would "let them know they're not alone."[25] The comment had immediate meaning for Poitras, who had to move to Berlin to continue her investigative reporting without interference from the U.S. government.

The biggest honor of all in journalism, the Pulitzer Prize for Public Service, then went to *The Guardian* and the *Washington Post*. The citations were almost the same, praising both papers for articles based on the Snowden documents: "Awarded to The Guardian US for its revelation of widespread secret surveillance by the National Security Agency, helping through aggressive reporting to spark a debate about the relationship between the government and the public over issues of security and privacy."

The Freedom Act

Debates in the journals and newspapers were mirrored on Capitol Hill. By the end of summer 2014, Congress had not acted upon any legislation to curb (or reform) the NSA programs that Edward Snowden had revealed more than a year earlier. Writing in the *Washington Post* on the thirteenth anniversary of 9/11, Aaron Blake argued that fears about the rise of the Islamic State had meant people were now willing "to cash in some of their civil liberties in exchange for peace of mind when it comes to their safety." Polls showed that the pro-security position of the

American people had undergone a rapid change. Now 50 percent of Americans said that the government had not gone far enough to protect security, while 35 percent were worried about it going too far in restricting civil liberties.[26]

When the president's committee reported on the NSA wiretapping programs in December, the White House had "arranged closed-door briefings with lawmakers in a bid to contain the damage." At one of these sessions, an exasperated Robert S. Litt, the never shy general counsel of the agency, challenged them to own up to their own role. "Well, you're the ones who passed it," he said in a reference to the Patriot Act, the rationale for the programs that collected phone records of virtually every U.S. citizen. "And if you don't like it, you can always repeal it."[27]

The statement was a perhaps unconscious echo of the challenge President Lyndon Baines Johnson put to dissenting congressional figures during the Vietnam War. You authorized it with the 1964 Gulf of Tonkin Resolution, he would say, putting a finger on the chest of anyone who dared to challenge him. If you don't like your war, repeal it! Wisconsin representative Jim Sensenbrenner, an author of Patriot Act, took up Litt's challenge and now pushed for the Freedom Act. The administration had distorted his earlier efforts into something quite different than he had intended, he said. "The phone records of innocent Americans do not relate to terrorism whatsoever, and they are not reasonably likely to lead to information that relates to terrorism. Put simply, the phone calls we make to our friends, our families and business associates are private and have nothing to do with terrorism or the government's efforts to stop it."[28]

Here again was a similarity between the report on the torture program and the one on the NSA metadata programs: when examined closely, neither program had done anything to improve national security. Like any other bureaucracy, the intelligence agencies simply wanted to expand unimpeded and depended upon simply outlasting critics and particularly upon always having the national security trump card to play.

An earlier NSA lawyer and general counsel, Stewart Baker, also defended the program in absolutist terms. "The only way you're going to find some numbers is if we collect them all," he said. "If you put limits on what the government collects, it will miss the calls that are most important." Sensenbrenner thought that was nonsense and a false interpretation of the Patriot Act. "If everything is relevant, then the term 'relevance' ceases to have any legal significance. If Congress intended to allow bulk collection, it would have authorized bulk collection. Instead, we attempted to set limits on what the government could obtain."[29]

When Sensenbrenner introduced a reform bill to limit the scope of NSA collections to specific targets and named it the Freedom Act, a struggle was in the offing over potent symbols. At first the Republican National Committee lined up behind him and approved on a voice vote a resolution condemning the NSA and asking GOP lawmakers to "immediately take action to halt current unconstitutional surveillance programs." Prominent Republican "intelligence officials" then sent a letter of protest to the RNC chair Reince Priebus, saying, "Count us out." If nothing else, Snowden's revelations were a nightmare for both Republican and Democratic whips trying to maintain party discipline.

Not surprisingly, the man who led the executive branch team in discussions with a committee of lawmakers was Robert Litt. As a result of his work, the original bill bore little resemblance to the final product the full House voted on. The original approved by the Judiciary Committee had restricted data collection with a qualifier to a "specific selection term," such as a "person, entity or account." The revised version substituted the phrase "a discrete term," something the FBI wanted so it could continue to obtain business records in ordinary ways, like obtaining all records of hotel guests. The new language would allow the government under that "discrete" rubric to obtain vast amounts of records so long as there was "some kind of limit"—say, all records from a single ZIP code.[30]

The changes in the bill also weakened the requirement that

"a special advocate" appear in the FISA Court to argue against a government petition for a warrant. The presiding judge in the changed version could decide whether or not a special advocate was needed, and the ruling was not appealable. In a letter to Congress, a committee from the Constitution Project concluded, "We believe H.R. 3361 will produce a negligible increase in adversarial presentation before the FISC." That elimination of public representation pertained to a warrant for not just an individual target, but also, given the watering down of the selection term, de facto bulk records collection as well.[31]

Adding to the pressure, several major tech firms said the bill was just not enough to satisfy their customers. Facebook, Google, and Apple executives issued a statement calling the House bill inadequate and underwhelming. "While the House bill permits some transparency, it is critical to our customers that the bill allow companies to provide even greater detail about the number and type of government requests they receive for customer information."[32]

The revolt of the techies was unprecedented, but that was not all. Verizon, which had figured in the first Snowden-inspired articles as the subject of an NSA order to hand over its metadata, now attacked President Obama's plan to have the records kept with the companies for some specified period, still accessible to the government by individual warrants. A Verizon vice president had testified that forcing the phone company to keep the records for NSA perusal made it an arm of the government. "Any constitutional benefit of having the data held by private entities is lost when, by compelling retention of that data for non-business purposes, the private entity becomes a functional surrogate of the government."[33]

The revised bill passed 303 to 121, even after several supporters abandoned hope and turned to the Senate to take corrective action. There was enough momentum, however, behind the reformist urge to provide Representative Sensenbrenner with reasons to vote for it. Whatever the concerns, the bill would end "bulk collection" by law. It also would prohibit targeting people more than two hops away from an identified suspect. "Don't let the perfect become the enemy of the good," Sensenbrenner said as he cast his yea vote.

After the House bill passed, former NSA general counsel Stewart Baker belittled the results. In his view, the Freedom Act was really an effort to reject the new technology, to sweep back the tide. His testimony before Congress was a curious mixture of condemnation and counterthrust against critics by belittling their efforts. The new technology was one of the best ways the nation had to track down terrorists. The bill might deny bulk collection power to NSA, so reformers could congratulate themselves. But what else was it useful for? "Ending NSA's program will not end bulk collection of data in the private sector or by government agencies using other authorities, here and abroad."[34]

Now it was up to Senator Patrick Leahy to take up the burden of revising the Freedom Act to make it stronger, more like the original Sensenbrenner draft, and to educate the public as to the stakes involved. Even before the president's speech in January, he had said, "We're really having a debate about Americans' fundamental relationship with their government."[35] But Baker's hints about other methods of data collecting, no matter what Congress did or did not do, took on added meaning when a former State Department official, John Napier Tye, wrote an op-ed piece for the *Washington Post*, "Meet Executive Order 12333: The Reagan Rule That Lets the NSA Spy on Americans." There had been many references to EO 12333 as the Snowden/NSA story developed over the year past, but none that so fully explained the phrase "using other authorities."

In March 2014, Tye related, he had been instructed to write a speech for his boss on the impact of the Snowden disclosures on surveillance practices and U.S. Internet freedom policies. His draft had included the statement that if U.S. citizens "disagree with congressional and executive branch determinations about the proper scope of signals intelligence activities, they have the opportunity to change the policy through our democratic process"—the Litt/Baker position, in other words. The White House counsel's office told him that that wasn't so, and he was instructed to amend the line by making a general reference to "our laws and policies" rather than intelligence practices. Lest anyone miss the point of his opening paragraph in the op-ed article, Tye then wrote, "Even after all the reforms President Obama has announced, some intelligence practices remain so secret, even from members of Congress, that there is no opportunity for our democracy to change them." [36]

Strong words. And Tye backed them up by saying he had been cleared in his job to receive top secret and even "sensitive compartmented" information. "Based in part on classified facts that I am prohibited by law from publishing," he wrote, "I believe that Americans should be even more concerned about the collection and storage of their communications under Executive Order 12333 than under Section 215 [of the Patriot Act]." In fact Section 215 contained some protections—even as interpreted by the NSA and the FISA Court—that Executive Order 12333 did not. Issued by President Ronald Reagan in 1981, it authorized the collection of the contents of communications, not just metadata, "even for U.S. persons." While data could not "be individually targeted under 12333 without a court order, . . . if a U.S. person's communications were 'incidentally' collected (an NSA term of art) in the course of a lawful overseas foreign intelligence investigation, then Section 2.3(c) of the executive order explicitly authorizes their retention." [37]

Tye had been careful to state that he was revealing no classified information in the op-ed and to add that he had filed complaints with the department's inspector general arguing that the EO's use and collections of data under the current system violated the Fourth Amendment. This set him apart, legally, from Edward Snowden. But like him, Tye closed the article by invoking his oath to protect the Constitution as his reason for coming forward. When is a leak not a leak, in other words? When you only assert something without proof? But without Snowden's revelations, who would have believed Tye or paid much attention? The first ten amendments had become an intellectual battlefield in the war on leakers.

"The Government Has Unchained Itself from the Constitution"—Where to Now?

Patrick Leahy's leadership in restoring many of the provisions of the original Freedom Act before it was gutted under pressure from the White House and intelligence community evoked favorable attention in some quarters and fear in others. The Senate-revised version rescued the specific-target requirement and also provided for more transparency in the FISA Court by requiring it to make public the reasons for its decisions. The bill would cause a lot of information about U.S. signals intelligence activities to become public, wrote a staunch defender of the NSA programs, Benjamin Wittes, "a huge amount more than any country has ever, to my knowledge, released about what it is doing in the way of electronic surveillance."[38]

But it was not all bad to conservatives' way of thinking. For one thing, it would have put a proper legal basis under the programs that had become controversial because of strained interpretations of the Patriot Act's various provisions, especially sections 215 and 702. Requiring more disclosure and more adversarial procedures in the "FISA process will tend to enhance the legitimacy of decisions," wrote Wittes, "that will, at the end of the day, still allow a great deal." Thus, while bulk collection of metadata under Section 215 would have been banned, the Leahy version of the bill would not have changed the government's ability to engage in warrantless collection of electronic communications by Americans to foreign countries under Section 702, leaving open a huge loophole for "incidental" searches pertaining to ongoing investigations and not limited to supposed terrorist activities. Neither did the bill require the intelligence agency to report annually on the actual number of times Americans' communications were swept up in this way. Senators Mark Udall and Ron Wyden issued a joint statement regarding the importance of the incidental-access loophole: "Congress clearly intended this authority to be used to collect the communications of foreigners—not Americans—yet the Director of National Intelligence recently confirmed that the NSA, CIA and FBI conduct warrantless searches of communications of Americans that are swept up under this authority." The Leahy version was little more than a codification of the status quo.

Even if the NSA were to feel hampered in any way by the Freedom Act, there are always, as Stewart Baker had told a congressional committee, other ways to receive a White House blessing—in particular Reagan's Executive Order 12333, about which no version of the Freedom Act had said anything. There is even another layer of secret presidential directives behind EO 12333, something called the President's Surveillance Program (PSP) or simply the Program, established in a document President George W. Bush signed on October 4, 2001, which permitted electronic surveillance "during a limited period to detect and prevent acts of terrorism within the United States." In 2004 the Office of Legal Counsel released a memo that even with substantial redactions included this claim: "The President has inherent constitutional authority as Commander in Chief and sole organ for the nation in foreign affairs to conduct warrantless surveillance of enemy forces for intelligence purposes to detect and disrupt armed attacks on the United States. Congress does not have the power to restrict the President's exercise of this authority."[39]

The assertions in this paragraph alone suggest why it is so difficult for any other branch of government—the legislative, the judicial, or even the executive—to take back control from the intelligence agencies. In the aftermath of 9/11, the Bush administration, with Vice President Dick Cheney in the lead, had seized the opportunity to "correct" what it believed had been congressional usurpations of presidential powers in foreign affairs dating back to the end of the Vietnam War and passage of the War Powers

Act. In fact, the WPA had proven useless in restraining the executive. Congress looked the other way when presidents redefined
war to avoid the requirement to seek legislative approval for acts
normally understood as constituting warfare. Congress also had
failed to play its role as watchdog to prevent the kinds of abuses
that had surfaced during the Church Committee hearings—such
as domestic spying, medical and psychiatric experiments on unwitting human subjects, and numerous assassinations of foreign
leaders. We must assume that there is more and worse, as much of
the testimony before the committee remains classified.

What many supporters of the Bush White House had not expected, however, was that a future president could use those same
powers, and that the intelligence community would become the
unacknowledged supreme master of the federal government. As
Thomas Drake pointed out, the incorporation of the PSP into the
FISA Amendments Act of 2008 makes it legal on a permanent
basis. "That's why you can't have secret laws and secret orders in
a constitutional order; it's anathema. . . . Those who have tried to
expose it were charged with espionage, like me. The government
has unchained itself from the Constitution."[40]

Whether the revised Leahy version of the Freedom Act would
do anything more than take the heat off the intelligence community was, therefore, very much in doubt. Since the nineteenth century, the press has been called the Fourth Estate, a check on the
other three—the church, the aristocracy, and the commoners. By
analogy, Americans sometimes refer to it as a fourth branch of government, guarding against abuses of power by the other three—
a mandate derived from the First Amendment. Now, however, the
secretive fifth branch, the espionage establishment, determines
more and more what the others can and cannot do. In late July
2014, it was said that Senate negotiators were "within inches" of
an agreement on a bill to place real restrictions on the intelligence
agencies. Leahy himself said he had been encouraged by conversations with the administration, which had understood why there
had been a negative reaction to the watered-down House bill.[41]

Leahy even received a letter signed by Attorney General Eric Holder and Director of National Intelligence James Clapper, which read, "Overall, the bill's significant reforms should provide the public greater confidence in our programs and the checks and balances in the system." Was this the momentum shift that would mean restraining the intelligence community or mere cosmetic steps to "provide the public greater confidence"?—the objective President Obama had been talking about ever since his first press conferences after the Snowden revelations, when he'd claimed that the balance between national security and privacy was pretty good and just needed fine tuning. The bill still lacked any standing for special advocates in the FISA Court to make appeals or to block those "incidental" searches under Section 702, but it laid out guidelines. Yet beyond the specifics of the Senate version loomed the question of how it would be interpreted. Would Obama issue a signing statement as President Bush had so often done, to "clarify" what the White House would enforce and what it would ignore as an encroachment on presidential powers under, say, Article II of the Constitution, or under a superior grant from Congress under the 2001 and 2002 Authorization to Use Military Force (AUMF) against Al Qaeda "and its affiliates"?

Whether the Leahy bill would even pass the Senate became more and more doubtful as the political clock's hands moved closer to the midterm elections and, more important, after the sudden rise of the Islamic State of Iraq and al-Sham (ISIS). The power and determination of this group, numbered at just over thirty thousand fighters, blindsided Washington, which, as President Obama admitted at one point, had not decided on a strategy for dealing with the new threat. What that threat meant was also a big question mark, as it occupied territory inside Iraq and on the borders of Syria, where a civil war had raged for three years. But more than the land it occupied was the sheer brutality ISIS exhibited toward anything or anybody in its path. The videotaped beheading of two American newsmen stirred outrage even among those who wanted nothing more to do with Middle Eastern wars and continued to oppose sending ground forces back into Iraq. ISIS spokesmen took advantage of that conundrum with a clever media campaign that called Barack Obama "vile" and "more foolish" than his predecessor. Do what you will, Abu Mohammed al-Adnani said in one broadcast, "You will be defeated." Americans and Europeans will pay the price "as you walk on your streets, turning left and right, fearing the Muslims. . . . You will not feel secure even in your bedrooms."[42]

"If people don't get what we're saying about the threats to our homeland now," said Senator Lindsey Graham, a revitalized critic of any reform, "shame on the Congress." He went on, "When you've got a terrorist that you're monitoring, I want to know who they're calling. I want oversight, I want judicial review. But now is not the time to degrade our capability to pick up an attack before it happens." Senator Ron Wyden rejoined that there simply wasn't any evidence that collecting millions and millions of phone records on law-abiding Americans "was going to in some way affect our ability to deal with that threat." He was surprisingly relaxed about the prospect that nothing would be done before the midterms. The opponents faced their own problem, because Section 215 of the Patriot Act was set to expire in 2015, and it could not be renewed without an overall reconsideration of the entire law. "This is the first time since I've been at intelligence where the clock [has] favored the reformers."[43]

"We're always going to face threats," added Leahy. "The biggest one we can face is the threat to our own liberties and our own privacy." In all of this crossfire, Edward Snowden seemed to be the forgotten exile, despite his role in setting off the whole debate. Moreover, there was apparent confusion in the top ranks of the intelligence community about what he had wrought. On September 17, 2014, the new NSA chief, Admiral Michael Rogers, said in a speech that he rejected the premise of the question whether NSA was any longer in a position to do its job. Its relationship with foreign counterparts was solid, and likewise with the American corporate sector. Moreover, he pledged to follow the law. "We follow the rule of law. When we make a mistake, we stand up and say we got it wrong." A day later, however, DNI James Clapper asserted that Snowden's leaks had created a "perfect storm," degrading the intelligence community's capabilities. In many cases, he said, specific programs had been cut, and documents had been declassified. These entailed risks. "All of those are good choices," he admitted, "as long as we recognize that we as a nation have to manage the attendant risks."[44]

The Freedom Act—even as watered down in negotiations with the White House—went down to defeat in mid-November 2014 after midterm elections returned both houses of Congress to Republican control. Florida Republican senator Marco Rubio prophesied about the consequences of passing the Freedom Act. "God forbid," said the presidential hopeful, "we wake up tomorrow and Isil is in the United States."[45]

In September 2014, James Bamford, author of the undisputed premier history of the NSA, *The Puzzle Palace*, went to Moscow to interview Snowden. He came away with a dramatic story. When Snowden had been working for the agency, he discovered that the NSA was "routinely passing along the private communications of Americans to a large and very secretive Israeli military organization known as Unit 8200." The materials included the contents of communications as well as the metadata about who was calling whom. Veterans of Unit 8200 confirmed Snowden's accusation, complaining in a letter to Prime Minister Benjamin Netanyahu that the information collected in this fashion had been used against innocent Palestinians for "political persecution."[46]

This information from domestic spying not only had been used for political purposes by the Israeli military, Bamford wrote, but it also may be being used similarly in the United States. A 2012 document he had seen in Snowden's leaked files noted that the then director of the agency, General Keith Alexander, confirmed that the agency had been compiling records of visits to pornographic websites to use the information to damage the reputations of people whom the *agency* considered "radicalizers"—not necessarily suspected terrorists but people attempting to radicalize others by incendiary speech. In Moscow, Snowden told Bamford that the document reminded one of the FBI's overreach in the days of J. Edgar Hoover, when it used its powers to monitor and harass political activists. "It's much like how the F.B.I. tried to use Martin Luther King's infidelity to talk him into killing himself," he said. "We said those kinds of things were inappropriate back in the '60s. Why are we doing that now? Why are we getting involved in this again?"[47]

8

Afraid of Our Shadow (Government)?

This year, a new Republican majority in both houses of Congress will have to extend current authorities under the Foreign Intelligence Surveillance Act, and I urge my colleagues to consider a permanent extension of the counterrrorism tools our intelligence community relies on to keep the American people safe.
— Senator Marco Rubio, "Obama's Terror Strategy Is Failing: U.S. Must Heed Lessons of 9/11," Fox News, January 27, 2015

I'm going to say this one more time because you're going to hear about it for months and months to come as we attempt to reauthorize the FISA program. Our government does not spy on Americans—unless they are Americans who are doing things that frankly tip off our law enforcement officials to an imminent threat. It was our law enforcement officials and those programs that helped us stop this person before he committed a heinous crime in our nation's capital.
— Speaker John Boehner on the arrest of Christopher Lee Cornell, January 15, 2015

Let me be clear: I continue to believe CIA's actions constituted a violation of the constitutional separation of powers and unfortunately led to the CIA's referral of unsubstantiated criminal charges to the Justice Department against committee staff. I'm disappointed that no one at the CIA will be held accountable. The decision was made to search committee computers, and someone should be found responsible for those actions.
— Senator Dianne Feinstein, January 15, 2015

With the defeat of the Freedom bill, attention in Congress turned to the upcoming deadlines for reauthorizing important sections of the Patriot Act. The pendulum had reached its farthest point, and with a push from events in Paris and Syria and Iraq and a decision in a federal courthouse in Alexandria, Virginia, it was swinging back hard. Polls showed that the electorate put two things at the top of its wish list, jobs and better defense against ISIS. Even better for the once besieged agencies at McLean and Fort Meade, one poll showed that in the under-thirty generation, about six in ten viewed the NSA favorably, while among those sixty-five and older, only 40 percent did so. Overall, Democrats had a much higher opinion of the NSA, 58 percent to 31 percent, than Republicans, who favored it only by 47 percent to 42 percent.[1]

Of course, such polls usually show support for the party occupying the White House, but the results for the under-thirties were particularly encouraging to surveillance proponents. Retired general Michael Hayden, the outspoken former head of the NSA, could feel satisfaction that his efforts to woo bright undergraduates while dressed in an open shirt and jeans had paid off. It was a good season for intelligence agencies. Another retired general, Michael Flynn, former head of the Defense Intelligence Agency, let loose a barrage of criticism against President Obama's supposed paralysis in the fight against Islamic militancy. What the nation needed was to mobilize for a decades-long fight against the new enemy, which was "committed to the destruction of freedom and the American way of life."[2]

Flynn's departure from his position was said to be because he had become too committed to raising awkward questions about getting tough with the enemy. "There is no substitute, none, for American power," he said to cheers and a standing ovation from a crowd of intelligence officers and friendly supporters from industry at a Washington conference. "You cannot defeat an enemy you do not admit exists." The enemy, in their view, had been aided by Snowden, but there were healthy signs that his ilk had lost the battle for the nation's heart and mind.

The Senate Intelligence Committee, for example, had just come through a fight to have the Justice Department investigate the CIA's spying on its staff as it worked through the problems of declassifying its own report on torture interrogations in the George W. Bush administration. In the course of its research, the committee's staff had seen a copy of an internal review by the agency, the so-called Panetta Review, which confirmed what it was finding on its own. This was very bad news for the CIA, because its fallback position in the discussions between the White House and the committee had depended on keeping the torture details secret, at worst allowing only a redacted executive summary to be published, so the agency could then join in disparaging what was released as biased and not the full story. And thus did General Hayden label the result the "Democrats' report" and assert that it was "probably the classic definition of political." But venting his displeasure at the tainted "politics" behind the Senate committee's determination to release the information in whatever form it could was not enough, and he accused the committee of reckless endangerment: "The final outcome of this report is going to be an American espionage service that is timid and friendless and really is a danger to the U.S."[3]

Hayden neatly reversed here the contention by the Snowden-ites that the danger to Americans came from the NSA's eavesdropping and storage of metadata gathered by warrantless sweeps of millions of items a day. Hayden had become the most reliable go-to guy for pithy comments against the Senate committee and its chairperson, Dianne Feinstein. As a "retired" official he could say what he really thought about the motives and actions of the committee and all other "enemies" of the intelligence community. When the attack on the Paris offices of *Charlie Hedbo* shocked the world, he suggested with grim satisfaction that the French would come running to the NSA to ferret out other plots. Outraged by cartoons of Muhammad the magazine had often run on its cover to mock the savagery of his worst followers, the raiders murdered twelve at that site and four hostages at a kosher market in another part of the French capital. "I wouldn't be surprised," he said on MSNBC, "if French services picked up cellphones associated with the attack and asked Americans: 'Where have you seen these phones active globally?' "[4]

Looked at closely, neither Hayden's quick response nor the Paris tragedy really demonstrated the effectiveness of his favorite haystack analogy. The Kouachi brothers had been under targeted surveillance for several years, but telephone, Internet, and physical monitoring had turned up no evidence they had been connected to a radical Islamist movement. But that did not prevent the tragedy from becoming a powerful image for linking the assault to a global conspiracy that needed all the watching the NSA or other agencies could do. Certainly it provided an excuse for lawmakers to push questions about the programs back behind closed doors. After the 2014 midterm elections, Republican Richard Burr replaced Dianne Feinstein as chair of the Intelligence Committee. The committee report, he told reporters (and anyone listening at Langley), was nothing more than a blatant attempt to smear the Bush administration under the pretense of "oversight" responsibilities. He was writing the White House at once, he added, to demand a return of all copies of that document and the Panetta Review. Echoing the words of CIA director John Brennan, Burr declared the report was never intended for the committee and should be sent back at once to its keepers at the CIA. By merging the two in his comments, the senator effectively blurred the basic issue of whether the committee's whole report would ever be declassified. In effect, he was saying that the Panetta Review had been leaked to the committee, and putting the genie back in the bottle before it caused trouble was an urgent matter. He used the same justification government officials claimed about the Snowden documents and would claim in the Jeffrey Sterling trial about to come to a conclusion. It "only endangers our officers and allies," he said in demanding the return of all copies from the White House. Maybe it was too late for Burr, because the American Civil Liberties Union immediately went to court to oppose his attempts to seal off the reports from public scrutiny.[5]

Attorney General Eric Holder, meanwhile, under intense

pressure from journalist groups, had finally decided against jailing reporter James Risen for refusing to testify at the trial of former CIA agent Jeffery Sterling, charged in an Alexandria, Virginia, courthouse with violating the Espionage Act. Holder also expressed concerns from time to time that perhaps the Justice Department should mend its ways about aggressive pursuit of journalists "doing their job." This also signaled a bigger decision—to separate the leaker from the journalist, after the backlash that had developed when James Rosen of Fox News was charged as a co-conspirator in an earlier leak case. Even so, the label of co-conspirator floated above the Sterling jury like a blinking sign on a dirigible. Prosecutors distributed blame for leaking the Merlin secret almost equally between Risen and Sterling. "Jeffrey Sterling was the hero of Risen's story," prosecutor Eric Olshan admonished the jury in his closing statement at the trial. "Don't let him be the hero of this one." Victory in the Sterling trial was a big deal for the government. It marked the second time (Manning's case was the first) that the Espionage Act had been the winning card. Moreover, Holder heralded the outcome as a cautionary lesson about what harm leaking could do and declared that Sterling's disclosures had "placed lives at risk"—the essential justifier for use of the Espionage Act, even though neither Risen nor Sterling had ever been in contact with an enemy agent.

The Irrelevance of Reform?

The day after the midterm election, supporters of the draft Freedom Act urged the Senate to vote on it before the Republicans took control of both houses of Congress. It was not as though supporters knew that the parties were perfectly aligned on one side or the other of the question, because there were widely varying opinions on the need for this bill—or any other restrictive measure Congress could enact. There were Republicans and Democrats who feared the bill would not go far enough to rein in NSA eavesdropping and many who believed it went too far—Senator Dianne

Feinstein, for example—but she gave it tepid support out of party loyalty. On the other hand, Senators Ron Wyden and Mark Udall insisted that the measure should include a requirement that the government obtain warrants for backdoor searches of Americans' Internet data.

If the lame-duck session after the election didn't see an up-or-down vote, supporters feared, the new Congress would already feature previews of presidential politics on the big screen—a bad situation for getting an honest vote. Outgoing majority leader Harry Reid moved to bring the bill to a vote on November 12, needing sixty votes to end debate. Its supporters included one Republican hopeful, Ted Cruz, of Texas, a co-sponsor of the legislation that Patrick Leahy had invested so much time and effort in. Supporters wanted no more amendments and asked for passage of an "undiluted" bill, but that was something of a misnomer, because it had been watered down in various negotiating arenas since the president's speech back in January.

The Senate bill did restore some of the changes the House had made when it passed a version of the Freedom Act, but since that time the bill had lain dormant. Senator Leahy voiced a common concern as the bill neared a vote on whether to end debate. "The American people are wondering whether Congress can get anything done," he said. "The answer is yes. Congress can and should take up and pass the bipartisan USA Freedom Act, without delay." For Leahy the Freedom Act had a very personal meaning. After being elected in 1975, his first vote had been to establish a special Senate committee headed by Idaho Democrat Frank Church to investigate CIA abuses of individual rights during the Vietnam War. The Church Committee had produced evidence of widespread snooping on peace activists, and its report led to the establishment of the Senate Select Committee on Intelligence, now the central player in the tug-of-war over the competing claims of privacy and national security.[6]

From one point of view, NSA stood to gain from passing the bill, which would forestall another fight in June when the legislative authority for the NSA program expired. But whoever bet on that outcome lost. On the day of the vote, the intelligence community's town crier Michael Hayden wrote in the *Wall Street Journal* that passing the act would cost lives by blinding the intelligence agencies. He and his co-author, Michael Mukasey, a former attorney general in the Bush administration, commented sarcastically, "Back in the bad old days, as during World War II and the Cold War, intelligence of all sorts directed at protecting national security was gathered by the executive without supervision by judges who, after all, know nothing about the subject and cannot be held to account for adverse outcomes." The authors were especially exercised about a requirement in the bill that a public advocate appear before the FISA Court to challenge the government's applications for wiretap authority on American citizens. Such a provision would violate the "separation of powers principles" and even the Constitution. A former FISA Court judge, John D. Bates, had written an extraordinary piece, they said, pointing out that the very presence of such an advocate, "who cannot conceivably be aware of all the facts," would only impose added burdens on the court, as well as delays that "wind up sacrificing both national security and privacy."[7]

Their article was the umpteenth variation on the old "if you knew what I knew" theme, with the inevitable follow-up "but of course I can't tell you." In the Senate debate that day, 9/11 was mentioned over and over, along with ISIS as the replacement for Osama bin Laden. Fearmongers were responsible, said an angry Senator Leahy: "Fomenting fear stifles serious debate and constructive solutions. This nation deserves more than that."[8]

Nevertheless, lawsuits featuring the Snowden documents were being used to challenge the constitutionality of the NSA collection programs. A suit by the Electronic Frontier Foundation, which had actually first been filed in 2008, used the documents as evidence that "the eyes and ears of the government now sit on the Internet." The case began when a former AT&T employee revealed that the NSA was routing copied Internet traffic to a secret room in San Francisco. The lawyers pointed out that by doing this "the government is operating a digital dragnet . . . that makes it impossible for ordinary Americans not suspected of any wrongdoing to engage in a fully private online conversation."[9] The presiding judge, Jeffrey S. White, wondered if there was enough evidence on either side to make a constitutional determination. After hearing oral arguments, however, he wondered if the filtering and destruction of this information was really as "automatic" as the government claimed. "It's concerning that, given the digital age, if the government can't do something directly, but can do it by a machine, does that open the door to get around whether there was illegal search and seizure?"[10]

There was other Snowden fallout as well, in the form of so-called Fourth Amendment protection bills in several state legislatures—perhaps surprisingly, mostly in red states and sponsored or supported by Republicans—that would shut off water supplies and electricity to NSA facilities. The enormous federal data center in Bluffdale, Utah, was built with expandable capacity to permanently store all global digital communications into the foreseeable future; it requires millions of gallons of water a month to cool its computer systems. In California, a blue state, the sponsor of such a bill, Republican David Taylor, explained that he feared Congress's failure to act on a "death knell" bill to end the NSA programs had emboldened local, state, and federal law enforcement agencies to move forward more rapidly with their own secret warrantless data collection schemes.[11]

The ongoing debate in Congress demonstrated that the controversy and its cross-party alliances continued despite failure to secure an up or down vote in the final days of the legislative session. Meanwhile, the antireform forces had gained strength from the *Charlie Hedbo* massacre. Republican senators were relieved that now there was a way to avoid a final vote, given the continuing evidence that Republican state legislators remained more than skeptical about the NSA's intrusions into private communications. Tennessee's Bob Corker, now chair of the Foreign

Relations Committee, said, "Congress having oversight certainly is important, but what is more important relative to these types of events is ensuring we don't overly hamstring the NSA's ability to collect this kind of information in advance and keep these kinds of activities from occurring." He feared that fading support for the NSA in recent months would pose a "dangerous prospect for stopping future terrorism plots." [12]

Geoffrey Stone, the law professor from the University of Chicago who sat on President Obama's review committee along with Richard Clarke, took the opposite position, saying that whatever usefulness the NSA program had had, its effectiveness now had probably gone by the board. Renewing it was not really an important question, except to save face. Stone offered a shrewd explanation for what was going on in the Capitol Hill debate: "I can imagine that the resistance both from the NSA and the White House might have for ending the program completely might be the fact that it would give the impression that was Snowden's victory." [13]

The debate over the Freedom Act resumed in 2015 in an atmosphere already singed by election politics. Among the first to declare himself was Florida senator Marco Rubio, who wanted everyone to know where he stood. Rubio called for legislation to make permanent "the counterterrorism tools our intelligence community relies on to keep the American people safe." [14] Meanwhile, another debate about limits on the intelligence agencies had arisen amid accusations exchanged by Congress and the Central Intelligence Agency.

The CIA Versus Congress

When Obama's nominee to replace Eric Holder as attorney general, Loretta Lynch, defended the NSA program in her Senate confirmation hearings, she noted that "recent events" had underscored the "importance of this as an issue in the war on terror." She began her prepared statement by saying that she viewed the spy programs as "constitutional and effective." If there were to be changes to FISA, she said, they must be approached with "full and complete understanding of the risks that are . . ."—here she paused—"that we are still facing." In other words, FISA was here to stay with perhaps only minor modifications.

After the failure of the Senate to pass the Freedom Act in the postelection session, Patrick Leahy took another tack that he hoped would help Congress understand the ramifications and interconnections of the debate. He was interested, he told the nominee, in talking about a related issue that he hoped would focus attention on the dangers of letting the NSA and CIA set the rules." "Do you agree that waterboarding is torture and that it's illegal?"

Lynch replied, "Waterboarding is torture, Senator."

"And thus illegal?"

"And thus illegal."[15]

The question was highly relevant because the surveillance community had just won its battle over the Senate Intelligence Committee's report on CIA enhanced interrogation techniques (EIT) after 9/11. At first, CIA director John Brennan had been put on the defensive by exposure of the fact that the spies had spied on the spy committee by hacking into its computers. The agency had maintained that the Panetta document—a secret internal CIA document that verified what the committee's secret long report said—had been illegally accessed by congressional staff. Here was a clear-cut challenge that could not be voted up or down like the Freedom Act. Did the Senate committee charged with oversight of the CIA have the right to "access" a CIA document, or would that breach separation of powers under the Constitution?

As accusations flew back and forth, both sides had appealed to the Department of Justice to pursue the question of who broke the law. The climactic moment came, we will see, in Dianne Feinstein's March 2014 speech on the Senate floor. Obama had fervently hoped this moment would never come. But the torture questioned had pursued him from the moment he entered office and tried to turn the page. He had ended many policies of the Bush administration, promising to shut down the trial-free Guantánamo prison and reclaim the American role as moral leader. The torture question was particularly difficult because, with the economy spinning downward, to enter into a lengthy fight over what had happened in the past when anger over 9/11 was white-hot risked both dividing the country and charges that he had launched a partisan attack on Republicans. There were, to his mind, no upsides to that fight, only downsides when he needed congressional support to pass antirecession measures and his health insurance program. But after passage of the health insurance bill, immediately labeled Obamacare by opponents, the administration faced continual challenges from almost every direction. The Bush years had left a legacy of bitter partisanship that would not go away. That legacy was such an important issue in the public mind because there seemed no way to avoid conflict over what the Great War on Terror had done to protect the country or, as others said, undermine democracy.

Senator Leahy had come forward to suggest a truth-and-reconciliation commission like the one that exposed the police abuses of apartheid South Africa. Some White House officials proposed instead a commission headed by former Supreme Court justice Sandra Day O'Connor to examine the evidence without public hearings or prosecutions. Obama rejected all options of disclosure, but the Senate Intelligence Committee's staff continued working on a report that eventually documented the torture program in detail. Although the full report is still highly classified, hints of what it contains kept leaking out, and qualms about torture merged with those about secret domestic spying. Enough had been known about the EIT program even without the new report to doom John Brennan's original nomination in 2009 to head the Central Intelligence Agency. President Obama had then named him a special counselor and kept him close by in the White House, where he was to provide direction to the drone program for eliminating terrorists by "surgical strikes."[16] As dronemaster, Brennan had claimed at one time that there were no confirmed civilian casualties from these attacks. It was no help to his credibility in discussing other questions, particularly those about the torture report and CIA hacking.

When Edward Snowden's revelations broke into the headlines, it was inevitable that the NSA program would be connected in people's minds with the war on leakers and the fight between the CIA (now finally led by Brennan) and the Senate Intelligence Committee over declassification of the torture report, with the White House trying its best to seem neutral. Before Brennan's confirmation hearing in February 2013, the committee had given him a copy of its draft to read and comment on. No one else could see it at this point, but that didn't prevent questions from senators about what it contained. In response, the director-designate said that he now had come to doubt whether the EIT techniques had yielded valuable intelligence. He said it raised "serious questions about the information that I was given." Brennan always claimed he was simply a bystander while in the CIA during these years. "I do not know what the truth is," he said at his confirmation hearings.[17]

But there was now a bigger issue that concerned not merely the report on torture, but the very basis of congressional authority to know what the agency does. This question had been simmering ever since the committee chair, Senator Dianne Feinstein, had formally requested a copy of the Panetta Review. In early March 2014, Feinstein—a tried-and-true friend of the intelligence community—stood up on the Senate floor to tell her startled colleagues that the CIA had hacked into committee staffers' computers. She denied a CIA charge that committee staff had illegally obtained a copy of the Panetta Review.

But now she criticized John Brennan: "Based on what Director Brennan has informed us, I have grave concerns that the CIA's search may well have violated the separation of powers principle embodied in the United States Constitution, including the speech and debate clause. It may have undermined the constitutional framework essential to effective congressional oversight of intelligence activities or any other government function."[18]

No charges of domestic malfeasance as grave as this had officially been made against the CIA since the 1970s and the Church Committee's revelations of a toxic stew of CIA, NSA, and FBI domestic spying, political sabotage, and hidden propaganda in all media, all dating back to the 1950s and all used against dissidents during the Vietnam War. Feinstein seemed to realize that the question now was: who actually controls the government? She explained the origins of the current dispute. The torture program had begun in 2002, but it was not until September 2006 that the chairman and vice chairman of her committee had been told about its existence by director Michael Hayden—a few hours before President George W. Bush disclosed it to the public.

A year later, she said, the *New York Times* published an article about the destruction of videotapes of the "so-called enhanced techniques [waterboarding]." When the committee raised questions about the videotapes, Hayden had "assured us" this was not really destruction of evidence, because there were descriptive cables that could be provided to the committee. The committee sent over staffers to review these cables, a process that took many months. "The resulting staff report was chilling. The interrogations and the conditions of confinement at the CIA detentions sites were far different and far more harsh than the way the CIA had described them to us." [19]

The committee staffers struggled to deal with what Feinstein called a "document dump" of immense proportions, but gradually began to sift out the material needed for the comprehensive report. Then two things happened in 2010. Documents that had been made available by electronic means and had been used in compiling a draft of the report began to disappear from the computer used for the work, in violation of the agreement reached with the director about untrammeled access. When Feinstein went to the White House to complain, she was assured that this behavior would stop. Meanwhile, among the documents the CIA had provided was the Panetta Review. As the staffers worked to complete their report, they noted that the conclusions of the Panetta Review bore out their own findings. As Feinstein remarked, "The staff did not rely on these internal Panetta review documents when drafting the final 6,300-page committee study. But it was significant that the internal Panetta review had documented at least some of the very same troubling matters already uncovered by the committee staff, which is not surprising, in that they were looking at the same information."

By erasing the documents from the computer the staffers used, the CIA was apparently engaging in a kind of preemptive strike, deleting what it must have assumed would be crucial documentation from the final committee report. But Feinstein's comment that the similarity was not "surprising in that they were looking at the same information" took on a greater significance with the Snowden documents and articles in the press. A federal judge, Richard Leon, had recently ruled that the government could no longer make the argument that those who had begun suits against government surveillance lacked standing because they could not prove they were being spied on. Snowden's revelations had provided evidence of the NSA's sweeping programs, forcing the government into the position of having to prove that the specific plaintiffs were somehow *not* being spied on. In the same way, the Panetta Review undermined CIA rebuttals of the Senate Committee report. With the Panetta Review at hand, it was awfully hard to argue that the committee's review was not accurate. Instead, everything kept coming back to the central issue of executive privilege in deciding what the public could know, had any right to know.

"Some of these important parts that the CIA now disputes," Feinstein said in her speech, "are clearly acknowledged in the CIA's own internal Panetta review. To say the least, this is puzzling. How can the CIA's official response to our study stand factually in conflict with its own internal review?" Feinstein was rightly afraid that the next step the CIA would take would be to make the documents cited in the Panetta Review disappear. "As I have detailed, the CIA has previously withheld and destroyed information about its detention and interrogation program, including its decision in 2005 to destroy interrogation videotapes over the objections of the Bush White House and the director of national intelligence. Based on the above, there was a need to preserve and protect the internal Panetta Review in the committee's own secure spaces."

In late 2013 Feinstein had requested in writing that the CIA provide a "final and complete version of the Panetta review." The new CIA director, John Brennan, refused and, in a very different mood from the questioning of the nominee at his hearing, asserted that the document was deliberative and privileged, only tentative and still not an agreed-upon official product but definitely secret. Feinstein refused to accept this answer and cited the Senate legal counsel's opinion that Congress did not recognize such claims when it comes to documents requested by oversight committees. Brennan still refused and then, at an emergency meeting, told Feinstein that CIA personnel had also conducted a "search" of the committee's computers at the staff's off-site facility!

Brennan then told Feinstein that he was making an official complaint to the Department of Justice suggesting that the committee staffers had used illegal methods to obtain the Panetta Review. The director wanted to have it both ways. While he told Feinstein in private about the search, in public comments he seemed to deny that it had happened. In an appearance at the Council on Foreign Relations in March 2014, he said, "As far as the allegations of CIA hacking to Senate computers, nothing could be further from the truth. I mean, we wouldn't do that. I mean, that's . . . that's just beyond the scope of reason in terms of what we would do." In her speech, Feinstein demanded an apology, and declared,

> We're not going to stop. I intend to move to have the findings, conclusions and the executive summary of the report sent to the president for declassification and release to the American

people. The White House has indicated publicly and to me personally that it supports declassification and release.

If the Senate can declassify this report, we will be able to ensure that an un-American, brutal program of detention and interrogation will never again be considered or permitted. . . . How Congress responds and how this is resolved will show whether the Intelligence Committee can be effective in monitoring and investigating our nation's intelligence activities, or whether our work can be thwarted by those we oversee.

I believe it is critical that the committee and the Senate reaffirm our oversight role and our independence under the Constitution of the United States.

Brennan then did a side step, explaining that in a subsequent report the CIA's general counsel had informed him that his investigation *had* revealed improper activities by agency personnel. He apologized to Feinstein and Republican Saxby Chambliss and announced the appointment of a special investigative committee under the leadership of former senator Evan Bayh. That didn't stop some senators, longtime critics like Mark Udall and others, from calling for his resignation.

That wasn't about to happen. Brennan and Obama had been closely linked from the very outset of Obama's presidency. In the interim between the 2008 election and the inaugural address, Brennan had been Obama's tutor on the specifics of drone warfare and, perhaps more fatefully, on the theory and rationales for a just war. The president's Nobel Prize speech seemed almost a condensation of what he had "learned" from Brennan. He had wanted him for his CIA director then, but questions about waterboarding stuck to Brennan, and Obama gave up trying to force him on Congress. Instead, he appointed him a special adviser with an office in the White House.[20]

Brennan's brief tenure had been filled with the hacking scandal and the mutual accusations by the CIA and the Senate Intelligence Committee. At a press conference in early August 2014, the president tried to calm things down by saying Brennan was the one who had called for the inspector general's report, "and he's already stood up a task force to make sure that lessons are learned and mistakes are resolved." The pattern was already clear. Just as in the case of the original Snowden revelations, the White House had edged up to the brink of doing something concrete, but it never got out of the cement mixer. Moreover, he even accepted the CIA's basic contention that the Panetta Review had somehow got to the Senate improperly. "I have full confidence in John Brennan," he said. "I think he has acknowledged and directly apologized to Senator Feinstein that C.I.A. personnel *did not properly handle* [italics added] an investigation as to how certain documents that were not authorized to be released to the Senate staff got somehow into the hands of the Senate staff." [21]

Did not properly handle? It was hardly surprising that Feinstein was not at all reassured by the president's anodyne comments and his assurance that what the White House approved for declassification for its report would clear the air. She said that "a preliminary review of the report" they had sent to the White House "indicates there have been significant redactions. We need additional time to understand the basis for these redactions and determine their justification." She would not approve its release to the public until these matters were resolved, she announced, hoping to up the pressure on the CIA. As in the case of Brennan's refusal to name who was responsible for the hacking, the question came down to naming those responsible for torture interrogation methods. On the hacking question, meanwhile, the Department of Justice, also not surprisingly, decided there was nothing in the CIA inspector general's report to warrant pursuing criminal charges.

The ground between the committee and the CIA now seemed like no-man's-land between two barbed-wire-protected trenches. The CIA insisted that even pseudonyms listed in the report could not be released, nor could the location of still secret rendition sites. Citing dangers to personnel and to the governments of countries that had cooperated with the agency after 9/11—many of them former Russian satellites where such techniques were standard operating procedure—the CIA dug in its heels. And it began to mobilize a backlash against the Senate committee by former officials who would soon claim that the report, still unseen by the public, was motivated by politics rather than a search for the truth. Senator John McCain—by dint of personal experience a dissenter from his Republican colleagues on this one issue, on which he had never ceased a drumbeat of criticism of Obama—demurred. "The minority report [a rebuttal to the version approved by the committee] will say that certain information was gained. First of all, I reject those on their face. But second of all, even if there was some truth in it, the damage done to the United States of America's reputation is incalculable."[22]

Leaks about what the committee report contained concerning divisions within the CIA over the torture techniques—even an instance when employees left a prison site in Thailand in protest—had been circulating for months. The chief fear in the higher echelons of the CIA concerned discrepancies between what field agents were saying and the things top officials said to Congress and the White House. The report said that the torture had little or nothing to do with the big success of the Obama administration, the killing of Osama bin Laden in 2011. It had suited the administration not to challenge the original claim that torture worked rather than cause a controversy about the president's signal victory in the Great War on Terror and cloud his hopes of ending the Iraq and Afghan involvements. More and more, the White House was caught out in that no-man's-land with shells landing all around.[23]

When these leaks began, Michael Hayden claimed that Senator Feinstein had prejudged the issue and ordered up a scathing report. Feinstein had called torture "un-American" and "brutal," terms that apparently indicated to Hayden some sort of hysterical mental state. "Now, that sentence, that motivation for the report . . . may show deep emotional feeling on the part of the senator. But I don't think it leads you to an objective report."[24]

As Amy Davidson pointed out, Hayden had overlooked the

facts of the situation. Feinstein had not "ordered" the report to make sure such a brutal program was not repeated; she had said it should be *declassified* for that reason—a crucial distinction. Hayden's purpose, Davidson surmised, was to suggest that the report was evidence that a certain femininity, "the wilting kind," can be "ascribed to those who doubt that torture is good for America."

Besides Dick Cheney—who loudly proclaimed he would do it again in a minute—one other man who had no doubts that the interrogation program was good for America was George Tenet, the former CIA director who had wagged a finger at a CBS correspondent in 2007 when asked about the interrogation program, saying, "We don't torture." The correspondent had still seemed skeptical, and Tenet exploded. "No, listen to me. No, listen to me. I want you to listen to me. Everybody forgets one central context of what we lived through: The palpable fear that we felt on the basis of that fact that there was so much we did not know. I know this program has saved lives. I know we've disrupted plots." [25]

When the Senate Intelligence Committee voted to declassify its report, Tenet began mobilizing former CIA figures to plan a rebuttal. John Brennan then convened a meeting of these "old boys" to plan strategy. At the meeting, the current head of the counterterrorism center told Brennan that the Senate report would list at least two hundred people who had been part of the EIT program at one point or another. How was Mr. Brennan going to protect them? Brennan's answer was a letter to Dianne Feinstein asking that former senior CIA officials be allowed to read an unredacted copy of the report before it was declassified. To the dismay of some of the senators, President Obama agreed that that was a good idea; it could be read in a secure room at the office of the director of national intelligence. The report was being vetted by those named in it.

Finally, on December 9, 2014, a brief cease-fire came into effect when the committee released a five-hundred-page executive summary, less than a tenth of the whole report. But now that was not enough for Brennan or his loyal two hundred. He now said that his apology for hacking committee computers had been mischaracterized. What he'd said, he now insisted, had actually been in response to a question about whether the *intention* had been to thwart the committee's investigation; no, that was never the intention, he said. Although he didn't address the question of the removal of documents from those computers or the relationship the Panetta Review had to the CIA snooping, Brennan cast himself as a someone who really wanted to have everything out in the open. "What I've said to the committee and others is that if I've done something wrong, I'll stand up and admit it, but I'm not going to take, you know, the allegations about hacking and monitoring and spying and whatever else, no. . . . When I think about that incident, I think there are things on both sides that need to be addressed."[26]

The interrogation program did save lives, Brennan now insisted, reversing himself yet again. "The intelligence gained from the program was critical to our understanding of al-Qaeda and continues to inform our counterterrorism to this day." Here was a new claim. Not only did the torture program produce information about Al Qaeda, but that information is still vital to preventing future attacks a decade and a half later![27]

In Brennan's "reconsideration" speeches, he could not even bring himself to utter the word *torture*. Asked if waterboarding was torture, he gave this response:

I certainly agree that there were times when CIA officers exceeded the policy guidance that was given and the authorized techniques that were approved and determine to be lawful. They went outside of the bounds in terms of their actions as part of that interrogation process, and they were harsh. As I said in some instances, I considered them abhorrent, and I will leave to others how they might want to label those activities. But for me it was something that is certainly regrettable but we are not a perfect institution, we [*are*] made up of individuals and as human beings we are imperfect beings.[28]

The intelligence community's nemesis was among the next to speak out. Asked about his opinion of the revelations in the declassified executive summary, Edward Snowden spoke to a Paris conference organized by Amnesty International by videolink that he was "deeply saddened and to a great extent angered by what I read." Like other readers, he was upset at the executive summary's record of "inexcusable crimes," including rectal feeding, shackling to floors, nudity in cold cells, and other forms of mistreatment. Some prisoners lost their lives. Yet no one had ever been punished for these acts. "These are things that leave a stain on the moral authority of the United States government," he told the Paris audience. "If the US can allow its officials to torture and not hold them to account, what does this mean for other more totalitarian states, in Asia and in Africa and elsewhere around the world?" [29]

In fact, the committee report went easy on the Bush White House, charging that the CIA had deliberately kept the president in the dark. "The C.I.A. repeatedly provided incomplete and inaccurate information," the report concluded. Not only that, it overstated the effectiveness of the interrogations in obtaining information that could not be gained elsewhere. Finally, specific questions "were not answered truthfully or fully." An internal CIA e-mail in July 2003 noted that the White House "is extremely concerned [Secretary of State Colin L.] Powell would blow his stack if he were to be briefed on what's been going on." [30]

These accusations caused consternation among former Bush administration officials. On one side there were those who wished to use the report to distance the former president from the CIA's programs, especially waterboarding and rendition; on the other were those, like former vice president Dick Cheney, who saw the perils in repudiation all too clearly. He was insistent that the president knew all about the programs—knew they were appropriate and effective. "It produced results and saved lives." The inquiry and report had been a Democrat-controlled project, he argued. "They didn't interview the people who were involved in the program." [31]

Senator Feinstein responded to the intelligence community's criticism (and that of Republican defenders of George Bush) by saying she could understand the impulse to "gather intelligence and remove terrorists from the battlefield." But such well-intended motives could not "justify, temper or excuse improper actions taken *by individuals or organizations* in the name of national security."[32] That was really the crux of the matter, not a few misdeeds, but questions of institutional ethos and power—and whether these did not now threaten the integrity of the republic's founding principles. President George W. Bush had been fond of saying that the 9/11 terrorists and their allies hated what America stood for and were determined to destroy the nation's freedoms. Senator Feinstein's speech posed a different question: what *did* America stand for?

As an indication of how the CIA had put the nation in peril of violating its own core values, its laws, its Constitution, and its claims to moral leadership in the struggle with terrorism, the United Nations' special rapporteur on counterterrorism and human rights, Ben Emmerson, said the committee report could not be just swept under the rug as past mistakes. Officials connected with the waterboarding episodes had to be prosecuted, he said. "The fact that the policies revealed in this report were authorized at a high level within the U.S. government provides no excuse whatsoever. Indeed, it reinforces the need for criminal accountability."[33]

Inside the United States, Senator Mark Udall, a longtime critic of the NSA's surveillance program and the CIA's secret interrogation programs, now demanded that the president "purge his administration of high-level officials" complicit in the torture program—but not only those directly responsible. He said the main person to go should be John Brennan, whom the president had declined to rein in even after his admission (under duress) that his agency had broken into committee computers. So far, he said, no one had been held accountable. And the director, protected by the president, was "continuing to willfully provide

inaccurate information and misrepresent the efficacy of torture."
Now the CIA was claiming that the Panetta Review was nothing
more than "short summaries" of documents that left the wrong
impression. That was not so, and the agency knew it. "In my view,
the Panetta review is a smoking gun." It directly refutes the CIA's
formal responses to the report, and is "refreshingly free of excuses,
qualifications, or caveats." And finally White House complicity
in obscuring the torture record jeopardized Obama's antitorture
stance and undermined the president's pledge to run a transparent administration. Finishing what was likely to be his last speech
on the Senate floor, Udall reminded the president, "Actions speak
louder than words."[34]

From prison in Pennsylvania, the only man who had served
time for the activities in CIA prison sites, the whistleblower John
Kiriakou, said, "I think it's clear from the Senate torture report
and also from Director Brennan's comments that crimes were
committed, and I think that the officers who committed those
crimes ought to be prosecuted." From his experience as a witness
to the results of waterboarding, he said, the prisoners were willing to say anything you want to know to get the torture to stop.
"But there's a deeper issue here . . . we should be asking ourselves
whether or not the techniques were right or moral."[35]

The CIA's inspector general David Buckley had previously
issued a report—often cited as an example of CIA integrity and
proper dealing with the committee—that singled out five individuals for improperly carrying out the computer searches and
then made recommendations to prevent repeats. In following
up, Brennan appointed a panel of three CIA agents and two
outsiders, which then repudiated the IG's report and concluded
that the searches had been lawful and in some cases done "at
the behest of John O. Brennan, the C.I.A. director." Apparently,
the director's admission that there had been wrongdoing was now
inoperative (one of Nixon press secretary Ron Ziegler's favorite
words whenever his boss got caught in a lie), because the panel
had found notes of a phone call in which he gave approval. Next,

the inspector general announced that he would resign effective January 31, 2015, to "pursue an opportunity in the private sector." Officials at the agency assured reporters that his departure was unrelated to politics or anything he had investigated. At this moment, Dianne Feinstein, outgoing chair of the Intelligence Committee, recommended an increase in the inspector general's powers to oversee interrogations.[36]

The portcullis had already fallen with the election of 2014 that gave Richard Burr the chairmanship of the Senate Intelligence Committee. The North Carolina senator said he considered the whole matter—Brennan's zigzagging, the inspector general's report, and the Brennan panel's reversal of that report—a closed issue. "What happened happened. Everybody's got their own interpretation." Burr sent a letter to the White House saying that his predecessor should never have transmitted the entire 6,700-page report to numerous departments and agencies within the executive branch. He wanted them "returned immediately." The Panetta Review was to be returned to John Brennan for deep-sixing. Obama had missed yet another chance to free himself from the worst fallout of the Bush War on Terror.

The Risen Subpoena

As the Intelligence Committee–Brennan fight ended with referee Barack Obama outside the ring, the trial of Jeffrey Sterling was the next attraction. In this fight, Obama was not merely an inheritor, but a champion of the Espionage Act indictments and trials. The Risen case (for it was always about Risen's investigative skills) became a crucial test of the government's ability to go beyond using the Espionage Act not only to convict leakers, but also to intimidate reporters. Anyone who talked with someone accused under that act—let alone published the results—would have to answer for it.

On June 2, 2014, the Supreme Court had rejected Risen's appeal against a court order to testify at the trial of Jeffrey Sterling after the U.S. Court of Appeals had reversed a lower court judge's decision to quash the subpoena. "A criminal trial subpoena," Judge Leonie M. Brinkema had ruled, "is not a free pass for the government to rifle through a reporter's notebook." The appellate court had overruled her decision, and now the Supreme Court issued a one-line order siding with the government. "I will continue to fight," Risen said. His defense attorneys said the ball was now in the government's court, whether to seek to have him held in contempt "for doing nothing more than reporting the news and keeping his promises."[37]

Attention shifted to Attorney General Holder. Even before the Supreme Court ruling, Holder had said at a meeting with journalists on May 27, 2014, to discuss press freedom, "As long as I'm attorney general, no reporter who is doing his job is going to go to jail. As long as I'm attorney general, someone who is doing their job is not going to get prosecuted." That was not completely definitive, of course, as it left open the definition of "their job." Did it include publishing stories based on classified materials?[38]

The threat that he would be jailed had not been removed. "They just keep coming at me." But in August 2014, the Risen case came up in a gotcha moment for Obama as he reacted to events surrounding the police killing of an eighteen-year-old black youth in Ferguson, Missouri. It happened when President Obama criticized the local police for arresting two reporters covering the story. "Here in the United States of America, police should not be bullying or arresting journalists who are just trying to do their jobs." The two had been quickly released, but just after the president finished his news conference on Martha's Vineyard, a coalition of journalism organizations at the National Press Club began its own press conference condemning the administration for its attempts to compel Risen to testify and identify his confidential source. The coalition presented a petition signed by more than 125,000 people calling on the DOJ to end its six-year effort to force Risen to testify against his source. Before the journalists began their press conference, the distinguished *Washington Post* reporter Dana Priest issued a statement: "As Presidents George W. Bush and Barack Obama classified more and more of the government's actions over the last 14 years, denying the public critical information to judge how its democracy is faring, it has fallen to reporters like Risen to keep Americans informed and to question whether a gigantic government in the shadows is really even a good idea." The meeting was held in the Zenger Room—named for the colonial journalist John Peter Zenger, who had been jailed by British authorities for refusing to stop printing criticisms of New York's royal governor.[39]

The problem for the government was that all it has as an alternative to Risen's testimony was circumstantial evidence—unless it was to reveal the content of telephone and e-mail messages that had been obtained under a wiretap. That would be difficult, because the legality of the NSA metadata programs had been challenged and then had been revealed by Snowden as going far beyond what even critics had previously charged. The DOJ would have to admit that the evidence had been gathered through the NSA's PRISM program. "How would it look for the government to accuse a man of domestic espionage," wrote one commentator, "using evidence gathered by means of, well, domestic espionage?"[40]

Probably it would look something like the modern version of Nixon's Plumbers in Daniel Ellsberg's psychiatrist's office. As Risen remained under subpoena, he was eager to give interviews about why he was refusing to cooperate with the effort to convict Jeffrey Sterling under the Espionage Act for supposedly having supplied him with the information about Operation Merlin that appeared in his book. Lesley Stahl on CBS News asked him if he would ever divulge his source. "Never, no. Basically, the choice the government's given me is: give up everything I believe or go to jail. So, I'm not going to talk."

It All Comes Together—the Trial of Jeffrey Sterling

Meanwhile, preparations for the trial of Jeffrey Sterling neared their end. Attorney General Holder followed up his previous comments that no journalist would be put in jail for "doing his job" by reducing the subpoena to a demand that Risen testify only about what he had written, without saying anything about his sources. Risen appeared in a federal court in Alexandria, Virginia, on January 5, 2015, but reaffirmed that he would say nothing that would provide tiles for the mosaic the government was trying to put together to convict Sterling. Defense lawyers then moved that the charges against Sterling be dismissed, but the judge, Leonie Brinkema, not surprisingly ruled against them. They were trying to lay a foundation for arguing that the person on trial was not their client but James Risen, while the only one who would serve time was Jeffrey Sterling.

Opening statements took place on January 14, 2015. The government argued that Sterling's behavior "potentially" threatened many lives and that the plans Project Merlin gave to the Iranians were not flawed—only incomplete. In other words, the CIA had not committed another error like its estimate of Iraq's possession of weapons of mass destruction, but had laid out a sound scheme for disrupting the program. And no, prosecutors said, the Russian engineer had *not* discovered a problem and, fearful of being killed, told the Iranians of the deception—the central contention in Risen's book about the naïveté of the CIA planners. In a sense, Risen's absence from the trial actually *helped* the prosecution, because defense attorneys could not question the journalist about government contentions.

They did their best. "A criminal case is not a place where the CIA gets its reputation back," said defense lawyer Edward Mac-Mahon. Given the nature of the trial, nevertheless, the main effort was to show that Sterling had not been proven to be Risen's source. This was a necessary, if uncomfortable, position for defenders of leakers who act out of conscience. In previous trials, conscience had been ruled inadmissible, particularly in the Chelsea Manning case, in which the defense could introduce motive only at sentencing. To recognize conscience before the verdict would be to put the government on trial. Hence the separation of Risen and Sterling suited both sides, though for different reasons.

As shown by the Sterling trial and other trials going back to the passage of the Espionage Act in 1917, the espionage establishment and the White House want a risk-free environment—free of any possibility of criticism, let alone punishment, free of any public or congressional knowledge of government activities as a result of revelations and newspaper stories. In the Sterling trial, another aspect of this government demand was evident. Prosecutors presented their case by using the testimony of unidentified CIA witnesses who "testified" behind high partitions that prevented them from being seen by the jurors or the audience. The charade, for that is what it was, lent an aura of deep danger to the proceedings.

The lead prosecutor, Eric Olshan, finished his closing argument saying, "Jeffrey Sterling was the hero of Risen's story. Don't let him be the hero of this one." Sterling was convicted after the jury deliberated three days. Sentencing was put off until April 2015. A few days before the verdict, in the wake of the *Charlie Hedbo* attack, which focused attention on terrorist attacks on freedom of the press, Secretary of State John Kerry talked to the Journalist Security Conference in Washington. "We all know that journalism can be dangerous," he began. "There's no way to eliminate the risk completely, except by keeping silent, and that's what we call surrender. So that's not in the cards. The world obviously needs to be informed about what is happening. Silence gives power to dictators, to the abusers, to tyrants. It allows tryanny to flourish, not freedom."

It could have been the closing statement by the defense attorneys if the trial had proceeded under different ground rules or if Risen had sat at the defense table beside Sterling. But outside the courtroom, Eric Holder pronounced the guilty verdict a triumph. "This is a just and appropriate outcome." Sterling, he contended, had compromised operations undertaken to protect American national security. "The disclosures placed lives at risk." But best of all, he said, "This verdict proves . . . it is possible to fully prosecute unauthorized disclosures that inflict harm upon our national security without interfering with journalists' ability to do their jobs."[41]

Of course Holder didn't really mean what he said, for the whole trial was about shutting down the flow information to the public by using the Espionage Act to imprison sources and threaten reporters. The Obama campaigns in this war against transparency had become a central feature of his administration. In the course of these campaigns, the balance of power in the federal government had tilted in favor of the generals in the intelligence agencies and against the civilian political leaders who are by law supposed to control them.

There is no better witness to this struggle than Michael Hayden, who has shown himself to be the best expositor of how the battle began and how it has gone. His position is that 9/11, in effect, amended the Constitution. In a speech at Washington and Lee University, he explained that things he found unreasonable on September 10, 2001, struck him as reasonable the next day after the death of three thousand people. "I actually started to do different things. And I didn't need to ask 'mother, may I' from the Congress or the president or anyone else . . . the death of 3,000 countrymen kind of took me in a direction over here, perfectly within my authority, but a different place than the one in which I was located before the attacks too, place. So if we're going to draw this line I think we have to understand that it's kind of a movable feast here."[42]

The question remained hanging: who will draw the line? And how many times can it be redrawn before the Constitution is pushed over the precipice or simply erased?

Conclusion

Defending the Republic?

I would say the best part of the Obama administration would be his continuance of the protections of the homeland using the big metadata programs, the NSA being enhanced.
— Jeb Bush, April 21, 2015

We have it back. The statue is free.
— Snowden bust activists, May 7, 2015

The successful prosecution of former CIA agent Jeffrey Sterling for allegedly giving *Times* reporter James Risen information about the attempt to sabotage Iran's nuclear program was noteworthy for several reasons. Getting a conviction without forcing the journalist to reveal his sources in court let the administration off the hook for threatening the press but still opened a new door for prosecutions under the Espionage Act.

Holder's statement suggested that all had ended well for everybody. Sterling and his lawyers did not see it that way, of course, even though the sentence Judge Leonie Brinkema handed down on May 12, 2015—three and a half years in prison—was far less than the government had hoped. Some observers said the sentence was a rebuke to the Obama administration for exaggerating claims that Sterling's actions had put lives in danger and caused limitless damage to national security. But Sterling's lawyers believed that Risen had been on trial in absentia, and their client had been sentenced in his stead. Their strategy had been to avoid the whistleblower defense and plead innocent of all charges. As one defense lawyer put it, "The government has great lawyers. It has a great theory. It just made a great argument. What the government lacks is evidence."[1]

Sterling's plea avoided all debate about whistleblowers, which had complicated matters in recent years. He had been charged under the 1917 Espionage Act, like all others the administration had sought to punish for revealing classified information to reporters, but unlike the seven previous cases, his was the first to come to trial in a civilian court. Chelsea Manning had given hundreds of thousands of documents to WikiLeaks, but she was tried in a military court-martial. The others all came before judges with plea bargains. Brinkema had sentenced one, John Kiriakou, to thirty months for revealing the name of an undercover CIA agent to a freelance reporter, who in fact did not publish the name.

Moreover, Judge Brinkema said she imposed a slightly longer sentence on Sterling than Kiriakou because he had not pled guilty to the charges. So while the prosecution had hoped for a longer sentence as deterrent to future leakers, it gained (or at least seemed to at first blush) a clear-cut victory on a test of the Espionage Act's viability as a weapon against leakers as well as spies, thereby erasing long-term doubts after the failure to convict Daniel Ellsberg in the Pentagon Papers case more than forty years earlier. Given the short shelf life of front-page Washington politics, probably few thought about that dramatic moment in Nixon's downfall during the Sterling trial. But the Ellsberg case had left unanswered the question of whether the act could be used when there had been no contact with a representative of an enemy state. Recent cases had attempted to expand the law to include culpability even if the leaker had intended no harm to individual lives or that deliberately vague catchall "national security," and in doing so prosecutors went back to the beginning: the most famous prosecution under the Espionage Act, that of Eugene Debs in World War I. In that case, Judge David Westenhaver, in Canton, Ohio, declared in sentencing Debs to prison for his speeches against the draft that the prosecution did not even have to prove that he had actually had a direct influence on whether men disobeyed the law.

From the beginning, the Espionage Act has constituted a form of profiling, assuming that an opponent of any government activity must be a foreign agent and providing prosecutors with a pretrial edge even before any testimony was taken. To take advantage of that edge, Department of Justice lawyers constantly hammered on Sterling's character, arguing that his actions were not those of a whistleblower—even though he didn't claim to be one—but of a man who, embittered by his termination at the agency, had first tried to sue the government on grounds of racial discrimination and when that failed sought revenge by striking out regardless of the consequences to national security. The sentencing memorandum prosecutors gave to Judge Brinkema described Sterling as "vindictive" five times and "selfish" three times—just like the old debater's advice to a neophyte: when the case is weak, pound the rostrum hard.[2]

There was another big plus for the government, though one much less remarked upon: Risen's refusal to testify made it easier to convict on circumstantial evidence, in part because it was impossible to keep secret the fact that the government had a witness who couldn't be forced to appear in court. Without Risen on the stand, moreover, the defense had to concentrate on rebutting Sterling's supposed personal desire for revenge. It was a very peculiar situation. The government could hide behind a screen (literally) and malign the accused with anonymous testimony that the defendant is prohibited from rebutting.

To sum up, while fellow journalists celebrated Risen's brave stand and cheered when Holder finally backed off and withdrew the subpoena that had threatened to put him in jail, the defense lawyers were denied the chance to cross-examine a witness who might have cleared their client. The prosecution succeeded in Risen's absence by using metadata, records of phone calls placed and the duration of the conversations. Ironically, then, Risen's stand worked against Sterling because it denied his attorneys the chance to introduce the substance of those conversations. Instead of helping Sterling sustain his plea of innocence, then, Risen's absence hurt his case—especially if in fact the phone calls contained nothing about the Operation Merlin effort to sabotage the Iranian nuclear program.

Sterling's lawyers insisted that the only place he had discussed Operation Merlin, named for the Russian scientist the CIA had brought in to supply Iran with faulty information, was before the proper Senate oversight committee. Yes, Risen may have asked Sterling about Merlin during one of their phone calls about his discrimination suit, but their client had not told him anything. Perhaps the source was one or more of the congressional staffers or Merlin himself? Because the details of the effort to disrupt Iran's nuclear program were still classified, even though much had already been revealed in Risen's book, Sterling found it difficult to mount an effective defense against the parade of witnesses the government presented to the court.[3]

At the top of the list was Condoleezza Rice, who stuck to old talking points the more recent Bush administration had used before the Iraq War about the government's sacred duty to prevent nuclear proliferation. She described the Merlin operation as somehow a success. Without Risen on the stand, her testimony went unchallenged, as once again the mushroom cloud hovered over the courtroom. She said the Merlin operation "was very closely held, one of the most closely held programs during my tenure." It was known to hardly anyone. But "Bob," the manager of the program, then testified, from behind a screen to protect his identity like a Mafia witness, that more than ninety people knew about Merlin. He was the first in a parade of anonymous witnesses who followed Rice, all carefully blocked from view behind a gray retractable screen and using only first-name aliases, and who told the court about the great value of Merlin and the dangers Sterling's alleged revelations to Risen had caused for Merlin and his wife, "Mrs. Merlin," who were still under U.S. protection, despite his failing to follow instructions. When the defense got close to a challenge about her credentials and Iraq's fictional weapons of mass destruction, Judge Brinkema clamped down.[4]

The prosecution thus was effectively allowed to put James Risen on trial in absentia—much to the displeasure of defense attorneys. The government contended, in order to have it both ways, that Sterling was guilty of "causing" Risen to write about Operation Merlin in his book. It was a strange formulation, suggesting that Sterling somehow controlled what Risen would write. Merlin was a success, it was argued, and only "Jeffrey Sterling's spin is what appears in the book."[5]

The government said Sterling had sabotaged a brilliant effort out of spite, but even Brinkema was not fully convinced on that point, so by her relatively lenient sentence (three and a half years instead of a possible thirty-five), she sidestepped that argument. She said instead that her decision was based primarily on the possible danger to Merlin by revealing the code name of a covert operative. A *Times* editorial took that as a "significant rebuke to the Obama administration's dogged-yet-selective crusade against leaks."[6] Perhaps it was, but the victory chalked up for the Espionage Act in an open court test decided by a jury was a precedent of "limitless value" to the intelligence community. It was a forever gift, a magic wand to wave any time the secret agencies felt pressed by a critic inside or outside government.

The verdict not only affirmed the ability to use the Espionage Act without direct testimony, but also gave a boost to defenders of the NSA metadata haystack. Bruce Brown, executive director of the Reporters Committee for Freedom of the Press, said the conviction showed that forcing reporters to disclose sources was unnecessary and ill-advised. "The speed with which the jury reached its verdict shows that reporter's testimony was not needed for the government to make its case. I think going forward this is going to be a powerful precedent."[7]

Indeed it would be, if the classifiers have their way. The path back to the Wilson administration's practice of silencing opposition by prosecuting dissenters as spies under the Espionage Act had begun, one could argue, with the imprisonment of John Kiriakou for revealing the name of a retired participant in the

already defunct waterboarding interrogations. The Sterling conviction shortened the remaining distance and made the going
easier—a downhill jaunt, if not yet quite a ski slope. As the Sterling prosecutors had argued in their sentencing memorandum to
the court, "Although prosecutions of government employees under the Espionage Act have been few, no court has held that the
law does not apply to a person who discloses classified information
to the media or the public rather than to a foreign government."
Now one had. It was a chilling assertion. In effect, it was an attempt to define the American people as a foreign power, a perpetual enemy of their own government merely by virtue of their
desire to know what it's doing in their name.[8]

But Not Quite Yet

Speaking at the National Press Club shortly after the jury verdict,
Attorney General Holder replied to a question about Espionage
Act prosecutions by saying that the Obama administration had actually been quite restrained compared to what it might have done.
"We have turned away . . . [a] greater number of cases that were
presented to us where prosecution was sought," tacitly admitting
that many government employees have been sufficiently outraged
by what they have seen to start looking for a whistle. No one asked
him how many more there were than the record eight his department had pursued. Continuing, Holder then delivered a sponta-
neous lecture about what the press should do to restrain itself.
"I also think there's a question for you all, members of the press."
They should think about this. "As we've asked ourselves when it
comes to national surveillance, simply because we have the ability to do certain things, should we?" He said that he would give
an admittedly extreme example: Should reporters have leaked the
secret of the atomic bomb before it was dropped on Japan?[9]

There were actual spies in the Manhattan Project—people
who gave secrets to the Soviet Union—but what Holder was doing here was once again equating leakers with spies, apparently

emboldened to this level by Sterling's conviction. Risen answered Holder with a barrage of angry comments on Twitter, the twenty-first-century equivalent of a town meeting. These put him at the center of a new controversy about reporters' obligations to remain neutral even in their off-the-page comments. Holder had become the "nation's top censorship officer," Risen said in one tweet, and in another, the attorney general was making it look "okay" for dictators to jail journalists worldwide. After all, Holder had made it plain that there is no First Amendment "reporter's privilege." Risen vowed, "I plan to spend the rest of my life fighting to undo damage done to press freedom in the United States by Barack Obama and Eric Holder." [10]

"Risen's Rants" forced his readers to choose sides. Among the first to choose were the *New York Times* public editor, Margaret Sullivan, and its standards editor, Philip Corbett. They stood by their man—in surprisingly strong terms for the Gray Lady of American newspapers. Corbett said that the paper's reporters understand that they don't and shouldn't editorialize on issues, but because the *Times* was far from neutral on the question of press rights, "I would put this in a different category." Besides, "Jim has a very special and personal vantage point," as he lived for years under the threat of going to jail to protect his confidential source. "Maybe the tenor of Mr Risen's tweets wasn't very Timesian," added Sullivan. "But the insistence on truth-telling and challenging the powerful is exactly what The Times ought to stand for. Always." [11]

Sullivan's blogpost brought an immediate rejoinder from Jack Goldsmith and Benjamin Wittes, founders of the influential Lawfare blog. These two and their blog had often criticized government intrusions on privacy and morality, going back to Goldsmith's personal rebellion when he served in the Bush administration and challenged the legality of the infamous torture memos. However, both feared even more the dangers to "national security" that people like Snowden and Greenwald posed with their decisions to take into their own hands the question of what is rightfully classified and what is not. Risen's tweets, they wrote, were simply not truthful on many matters. They "wildly misdescribed" the facts of Holder's role in the decline of reporter's privilege, as well as in Risen's case. He had decided the right way in withdrawing the subpoena, but the press could not be the final arbiter in such disputes. The one powerful institution that Risen and Sullivan think should not be challenged, they wrote, is their own. Of Sullivan they said, "She's willing to describe a pattern of hyperventilating falsehoods as 'truth-telling.' " [12]

Amid all this furor, some were quick to point out the contrasts between the Sterling conviction and the Petraeus case. The once acclaimed savior general of the Iraq War, later head of the CIA, had been forced to resign because of FBI sleuthing that uncovered his leaks of classified information to his biographer and mistress. Two weeks before Judge Brinkema sentenced Sterling, Petraeus pled guilty to a misdemeanor for inappropriately removing government material and received a suspended sentence and what was for him a relatively small fine of $100,000. In addition, as critics noted, Petraeus retained his security clearances as an adviser to President Obama. The documents the general gave Paula Broadwell included his diary, as well as copies of operational plans and actual names of covert agents—not code names, as in the Sterling case. Moreover, Petraeus had admitted lying to FBI investigators, and the leniency of his plea deal was said to have infuriated many prosecutors and agents. [13]

The Petraeus "verdict" had one notable champion: John Kiriakou. Kiriakou continued to maintain that he had been targeted for exposing waterboarding, not revealing the name of a covert agent, but he thought the sentence for Petraeus was proper, because neither crime warranted invoking the Espionage Act. It was perhaps a tongue-in-cheek response. At the time of Kiriakou's sentencing, in October 2012, CIA director Petraeus had said, "Oaths do matter, and there are indeed consequences for those who believe they are above the laws that protect our fellow officers and enable American intelligence agencies to operate with the requisite degree of safety." One might add here that government claims of potential "limitless danger" to national security in the leaker cases are never based on who receives the information. Instead, as the sentencing memorandum in the Sterling case would have it, there is no distinction between a member of the media and a foreign agent.

To justify their practices, the intelligence community and President Obama have consistently argued that the government has struck just about the right balance between protecting national security and honoring individual rights under the Constitution. It is always put as a matter of balancing risks. How much are we prepared to risk by reining in the NSA, against how much are we willing to risk losing our constitutional rights? Every time "reform" nears the top of the legislative agenda, Congress predictably tilts heavily toward the position that the danger to individual rights is really trivial, after all. As the Patriot Act neared a deadline for reauthorization at the end of May 2015, for example, Senator John McCain, now chair of the Armed Services Committee, complained, "People seem to have forgotten 9/11. We have to have the ability to monitor these communications. It's pretty clear that 9/11 could have been prevented if we had known about some of the communications that were linked to those who committed the terrible atrocity of 9/11."[14]

Was that really so? As we have seen, various authors, including Lawrence Wright, a longtime student of the road to 9/11, have refuted McCain's assertion and others like it. He concludes the blame falls on the intelligence community's two most involved agencies, the FBI and the CIA, and their failure to share information that could have set the government on alert and prevented the attacks. "Edward Snowden broke the law, and the Obama Adminstration has demanded that he be brought to justice. No one has died because of his revelations. . . . Its failure to share information from the Al Qaeda switchboard opened the door to the biggest terrorist attack in history. As long as we're talking abut accountability, why shouldn't we demand it of the C.I.A.?"[15]

It would be hard to imagine a clearer statement about the stakes in the war against leakers. Whether Senate Intelligence Committee chairman Richard Burr would achieve his goal of zero accountability, including return and destruction of all copies of the CIA's Panetta Review and the Senate Intelligence Committee's Torture Report, would depend on several things. On the cultural level, which is increasingly difficult to sort out from the political level, one sign that the Torture Report wouldn't become a "footnote to history," as he put it, was the Academy Award for documentary film for *Citizenfour*, Laura Poitras's work detailing Snowden's break with the NSA and his flight to Hong Kong, where he first laid out the story he was about to tell to reporters for *The Guardian*.

The award surprised no one on either side of the debate, but the vehemence of one desperate potential candidate for the the 2016 Republican presidential nomination was an indication of how much contemporary politics had evolved into a battle for control of Twitter, Facebook, and Hollywood. New Jersey governor Chris Christie delivered his "audition" foreign policy speech in New Hampshire, telling an audience, "We shouldn't listen to people like Edward Snowden, a criminal who hurt our country and now enjoys the hospitality of President Putin—while sending us messages about the dangers of authoritarian governments." Neither should we listen to Hollywood, "the guys who made our intelligence agencies the villains in practically every movie from the last twenty-five years."[16]

Christie probably would not be satisfied about Hollywood's intentions unless a new series of John Wayne lookalikes once again rode at the head of a cavalry troop singing "She Wore a Yellow Ribbon" as they headed into battle with Apache raiders swarming all over the fabled West. But serious issues were at stake. Obama and his former rival Hillary Clinton, now the favorite for the Democratic nomination, both visited the home state of the Oscars and the denizens of Silicon Valley on repair calls. Obama was there to patch up the "deepening estrangement" between old allies. As David Sanger and Nicole Perlroth reported in the *New*

York Times, "The long history of quiet cooperation between Washington and America's top technology companies—first to win the Cold War, then to combat terrorism—was founded on the assumption of mutual interest. Edward J. Snowden's revelations shattered that. Now, the Obama administration's efforts to prevent companies from greatly strengthening encryption in commercial products like Apple's iPhone and Google's Android phones has set off a new battle, as the companies resist government efforts to make sure police and intelligence agencies can crack the systems."[17]

The government position was that encryption weakens American responses to cyberwarfare launched by nations such as Iran, North Korea, and China. FBI director James Comey warned that encryption "threatens to lead us all to a very, very dark place." Meanwhile, the president accused China of plans to force tech companies to install backdoors in their products to allow government surveillance, something the Chinese multinational Lenovo was caught doing in February 2015. In reality, however, as a new release of Snowden documents showed, China was only following the U.S. lead, as the CIA had targeted Apple for years in efforts to hack into its security codes. "Tearing apart the products of U.S. manufacturers and potentially putting backdoors in software distributed by unknowing developers all seems to be going a bit beyond 'targeting bad guys,'" commented Matthew Green, a cryptography expert at Johns Hopkins University. "It may be a means to an end, but it's a hell of a means."[18]

Snowden's most recent documents showed that the CIA had been seeking for years to penetrate Apple encoding, studying potential flaws in its systems for iPhone, etc., without letting the company know. If the CIA or NSA could do it, explained Christopher Soghoian, principal technologist at the American Civil Liberties Union, it was quite likely that Chinese and Russian and Israeli researchers could also. "By quietly exploiting these flaws rather than notifying Apple, the U.S. government leaves Apple's customers vulnerable to other sophisticated governments."[19]

Asked about these revelations, Apple CEO Tim Cook

denounced government efforts to compel companies to provide backdoors into their users' data. "I want to be absolutely clear that we have never worked with any government agency from any country to create a backdoor in any of our products or services. . . . And we never will. . . . We all have a right to privacy. We shouldn't give it up. We shouldn't give in to scare-mongering."[20]

Meanwhile, an announced candidate now, Hillary Clinton was out in California trying to put some space between her and the administration on domestic spying. Earlier in the year, she had placed herself within striking distance of Christie's stance about leakers. Of Snowden, she said, "He spent time with the Russians in their consulate," leaving "our intelligence forces" to try to "understand exactly what was taken" that might have become available to Moscow. "It struck me as—I just have to be honest with you—as sort of odd." But now she was more circumspect as the administration attempted to reach out to tech companies who had a long-running debate with the White House over the NSA intrusions into the privacy of their customers—especially in the world market, where, on all other issues, the United States was doing all it could to promote exports.

After addressing a conference on women in Silicon Valley, she was asked if Snowden was a traitor. Previously she had assailed the NSA's bête noire, accusing him of "outrageous behavior," aiding terrorists and other foes of the United States. Now she said, more cautiously, that she could not "condone" his behavior. "He stole millions of documents . . . many of those documents had nothing to do with civil liberties." But apparently he was no longer guilty of aiding terrorists. Her major concern now seemed to be what Snowden's new revelations said about the behavior of the NSA. It needed to regain people's trust. "People felt betrayed," she said of the efforts to break into iPhone encryption. "You didn't tell us you were doing this."[21]

Despite all attempts to contain the Snowden effect, it was stronger than ever in places that counted. A hundred-pound bust of Snowden appeared atop a Revolutionary War memorial in a

Brooklyn park. It stayed there for only a few hours before being removed by park workers. That night the activists, an artist collective called the Illuminator, projected a hologram of the bust at the same site. After negotiations with the authorities and paying a $50 fine, the group, which had planned the caper for a year, got the material sculpture back. "The ideal that Snowden seemed to be fighting for with his actions," said one member, Andrew Tider, "seemed to be in line with the ideals the revolutionaries, who might also have been called traitors, were fighting for." The group announced that those with 3-D printers could produce their own for display anywhere. Another of the creators of the original bust, Jeff Greenspan, told reporters about the availability of software to make eight-inch replicas of the famous leaker striking a stern pose. "It would be great if people put these in public spaces and Instagrammed them, or put photos on Twitter and Facebook to project them around the world. Anywhere it can get people thinking about surveillance, your rights and liberties, it would be wonderful."[22]

The language the activists spoke was twenty-first-century, but their appeal to American history resonated in political circles. Senator Richard Burr's hope that the Torture Report would be only a "footnote" in that history was now unlikely to be fulfilled. A rapid series of high-politics events battered the pro-NSA redoubts in the Senate manned by Burr, Majority Leader Mitch McConnell, John McCain, John Cornyn, and others. First came a federal appeals court ruling that the NSA metadata program run under Section 215 of the Patriot Act was illegal. It was illegal because the act did not authorize the program. The court's ninety-seven-page opinion constituted a lecture on what Congress *ought* to have done if it had wanted to give such powers to the intelligence agencies, and what it *had not done*. It also showed the use of common sense: "We would expect such a momentous decision to be preceded by substantial debate, and expressed in unmistakable language. There is no evidence of such a debate." And logic: "Congress cannot reasonably be said to have ratified a program of which many members of Congress—and all members of the public—were not aware."[23]

The judges' unanimous ruling was delivered in a tone that threw Congress an unmistakable challenge to see what support might be out there if it did properly debate the issue. In ruling the NSA metadata spying program illegal, the judges said, "We do so comfortably in the full understanding that if Congress chooses to authorize such a far-reaching and unprecedented program, it has every opportunity to do so, and to do so unambiguously."

Snowden was interviewed after the ruling and said that before the leaks Amnesty International had attempted to bring a suit against government surveillance, but it was thrown out because Amnesty couldn't prove it had been spied upon. But now, using the materials he had made public through articles in *The Guardian* and other outlets, the courts had acted to declare it unlawful. The appeals court ruling, it could be said, was a Newtonian reaction to the jury decision in the Sterling case. It pushed back that advance in the government's ability to do whatever it could because it could, without oversight or specific authorization. Said Snowden at a Nordic Media Festival, "The argument where people say, 'If you have nothing to hide you have nothing to fear. I don't care if they look at me because I have nothing to hide.' That's no different than saying, 'I don't care about free speech because I have nothing to say.' "[24]

Snowden's virtual appearances at forums in Scandinavia, Princeton, and California, to list only those in May 2015, were all to "packed houses." He joked at these appearances that he must have seemed to many in the audience like Big Brother from Orwell's dystopian novel *1984*. In one sense, certainly, that was so, for he peered out from huge screens as an omnipresent figure in contemporary political life, an omniscient one who seemed to anticipate or decide what would come next, as in the release of the documents about government spying on Apple and other tech companies. The effort to silence him, like the removal of his bust from a Brooklyn park, had completely failed. Scott Shane wrote in the *New York Times* about his "victories" with a sardonic opening line, "For an international fugitive hiding out in Russia from American espionage charges, Edward J. Snowden gets around."[25]

The U.S. government, if it couldn't get him to leave Russia for another country where he could be "apprehended," certainly preferred that he be in a country that under Putin has a miserable record on civil liberties. The data cloud he controlled at least had that silver lining. For anyone who gave it any thought, however, his Hobson's choice of sanctuaries only pointed to who was responsible for keeping him there. And that realization could only highlight his career as defender in chief of personal privacy, which, it could be (and was) perversely argued, actually *had* harmed national security by depriving the government of the trust of its citizenry by enlightening their ignorance.

The elections of 2014 did not halt the progress of a Freedom Act in Congress. Previously, the Senate had defeated the Leahy bill by two votes, but now the House of Representatives voted overwhelmingly (in the wake of the appeals court decision) in favor of a new version of the proposed act that would halt the government's "haystack" operation being run under Section 215 of the Patriot Act. It would also place greater emphasis on prior court orders by the FISA Court and require an amicus curiae to represent the "other side." The limitations on the role of such a person was greater than in the Leahy bill, but there was also a provision, again limited, stipulating that the director of national intelligence would have to declassify internal legal reviews of opinions that "include a significant construction or interpretation" of any provision of law. Previously, lawyers in the intelligence community could issue opinions without any significant challenge that then had the effect of rewriting laws to suit the occasion.[26]

Critics of the House-passed bill on the libertarian right and the liberal left immediately complained that it did not go nearly far enough in curbing the government's ability to invade citizens' privacy, but the bill faced an uncertain future in the Senate, where the Republican leadership had now lined up in a determined stand to prevent any changes at all in the law. The remarkable thing about the House action, of course, was the new alignment of Tea Party–leaning Republicans with liberal Democrats to pass the bill. In the Senate, two Republican presidential hopefuls, Ted Cruz and Rand Paul, now stood in favor of reform.

Despite desperate attempts by Senate majority leader Mitch McConnell to sink the House Freedom bill and reauthorize everything in the Patriot Act, the new bill passed the upper house with nary a comma changed and became the law of the land. For all the bill's shortcomings and the warnings that the government had easy ways to circumvent the new law by using various other means at its disposal, its passage in effect gave permission to reformers to contemplate the next steps to halt government overreach. That point needs to be underscored in considering the importance of the votes in both houses. The odd-couple alliance that succeeded in getting the bill passed was not limited to the congressional debate over the Freedom Act. The American Civil Liberties Union and a top Tea Party organization were teaming up to pressure lawmakers by running joint TV ads in Washington, D.C., as well as in the early primary states of New Hampshire and Iowa. "The federal government surveillance program has collected records on nearly every Americans' phone calls, emails—your most private moments—without a warrant, without cause and without your permission," says a narrator. Among those communications, the ad implies, are those between doctors and patients, as well as between a soldier stationed overseas and his daughter. Polls in those states showed that voters overwhelmingly supported reforming the NSA.[27]

Perhaps the most remarkable political impact made by Edward Snowden was on Texas representative Michael Burgess, called by the American Conservative Union the "top conservative" in Congress. In 2011 he had voted to renew the Patriot Act, believing that surveillance powers were used only against would-be terrorists calling terrorists in other countries. That's what he had been told in briefings by intelligence officials. The Snowden revelations made him angry on both points, the scope of the surveillance and being misled by intelligence officials. In the House vote on the Freedom Act, he had cast a no vote—because it did not go far enough in reining in the NSA to protect the privacy of the American people. Instead, along with Democrat Justin Amash, Rand Paul, and civil libertarians from both parties, he favors allowing Section 215 of the Patriot Act to expire.[28]

Burgess said there had been a "visceral reaction" to the Snowden revelations in his district. In Texas, as in other red states, legislatures were considering bills to cut off NSA buildings from access to water and electricity. California had already passed what's been called a Fourth Amendment Protection Act, prohibiting the state from providing support to a federal agency "to collect electronically stored information or metadata of any person if the state has actual knowledge that the request constitutes an illegal or unconstitutional collection." The appeals court decision will surely be cited if a case comes up in the near future. Besides Texas and California, similar bills had been introduced in a total of fifteen states. The "actual knowledge" provision in the California law is a big loophole, but even so, said one of the leaders in the fight for the law, it was a "good first step."[29]

On May 19, 2015, a letter was sent to President Obama signed by representatives of more than 140 tech companies and dozens of civil liberty, human rights, and press freedom groups, as well as by former White House counterterrorism czar Richard Clarke, who had headed the president's review board on security policies after the Snowden revelations. (The key recommendations of that board had still not been acted upon a year and a half later. Obama had dodged the issues raised by calling upon Congress to take the lead in passing new legislation, even though the NSA metadata sweeps originated under "interpretations" of Section 215 and other provisions of the Patriot Act.) The letter's key point: "We urge you to reject any proposal that U.S. companies deliberately weaken the security of their products. We request that the White

House instead focus on developing policies that will promote rather than undermine the wide adoption of strong encryption technology."[30]

We have come full circle since passage of the Espionage Act. Woodrow Wilson used it to censor the press—closing down access to the mails for radical papers—and imprisoning Eugene Debs for publicly speaking against the draft. Decades later the Nixon administration attempted to imprison Daniel Ellsberg using the act, but failed in the Pentagon Papers case without gaining a decision whether the law had ever been intended to be used to silence whistleblowers. The Obama administration, following the Bush precedents, has made the Espionage Act its weapon of choice in the war against leakers. The backlash he now faces on multiple fronts presents him and his successors with difficult choices.

The real choices to be made are about what the government is obligated to tell its citizens about what it plans to do, is doing, or has done, just as the court said in its decision on Section 215 of the Patriot Act. Is constitutional protection of the right to privacy outdated in an age of worldwide mobility and the capacity of a few individuals to bring about a catastrophe like 9/11 or worse?

Retired NSA director General Michael Hayden, a tireless speaker on behalf of the intelligence community, whether boosting the mass surveillance program or chasing leakers with the Department of Justice attorneys, now thinks Congress has given its answer with the Freedom Act—and says it refutes the agency's critics. Speaking at a conference sponsored by the *Wall Street Journal*, Hayden said the "Snowden effect" had been a mountain revealed to be a molehill.

If somebody would come up to me and say "Look, Hayden, here's the thing: This Snowden thing is going to be a nightmare for you guys for about two years. And when we get all done with it, what you're going to be required to do is that little 215 program about American telephony metadata—and by the way, you can still have access to it, but you got to go to the court and get access to it from the companies, rather than keep it to yourself"—I go: "And this is it after two years? Cool!"

He did not always think this way. When the Freedom Act was under consideration, Hayden pointed to the rise of ISIS and insisted that the "last thing" Congress should be doing is considering "a major" new bill, like the proposed legislation, that would require the NSA to get a warrant before monitoring telephone metadata. Such a requirement would make it more burdensome for the government to obtain information on potential terrorist messages than in "a routine criminal case."[31]

Whatever Michael Hayden now thinks, it can be argued that passage of the Freedom Act, if not a dramatic reversal, might signal that other steps are in the offing and that "national security" claims cannot always go unquestioned. In mid-June 2015, barely a month after the passage of the Freedom Act, a Republican-dominated Senate settled the white-hot debate about the Torture Report by passing an amendment to the defense authorization bill, 78–21, banning all agencies from using interrogation techniques other than those specified in the Army Field Manual.

In a sense, the debate over the Torture Report was like that over the Pentagon Papers. At that time, Judge Murray Gurfein could find nothing in the Espionage Act that applied to the publication of the Pentagon Papers, arguing, "The security of the Nation is not at the ramparts alone. Security also lies in the value of our free institutions. A cantankerous press, an obstinate press, an ubiquitous press must be suffered by those in authority in order to preserve the even greater values of freedom of expression and the right of the people to know."

One could argue that no "next step" could be taken until the disposition of the Snowden case. A petition calling for a presidential pardon was submitted to the White House on June 9, 2013, with 167,954 signatures attached. Two years later, Obama commissioned Lisa Monaco, the White House official who had chaired the meetings devoted to snatching up the leaker and transporting him in a CIA plane back to the United States, to fashion a response. It was posted on the White House's "We the People" website. "Thanks for signing a petition about Edward Snowden," the post began, and went on to state that the Snowden case was an issue many Americans felt strongly about "because his actions have had serious consequences for our national security." Without a touch of irony as to her known role in plotting a rendition-like capture of Snowden, Monaco then described the president's efforts working with Congress to "secure appropriate reforms," which she insisted predated the Snowden leaks. This was a particularly interesting statement given that there had been no White House action on the suggested reforms offered by Obama's post-Snowden commission, let alone any indication of what he had actually attempted pre-Snowden beyond a single speech. Then came the blast at Snowden:

> Instead of constructively addressing these issues, Mr. Snowden's dangerous decision to steal and disclose classified information had severe consequences for the security of our country and the people who work day in and day out to protect it.
>
> If he felt his actions were consistent with civil disobedience, then he should do what those who have taken issue with their own government do: Challenge it, speak out, engage in a constructive act of protest, and—importantly—accept the consequences of his actions. He should come home to the United States, and be judged by a jury of peers—not hide behind the cover of an authoritarian regime. Right now, he's running away from the consequences of his actions.[32]

We live in a dangerous world, Monaco summed up the White House response, requiring the government to give the "intelligence community" all the lawful tools it needs to address the dangers. Was this simply one more Hayden-esque justification for what the NSA and other agencies had done? She ended with a statement that the balance between security and civil liberties "that our ideals and our Constitution require deserves robust debate and those who are willing to engage in it here at home."

That was just the point, of course: first, that the "balance" applied to the First and Fourth Amendments is different than "interpretation," and weighted in favor of whoever is writing the memos in the Office of Legal Counsel; and second, there simply was no debate "here at home" before Snowden, except over articles like those of James Risen that the White House occupants in successive adminstrations sought to squelch.

Yet the NSA announced in July 2015 that it would destroy millions of Americans' phone records collected under its surveillance program—perhaps in order to "balance" somewhat the treatment of Snowden, as the Freedom Act mandated. Telephone companies would still be required to keep records of phone calls, but these could not be accessed without a warrant from the FISA Court. It was still far short of what many had hoped for with passage of a reform act, and far more than what intelligence community stalwarts felt was needed—absolute control of the haystack.

From Debs to Ellsberg to Snowden, the history of the war against leakers shows that the government has become more and more determined to keep the press from finding out what it's doing—by charging leakers as spies under the Espionage Act. Now serving a thirty-five-year sentence for "aiding the enemy" by passing hundreds of thousands of documents to WikiLeaks, many of which were then printed in the *New York Times*, Chelsea Manning has called for a media shield law with teeth and substance as the only way to ensure that there is a check on government. "I believe," writes Manning from prison, "that when the public lacks even the most fundamental access to what its governments and militaries are doing in their names, then they cease to be involved in the act of citizenship. There is a bright distinction between citizens, who have rights and privileges protected by the state, and subjects, who are under the complete control and authority of the state."[33]

NOTES

Introduction

1. David Johnston and Charlie Savage, "Obama Reluctant to Look into Bush Programs," *New York Times*, January 12, 2009, www.nytimes.com/2009/01/12/us/politics/12inquire.html?pagewanted.

1. From the Espionage Act to the National Security State

1. "Russia Grants Snowden Three More Years of Asylum, Lawyer," *New York Post*, August 7, 2014, nypost.com/2014/08/07/russia-grants-snowden-three-more-years-of-asylum-lawyer/.

2. Julian Hattem, "US Should Hang Edward Snowden, Says Former Spy Panel Senator," *The Hill*, July 20, 2015, thehill.com/policy/national-security/248490-ex-top-spy-committee-senator-publicly-hang-snowden.

3. Thomas Fleming, *The Illusion of Victory: America in World War I* (New York: Basic Books, 2003), 96–97.

4. Christopher McKnight Nichols, *Promise and Peril: America at the Dawn of a Global Age* (Cambridge, MA: Harvard University Press, 2011), 209.

5. Quotes from Wilson's Flag Day speech, "The German Plot," given at Washington Monument, June 14, 1917, American Presidency Project, www.presidency.ucsb.edu/ws/?pid=65400.

6. "Wilson and Censorship of the Press," Woodrow Wilson Presidential Library and Museum, www.woodrowwilson.org/library-archives/wilson-elibrary/explore-featured-documents/wilson-and-censorship-of-the-press.

7. Rahul Sagar, *Secrets and Leaks: The Dilemma of State Secrecy* (Princeton, NJ: Princeton University Press, 2013), 37. This excellent study illuminates all sides of the debate.

8. During the Cold War, Secretary of State John Foster Dulles relied heavily on the agent theory of dissent, expanding it into an international agent theory of

revolution that caused the Third World—the Orwellian name for postcolonial non-Western states—untold trouble and turmoil. The idea that the Vietnamese, for example, could actually elect a Communist, Ho Chi Minh, in a free election was unthinkable to him. If that happened, it could only be because loyal Vietnamese had been tricked or forced into voting for agents of the "international Communist conspiracy." The agent theory was immune to evidence. After the French colonialists' defeat at Dien Bien Phu, when a CIA analysis predicted that Ho would get 80 percent of the vote in the national election promised in the 1954 Geneva Accords, the Eisenhower administration refused to sign the agreement, blocked reunification, and ratified the egregiously fraudulent election of Ngo Dinh Diem in the South, in which the number of votes cast far exceeded the number of eligible voters.

It was not always easy to convince America's Cold War allies that the agent theory of revolution explained everything, however. After the organizing meeting of the Southeast Asia Treaty Organization (SEATO) in February 1955, Dulles told reporters that he was disappointed that the draft of the original communiqué did not have the word "Communism" in it anywhere. He took steps to correct that problem. "I called attention to the fact that it seemed rather extraordinary, when we were making all this effort to combat something, that we couldn't even give it a name. And so the words 'international Communism.' I think that from now on it will be respectable in this circle to talk about International Communism." Lloyd C. Gardner, *A Covenant with Power: America and World Order from Wilson to Reagan* (New York: Oxford University Press, 1984), 155.

9. Ernest Freeberg, *Democracy's Prisoner: Eugene V. Debs, the Great War, and the Right to Dissent* (Cambridge, MA: Harvard University Press, 2008), 50. As will be evident, most of the argument in the following paragraphs is based upon evidence in Freeberg's book.

10. Richard Drake, *The Education of an Anti-Imperialist: Robert M. La Follette and U.S. Expansion* (Madison: University of Wisconsin Press, 2013), 188–90.

11. Ibid., 189.

12. Ibid., 196, 218.

13. Ibid., 57, 64.

14. Ibid., 104, 130.

15. Ibid., 46, 135.

16. Ibid., 298–99.

17. "Nationalism and Americanism," text of Harding's speech, www.learnnc .org/lp/editions/nchist-newcentury/4959?.

18. Thomas H. Eliot, "Did We Almost Lose the Army?," *New York Times*, August 12, 1991.

19. Lloyd C. Gardner, *Economic Aspects of New Deal Diplomacy* (Madison: University of Wisconsin Press, 1964), 171.

20. Ibid., 10.

21. Thomas Fleming, *The New Dealers' War: F.D.R. and the War Within World War II* (New York: Basic Books, 2001), 1–36. Fleming tells the story of the

leak and suggests that FDR himself had a role in its escape from War Department safes to the offices of the *Tribune*.

22. Thomas F. Troy, "Truman on CIA," CIA Historical Review Program, released September 22, 1993, www.cia.gov/library/center-for-the-study-of-intelligence/kent-csi/vol20no1/html/v20i1a02p_0001.htm. Much of what follows about the founding of the CIA is taken from this excellent monograph.

23. Louis Menand, "Wild Thing: Did the O.S.S. Help Win the War Against Hitler?" review of Douglas Waller, *Wild Bill Donovan: The Spymaster Who Created the OSS and Modern American Espionage* (New York: The Free Press, 2012), *New Yorker*, www.newyorker.com/arts/critics/books/2011/03/14/wild-thing-louis-menand.

24. Troy, "Truman on CIA."

25. Menand, "Wild Thing."

26. Troy, "Truman on CIA."

27. Tom Wicker et al., "C.I.A.: Maker of Policy, or Tool?," *New York Times*, April 25, 1966.

28. Jack B. Pfeiffer, *Official History of the Bay of Pigs Operation* (National Security Archive Briefing Book No. 355), vol. 3, *Evolution of CIA's Anti-Castro Policies, 1959–January 1961* (Alexandria, VA: Central Intelligence Agency, December 1979; CIA Historical Review Program, "release as sanitized 1998"), nsarchive.gwu.edu/NSAEBB/NSAEBB355/bop-vol3.pdf, p. 72.

29. Hayden B. Peake, "Harry S. Truman on CIA Covert Operations," *Studies in Intelligence*, Spring 1981. Much of what follows is taken from this source.

30. Ibid. And for a good summary of how the early CIA got into covert activities, see John Prados, *Presidents' Secret Wars: CIA and Pentagon Covert Operations from World War II Through the Persian Gulf* (Chicago: Ivan R. Dee, 1996), 13–29.

31. Dominic Rushe, "Intelligence Chair: NSA Leaker Edward Snowden May Have Had Russian Help," *The Guardian*, January 19, 2014, www.theguardian.com/world/2014/jan/19/edwrd-snowden-nsa-mike-rogers-russia.

32. Ibid.

33. Nick O'Malley, "Julie Bishop Welcomes U.S. Intelligence Reforms, Lashes Snowden," *Sydney Morning Herald*, January 23, 2014, www.smh.com.au/world/julie-bishop-welcomes-us-intelligence-reforms-lashes-edward-snowden-20140123-hv9j5.html#ixzz2rFWYxlwN.

2. Where Ellsberg Fits In

1. Interview with Mike Gravel, "Mike Gravel to Senator Mark Udall: Make Full Torture Probe Public Like I Did with Pentagon Papers," Democracy Now, December 16, 2014, www.democracynow.org/2014/12/16/mike_gravel_to_senator_mark_udall.

2. David Johnston and Charlie Savage, "Obama Reluctant to Look into Bush Programs," *New York Times*, January 12, 2009.

3. Ibid.

4. Craig Frizzell and Magen Knuth, "Mortal Enemies? Did President Kennedy Plan on Splintering the CIA?," undated, mcadams.posc.mu.edu/jfk_cia .html.

5. Thomas C. Reeves, A Question of Character: A Life of John F. Kennedy (New York: The Free Press, 1991), 276–78. Not surprisingly, Reeves's book did not find much favor with Kennedy fans, although there was no attempt to refute his position on the CIA or Mongoose.

6. Christopher A. Preble, John F. Kennedy and the Missile Gap (DeKalb: Northern Illinois University Press, 2004), 177.

7. Tim Weiner, "J.F.K. Turns to the C.I.A. to Plug a Leak," New York Times, July 1, 2007, www.nytimes.com/2007/07/01/weekinreview/01word.html. Weiner's article contains the transcript of the meetings held to discuss what to do about Baldwin and future leaks. The following paragraphs are taken from that article and the transcripts.

8. "In 1962, JFK Was Urged to Take 'Drastic Action' Against Leakers," Secrecy News blog, Federation of American Scientists, September 24, 2012, www .fas.org/blog/secrecy.

9. Weiner, "J.F.K.Turns to the CIA."

10. David G. Coleman, "JFK's War Against Leaks," History News Network, October 22, 2012, hnn.us/article/148870.

11. Monica Crowley, Nixon in Winter: His Final Revelations About Diplomacy, Watergate, and Life Out of the Arena (New York: Random House, 1998), 287.

12. John Herbst, "Nixon and the Policital Prospects," New York Times, August 18, 1973.

13. Daniel Ellsberg, Secrets: A Memoir of Vietnam and the Pentagon Papers (New York: Viking, 2002), 203.

14. Ibid., 47.

15. Roger Morris, "How Not to End Another President's War," 100 Days blog, New York Times, February 26, 2009.

16. Ibid.

17. Roger Morris, Uncertain Greatness: Henry Kissinger & American Foreign Policy (New York: Harper & Row, 1977), 94.

18. Rick Perlstein, Nixonland: The Rise of a President and the Fracturing of America (New York: Scribner, 2000), 419.

19. Morris, Uncertain Greatness, 155.

20. See Garry Wills, The Kennedy Imprisonment: A Meditation upon Power (Boston: Little, Brown, 1985), for the strongest statement of this hurdle JFK's successors had to overcome.

21. H.R. Haldeman, Inside the Nixon White House: The Haldeman Diaries, introduction and afterword by Stephen E. Ambrose (New York: Putnam's, 1994), 41.

22. See William Shawcross, Sideshow: Kissinger, Nixon, and the Destruction of Cambodia (New York: Washington Square Press, 1979).

23. Richard Reeves, President Nixon: Alone in the White House (New York: Simon & Schuster, 2001), 75.

24. Ibid.

25. Seymour M. Hersh, *The Price of Power: Kissinger in the Nixon White House* (New York: Summit Books, 1983), 90–92.

26. Ibid., 96.

27. "Context of 'June 19, 1972: Supreme Court Holds Warrantless Wiretapping of US Citizens Unconstitutional,'" History Commons, undated, downloaded April 26, 2014, www.historycommons.org/context.jsp?item=civilliberties_95.

28. "Elizabeth Holtzman Calls for Americans to Put Impeachment Where It Belongs—Back on the Table," December 11, 2006, www.truth-out.org/buzz flash/commentary/elizabeth-holtzman-calls-for-americans-to-put-impeachment -where-it-belongs-back-on-the-table/1114-elizabeth-holtzman-calls-for-americans -to-put-impeachment-where-it-belongs—back-on-the-table.

29. See Betty Medsger, *The Burglary: The Discovery of J. Edgar Hoover's Secret FBI* (New York: Knopf, 2014).

30. The publication of a new book by Ken Hughes, *Chasing Shadows: The Nixon Tapes, the Chennault Affair, and the Origins of Watergate* (Charlottesville: University of Virginia Press, 2014), documents how the Pentagon Papers episode reveals attitudes about leaks and fears about election results that often trump the ostensible issue of national security.

31. Medsger, *Burglary*, 234.

32. The sobriquet was given to Lansdale by readers of Graham Greene's 1954 novel *The Quiet American*, a book that described the actions of Alden Pyle, an American intelligence agent filled with the best intentions, who justifies means by ends and sets loose forces he cannot control. The association stuck even though Greene denied that Lansdale was his model, and in fact Greene wrote *The Quiet American* in 1952, after he had left Vietnam and before Lansdale arrived. Norman Sherry, in his 2004 biography of Greene, considered it much more likely that Lansdale was the prototype for Colonel Edwin Hillendale in William J. Lederer and Eugene Burdick's *The Ugly American* of 1958, a supposition supported by similarity of name and character.

33. Ellsberg, *Secrets*, 141–42.

34. Ibid., 206.

35. John Prados and Margaret Pratt Porter, eds., *Inside the Pentagon Papers* (Lawrence: University of Kansas Press, 2004), 6–7, 51.

36. Ellsberg, *Secrets*, 352; David Landau, "Kissinger: Facing Down the Vietnamese," *Harvard Crimson*, May 28, 1971.

37. Landau, "Kissinger."

38. Tape of Telephone Conversation, January 13, 1971, reproduced in Prados and Porter, *Inside the Pentagon Papers*, 90–91.

39. Tape of White House Meeting, June 24, 1971, reproduced in Stanley I. Kutler, ed., *Abuse of Power: The New Nixon Tapes* (New York: Simon & Schuster, 1997), 4–5.

40. Hersh, *Price of Power*, 384–85.

41. James Reston, *Deadline: A Memoir* (New York: Random House, 1991), 329.

42. Ibid., 329–30.

43. Ibid., 121.

44. Ibid., 168–69.

45. John Ehrlichman, *Witness to Power: The Nixon Years* (New York: Simon & Schuster, 1982), 300–302; Tape Recording, July 1, 1971, Nixon, Haldeman, Colson, and Ehrlichman, in Kutler, *Abuse of Power*, 10–14.

46. Kutler, *Abuse of Power*, 10.

47. Egil Krogh, "The Break-in That History Forgot," *New York Times*, June 30, 2007.

48. Ibid.

49. Lamar Waldron, *Watergate: The Hidden History, Nixon, the Mafia, and the CIA* (Berkeley, CA: Counterpoint Press, 2012), 487–91.

50. James Goodale, *Fighting for the Press: The Inside Story of the Pentagon Papers and Other Battles* (New York: City University of New York Journalism Press, 2013), 86–87.

51. Tape Recording, June 15, 1971, in Prados and Porter, *Inside the Pentagon Papers*, 108–9.

52. Ellsberg, *Secrets*, 432–33.

53. Douglas O. Linder, "The Pentagon Papers (Daniel Ellsberg) Trial: An Account," 2011, law2.umkc.edu/faculty/projects/ftrials/ellsberg/ellsbergaccount .html.

3. The Great Transformation

1. Brad Friedman, "Daniel Ellsberg: Edward Snowden Is a Patriot," June 14, 2013, *Salon*, www.salon.com/2013/06/14/daniel_ellsberg_edward_snowden_is _a_patriot_partner.

2. Mike Masnick, "Words Mean Something: How Eric Holder Pretends He Won't Put Reporters in Jail Without Actually Saying That," *Techdirt*, May 29, 2014, www.techdirt.com/articles/20140529/06543627390/words-mean -something-how-eric-holder-pretends-he-wont-put-reporters-jail-without-actually -saying-that.shtml.

3. Glenn Greenwald, "Obama DOJ Formally Accuses Journalist in Leak Case of Committing Crimes," *The Guardian*, May 20, 2013, www.theguardian .com/commentisfree/2013/may/20/obama-doj-james-rosen-criminality.

4. Ibid.

5. Glenn Greenwald, "NSA Collecting Phone Records of Millions of Verizon Customers Daily," June 6, 2013, *The Guardian*, www.theguardian.com /world/2013/jun/06/nsa-phone-records-verizon-court-order.

6. The story of the telephone call is described in detail in Luke Harding, *The Snowden Files: The Inside Story of the World's Most Wanted Man* (New York: Vintage, 2014), 127–32.

7. Ibid.

8. Ellen Nakashima, "Verizon Providing All Call Records to U.S. Under Court Order," *Washington Post*, June 6, 2013, www.washingtonpost.com/world /national-security/verizon-providing-all-call-records-to-us-under-court-order /2013/06/05/98656606-ce47-11e2-8845-d970ccb04497_story.html.

9. Glenn Kessler, "Clapper's 'Least Untruthful' Statement to the Senate," *Fact Checker* blog, *Washington Post* June 12, 2013, www.washingtonpost.com /blogs/fact-checker/post/james-clappers-least-untruthful-statement-to-the-senate /2013/06/11/e50677a8-d2d8-11e2-a73e-826d299ff459_blog.html.

10. Spencer Ackerman, "James Clapper: Obama Stands by Intelligence Chief as Criticism Mounts," *The Guardian*, June 12, 2013, www.theguardian .com/world/2013/jun/12/james-clapper-intelligence-chief-criticism.

11. Harding, *Snowden Files*, 96–97.

12. Lee-Anne Goodman, "Obama's Approval Rating Down amid NSA Scandal; Snowden Defends Himself," Canadian Press, June 17, 2013, news.yahoo .com/obamas-approval-rating-down-amid-nsa-scandal-snowden-190802515 .html.

13. Eli Sanders, " 'The Stranger' Asks Glenn Greenwald About Microsoft, Snowden, and What to Fear Now," *Slog* blog, *The Stranger*, June 17, 2014, slog .thestranger.com/slog/archives/2014/06/17/the-stranger-asks-glenn-greenwald -about-microsoft-snowden-and-what-to-fear-now.

14. Ibid.

15. I have discussed the rapid evolution of Barack Obama's national security policies or, perhaps more accurately, the perception of those policies, in *Killing Machine: The American Presidency in the Age of Drone Warfare* (New York: The New Press, 2013).

16. "President Obama Defends NSA Spying," *BuzzFeed*, June 17, 2013, www .buzzfeed.com/buzzfeedpolitics/president-obama-defends-nsa-spying.

17. Ibid.

18. Jeremy Herb and Justin Sink, "Sen. Feinstein Calls Snowden's NSA Leaks an 'Act of Treason,' " *The Hill*, June 10, 2013, thehill.com/policy/defense /304573-sen-feinstein-snowdens-leaks-are-treason.

19. Ibid.

20. Luke Harding, "How Edward Snowden Went from Loyal NSA Contractor to Whistleblower," *The Guardian*, February 1, 2014, www.theguardian.com /world/2014/feb/01/edward-snowden-intelligence-leak-nsa-contractor-extract. This is a handy excerpt from Harding's *Snowden Files*.

21. Ibid.

22. Peter Maass, "How Laura Poitras Helped Snowden Spill His Secrets," *New York Times Magazine*, August 13, 2013, www.nytimes.com/2013/08/18 /magazine/laura-poitras-snowden.html?pagewanted=all.

23. Ibid.

24. Lana Lam, "Snowden Sought Booz Allen Job to Gather Evidence on NSA Surveillance," *South China Morning Post*, June 24, 2013, www.scmp.com /news/hong-kong/article/1268209/snowden-sought-booz-allen-job-gather-evi dence-nsa-surveillance?page=all.

25. Associated Press, "US Authorities Got NSA Whistleblower Edward Snowden's Middle Name Wrong on Extradition Request, Says Hong Kong," *The Independent*, June 27, 2013, www.independent.co.uk/news/world/americas /us-authorities-got-nsa-whistleblower-edward-snowdens-middle-name-wrong-on -extradition-request-says-hong-kong-8676687.html.

26. Josh Gerstein, "Edward Snowden Charged with 3 Felonies," June 21, 2013, *Politico,* www.politico.com/story/2013/06/edward-snowden-charged-nsa-93179 .html.

27. Ibid.

28. Daniel Ellsberg, "Edward Snowden: Saving Us from the United Stasi of America," *The Guardian,* June 10, 2014, www.theguardian.com/comment isfree/2013/jun/10/edward-snowden-united-stasi-america.

29. Although the WikiLeaks source was Bradley when arrested, by the end of the trial a name change to Chelsea had been requested.

30. Marcy Wheeler, "What Does the Government Consider 'Protected' First Amendment Activities?," Emptywheel.com, July 17, 2013, www.emptywheel .net/2013/07/17. I have also drawn upon the YouTube video of the press conference, which shows the body language, facial expressions, and tone of voice of the exchanges.

31. Gardner, *Killing Machine,* 163–64.

32. Greg Miller, "Legal Memo Backing Drone Strike That Killed American Anwar al-Awlaki Is Released," *Washington Post,* June 23, 2014, www .washingtonpost.com/world/national-security/legal-memo-backing-drone-strike -is-released/2014/06/23/1f48dd16-faec-11e3-8176-f2c941cf35f1_story.html.

33. Max Frankel, "Where Did Our 'Inalienable Rights' Go?," *New York Times,* June 23, 2013, www.nytimes.com/2013/06/23/opinion/sunday/where-did -our-inalienable-rights-go.html.

34. Ibid.

35. Ibid.

36. Erik Wemple, "David Gregory Whiffs on Greenwald Question," blog, *Washington Post,* June 23, 2013, www.washingtonpost.com/blogs/crik-wemple /wp/2013/06/23/david-gregory-whiffs-on-greenwald-question.

4. Front Lines—Leakers and the New (Old) Journalism

1. "The Spies Who Lost Me: GCHQ Claims Snowden Cost Them Criminals," *Sputnik,* December 30, 2014, sputniknews.com/europe/20141229/1013328497 .html.

2. Marie Morelli, "Edward Snowden, Spying on Citizens and Freedom of the Press: A Conversation with Alan Rusbridger," Syracuse.com, www.syracuse .com/opinion/index.ssf/2014/10/edward_snowden_spying_on_citizens_and_ freedom_of_the_press_a_conversation_with_a.html.

3. Ibid.

4. Ibid.

5. David Folkenflik, "New York Times Editor: Losing Snowden Scoop 'Really Painful,' " June 5, 2014, National Public Radio, www.npr.org/2014/06/05/31 9233332.

6. Leonard Downie Jr. and Sara Rafsky, "The Obama Administration and the Press," Committee to Protect Journalists Special Report, October 2013, cpj .org/reports/2013/10/obama-and-the-press-us-leaks-surveillance-post-911.php.

7. Ibid.

8. Ibid.

9. Dana Milbank, "Eric Holder Stews in His Own Juices," *Washington Post*, May 21, 2013, www.washingtonpost.com/opinions/stewing-in-his-own-juices /2013/05/31/90e6bb0c-c9f9-11e2-8da7-d274bc611a47_story.html.

10. Judson Berger, "DOJ Invoked Espionage Act in Calling Fox News Reporter Criminal 'Co-conspirator,' " FoxNews.com, May 22, 2013, www.foxnews .com/politics/2013/05/22/doj-invoked-espionage-act-in-calling-fox-news-reporter -criminal-co-conspirator.

11. Michael Hastings, "The Runaway General," *Rolling Stone*, June 22, 2010. The quotation is from Hastings's follow-up book, *The Operators: The Wild and Terrifying Inside Story of America's War in Afghanistan* (New York: Blue Rider Press, 2012), 292–93.

12. Benjamin Wallace, "Who Killed Michael Hastings?," *New York*, November 10, 2013, nymag.com/news/features/michael-hastings-2013-11.

13. Michael Hastings, "Why Democrats Love to Spy on Americans," *BuzzFeed*, June 7, 2013, www.buzzfeed.com/mhastings/why-democrats-love-to -spy-on-americans.

14. Mike Hogan, "Was Michael Hastings' Car Hacked? Richard Clarke Says It's Possible," *Huffington Post*, June 26, 2013, www.huffingtonpost .com/2013/06/24michael-hastings-car-hacked_n_3492339.html.

15. "The Times and Iraq," *New York Times*, May 26, 2004; Joe Strupp, "Bill Keller Speaks Out on Judy Miller, Iraq War Coverage, and Fox News," blog, Media Matters, June 3, 2011, mediamatters.org/blog/2011/06/03/bill-keller-speaks -out-on-judy-miller-iraq-war/180289.

16. James Risen and Eric Lichtblau, "Bush Lets U.S. Spy on Callers Without Courts," *New York Times*, December 16, 2005, www.nytimes.com/2005/12/16 /politics/bush-lets-us-spy-on-callers-without-courts.html.

17. Jeremy Hobson, host, "New York Times Admits Reason for Delay in Delivering NSA Wiretapping Story," *Here and Now*, National Public Radio, May 24, 2014, hereandnow.wbur.org/2014/05/14/nytimes-wiretapping-delay.

18. Glenn Greenwald, "Climate of Fear: Jim Risen v. the Obama Administration," *Salon*, June 23, 2011, www.salon.com/2011/06/23/risen_3.

19. James Risen, *State of War: The Secret History of the CIA and the Bush Administration* (New York: The Free Press, 2006), 194–211.

20. Downie and Rafsky, "Obama Administration and the Press."

21. Greenwald, "Climate of Fear."

22. Steve Coll, "A Test of Confidence," *New Yorker*, September 2, 2013, 21–22, www.newyorker.com/magazine/2013/09/02/a-test-of-confidence.

23. Michael Calderone and Dan Froomkin, " 'Reporter's Privilege' Under Fire from Obama Administration amid Broader War on Leakers," *Huffington Post*, May 18, 2012, www.huffingtonpost.com/2012/05/18/reporters-privilege -obama-war-leaks-new-york-times_n_1527748.html.

24. Ibid.

25. Dina Rasor, "Conversation with James Risen: Can Journalists Protect Their National Security Sources?," *Truthout*, April 23, 2014, www.truth-out.org /opinion/item/23207-conversation-with-james-risen.

26. Ibid.

27. Tim McCarthy, "James Rosen: Fox News Reporter Targeted as 'Co-conspirator' in Spying Case," *The Guardian*, May 20, 2013, www.theguardian.com/world/2013/may/20/fox-news-reporter-targeted-us-government.

28. Dana Milbank, "In AP, Rosen Investigations, Government Makes Criminals of Reporters," *Washington Post*, May 21, 2013, www.washingtonpost.com/opinions/dana-milbank-in-ap-rosen-investigations-government-makes-criminals-of-reporters/2013/05/21/377af392-c24e-11e2-914f-a7aba60512a7_story.html.

29. Ibid.

30. Erik Wemple, "Eric Holder on Fox News's James Rosen: Weaselly Garbage," blog, *Washington Post*, June 20, 2013, www.washingtonpost.com/blogs/erik-wemple/wp/2013/06/20/eric-holder-on-fox-newss-james-rosen-weaselly-garbage.

31. Meenal Vamburkar, "Obama Admin Reportedly Fought to Keep James Rosen Search Warrant Secret," Mediaite.com, May 24, 2013, www.mediaite.com/online/obama-admin-reportedly-fought-to-keep-james-rosen-search-warrant-secret.

32. Rasor, "Conversation with James Risen."

33. Merrill Knox, "Former State Dept. Adviser Pleads Guilty in James Rosen Leak Case," TVNewser, February 7, 2014, www.adweek.com/tvnewser/former-state-dept-adviser-pleads-guilty-in-james-rosen-leak-case/213946.

34. David Ingram, "Stephen Kim Pleading Guilty for Leaking Classified Information," Reuters, February 7, 2014, www.huffingtonpost.com/2014/02/07/stephen-kim-guilty_n_4746710.html.

35. Ibid.

36. Sari Horwitz, "Justice Department Tightens Guidelines in Leak Investigations," *WashingtonPost*, July 12, 2013, www.washingtonpost.com/world/national-security/justice-department-tightens-guidelines-in-leak-investigations/2013/07/12/5927e16e-eb19-11e2-8023-b7f07811d98e_story.html.

37. Cora Currier, "Charting Obama's Crackdown on National Security Leaks," *ProPublica*, July 20, 2013, www.propublica.org/special/sealing-loose-lips-charting-obamas-crackdown-on-national-security-leaks.

38. Downie and Rafsky, "Obama Administration and the Press."

39. Mary Beth Sheridan, "Hillary Clinton: WikiLeaks Release an 'Attack on International Community,'" *Washington Post*, November 29, 2010, www.washingtonpost.com/wp-dyn/content/article/2010/11/29/AR2010112903231.html.

40. Amy Goodman, "Nomads of the Digital Age," *Truthdig*, July 10, 2014, www.truthdig.com/report/item/nomads_of_the_digital_age_20140709.

41. "Collateral Murder," July 6, 2010, collateralmurder.wikileaks.org.

42. Kevin Gosztola, "Daniel Ellsberg: Both Manning & Snowden Exposed Secrecy to Proper Debate," *Firedoglake*, June 5, 2014, shadowproof.com/2014/06/05/daniel-ellsberg-both-manning-snowden-exposed-government-secrecy-to-proper-debate.

43. Jonathan S. Landay and Marisa Taylor, "Experts: Obama's Plan to Predict Future Leakers Unproven, Unlikely to Work," McClatchy DC, July 9, 2013, www.mcclatchydc.com/news/special-reports/insider-threats/article24750850.html.

44. Ibid.

45. James Risen, "Snowden Says He Took No Secret Files to Russia,"*New York Times*, October 17, 2013, www.nytimes.com/2013/10/18/world/snowden -says-he-took-no-secret-files-to-russia.html.

5. Prosecutions and Principles

1. James Risen, "2014 Lovejoy Address," October 15, 2014, Colby College website, www.colby.edu/lovejoyaward.

2. Leonard Downie Jr., and Sara Rafsky, "The Obama Administration and the Press," Committee to Protect Journalists Special Report, October 2013, cpj .org/reports/2013/10/obama-and-the-press-us-leaks-surveillance-post-911.php.

3. Ibid.

4. Chelsea Manning, "The Fog Machine of War: Chelsea Manning on the U.S. Military and Media Freedom," *New York Times*, June 14, 2014, www .nytimes.com/2014/06/15/opinion/sunday/chelsea-manning-the-us-militarys -campaign-against-media-freedom.html.

5. Ibid.

6. Abby Ohlheiser, "Bradley Manning's Pre-Trial Hearing Enters 10th Day," *Slate*, December 10, 2012, www.slate.com/blogs/the_slatest/2012/12/10/brad ley_manning_pre_trial_hearing_alleged_wikileaks_whistleblower_charges .html.

7. Glenn Greenwald, "The Inhumane Conditions of Bradley Manning's De-tention," *Salon*, December 15, 2010, www.salon.com/2010/12/15/manning_3.

8. "Barack Obama on Bradley Manning: 'He Broke the Law,' " *Politico*, April 22, 2011, www.politico.com/news/stories/0411/53601.html; Glenn Green-wald, "WH Forces P.J.Crowley to Resign for Condemning Abuse of Manning," *Salon*, March 13, 2011, www.salon.com/2011/03/13/crowley_3.

9. Brennan Center for Justice, "Bradley Manning Confinement Ruled Ille-gal," press release, January 8, 2013, www.brennancenter.org/press-release/bradley -manning-confinement-ruled-illegal.

10. Glenn Greenwald, "President Obama Speaks on Manning and the Rule of Law: The President Invokes Incoherent and Factually Confused Claims to Justify the Whistle-Blower's Pre-trial Punishment," *Salon*, April 23, 2011, www .salon.com/2011/04/23/manning_10.

11. Greg Miller, "U.S. Officials Scrambled to Nab Snowden, Hoping He Would Take a Wrong Step. He Didn't," *WashingtonPost*, June 14, 2014, www .washingtonpost.com/world/national-security/us-officials-scrambling-to-nab -snowden-hoped-he-would-take-a-wrong-step-he-didnt/2014/06/14/057a1ed2 -f1ae-11e3-bf76-447a5df6411f_story.html.

12. Duncan Campbell, "CIA Rendition Jet Was Waiting in Europe to SNATCH SNOWDEN," *The Register*, www.theregister.co.uk/2014/06/13/cia _rendition_jet_was_waiting_in_europe_to_snatch_snowden.

13. Miller, "U.S. Officials Scrambled to Nab Snowden."

14. Ibid.

15. Ibid.

16. Noam Chomsky, "Is Edward J. Snowden Aboard This Plane?," *Truthout*, August 1, 2013, www.truth-out.org/opinion/item/17923.

17. "Former NSA Director Jokes About Putting Snowden on a 'Kill List,'" Says He 'Hopes' NSA Is Involved in Targeted Killings," TechDirt.com, October 3, 2013, www.techdirt.com/articles/20131003/09451524742/former-nsa-director-jokes -about-putting-snowden-kill-list. Obama quoted in Lloyd C. Gardner, *Killing Machine: The Presidency in the Age of Drone Warfare* (New York: The New Press, 2013), 92.

18. Gardner, *Killing Machine*, 92.

19. Amy Goodman, "Nomads of the Digital Age," *Truthdig*, July 10, 2014, www.truthdig.com/report/item/nomads_of_the_digital_age_20140709.

20. Sarah Ellison, "The Man Who Came to Dinner," *Vanity Fair*, October 2013, www.vanityfair.com/news/politics/2013/10/julian-assange-hideout-ecuador.

21. Ibid.

22. Jane Mayer, "The Secret Sharer: Is Thomas Drake an Enemy of the State?," *New Yorker*, May 23, 2011, www.newyorker.com/magazine/2011/05/23/ the-secret-sharer.

23. Thomas Drake, "Snowden Saw What I Saw: Surveillance Criminally Subverting the Constitution," *The Guardian*, June 12, 2013, www.theguardian.com /commentisfree/2013/jun/12/snowden-surveillance-subverting-constitution.

24. Tim Shorrock, "Obama's Crackdown on Whistleblowers: The NSA Four Reveal How a Toxic Mix of Cronyism and Fraud Blinded the Agency Before 9/11," *The Nation*, Mar. 26, 2013, www.thenation.com/article/173521.

25. Ibid.

26. Mayer, "Secret Sharer."

27. Ibid.; Shorrock, "Obama's Crackdown."

28. Shorrock, "Obama's Crackdown."

29. Scott Shane, "Obama Takes a Hard Line Against Leaks to Press," *New York Times*, June 11, 2010, www.nytimes.com/2010/06/12/uspolitics/12leak .html.

30. Mayer, "Secret Sharer."

31. Ibid.

32. Ibid.

33. Downie and Rafsky, "Obama Administration and the Press."

34. Mayer, "Secret Sharer."

35. Downie and Rafsky, "Obama Administration and the Press."

36. Kevin Gosztola, "Bureau of Prisons Throws CIA Torture Whistleblower John Kiriakou's Children Out of Visitors Room," *Firedoglake*, April 21, 2014, shadowproof.com/2014/04/21/bureau-of-prisons-throws-cia-whistleblower-john -kiriakous-children-out-of-visitors-room.

37. "No Charges in CIA Waterboarding Video Destruction," BBC News, November 10, 2010, www.bbc.com/news/world-latin-america-11723140.

38. Scott Shane, "Ex-Officer Is First from C.I.A. to Face Prison for a Leak," *New York Times*, January 5, 2013, www.nytimes.com/2013/01/06/us/former-cia -officer-is-the-first-to-face-prison-for-a-classified-leak.html?pagewanted=all.

39. Ibid.

40. John Kiriakou, "Obama's Abuse of the Espionage Act Is Modern-Day McCarthyism," *The Guardian*, August 6, 2013, www.the guardian.com/com mentisfree/2013/aug/06.

41. Shane, "Ex-Officer Is First from C.I.A. to Face Prison."

42. Kiriakou, "Obama's Abuse of the Espionage Act."

43. Catherine Hickley, "Cold War Spy Tunnel Under Berlin Found After 56 Years," Bloomberg News, August 20, 2012, www.bloomberg.com/news/2012-08 -20/cold-war-spy-tunnel-under-berlin-found-after-56-years.html.

44. John le Carré, "I Was a Secret Even to Myself," *The Guardian*, April 12, 2013, www.theguardian.com/books/2013/apr/12/john-le-carre-spy-anniversary.

45. "Snowden Letter Raises New Questions for Merkel," Strategic Culture Foundation Online Journal, November 19, 2013, www.strategic-culture.org /pview/2013/11/19/snowden-letter-raises-new-questions-for-merkel.html.

46. Alison Smale, Mark Marzetti, and David E. Sanger, "Germany Demands Top U.S. Intelligence Officer Be Expelled," *New York Times*, July 11, 2014, www.nytimes.com/2014/07/11/world/europe/germany-expels-top-us-intel ligence-officer.html.

47. "Embassy Espionage. The NSA's Secret Spy Hub in Berlin," *Der Spiegel* Online, October 27, 2013, www.spiegel.de/international/germany/cover-story -how-nsa-spied-on-merkel-cell-phone-from-berlin-embassy-a-930205.html.

48. Ibid.

49. "NSA Whistleblowers Testify in Bundestag Inquiry, Disclose 'Totalitarian' Surveillance," RT.com, July 3, 2014, rt.com/news/170276-germany-nsa -bundestag-inquiry.

50. Drake, "Snowden Saw What I Saw."

51. "United Kingdom Defends Detention of David Miranda, Glenn Greenwald's Partner," *Washington Post*, August 20, 2013, www.washingtonpost.com /world/national-security/united-kingdom-defends-detention-of-david-miranda -glenn-greenwalds-partner/2013/08/20/2c077142-09a8-11e3-b87c-476db8ac34 cd_story.html

52. Philip Rucker and Karla Adam, "U.S. Had Advance Notice of Britain's Plan to Detain Reporter Glenn Greenwald's Partner," *Washington Post*, August 19, 2013, www.washingtonpost.com/world/europe/uk-police-urged-to -explain-detention-of-reporter-glenn-greewalds-partner/2013/08/19/f2a3159c-08 d9-11e3-89fe-abb4a5067014_story.html.

53. Jack Mirkinson, "Jeffrey Toobin Compares David Miranda to a 'Drug Mule,'" *Huffington Post*, August 20, 2013, www.huffingtonpost.com/2013/08/20 /jeffrey-toobin-david-miranda-drug-mule-glenn-greenwald_n_3787770.html.

54. Leah McGrath Goodman, "David Miranda and the Human-Rights Black Hole," *Newsweek*, January 7, 2015, www.newsweek.com/2015/01/16/edward -snowdens-helpers-296988.html.

55. RT, "Canadian Spy Agency 'Dissected' Brazilian Energy Ministry," Global Research, October 7, 2013, www.globalresearch.ca/canadian-spy-agency -dissected-brazilian-energy-ministry/5353279.

56. David E. Sanger and Thom Shanker, "N.S.A. Director Firmly Defends Surveillance Efforts," *New York Times*, October 12, 2013, www.nytimes

.com/2013/10/13/us/nsa-director-gives-firm-and-broad-defense-of-surveillance
-efforts.html.

57. Lara Jakes and Julie Pace, "US Weighing Changes After Allies Object to Spying," Yahoo News via AP, October 29, 2013, news.yahoo.com/us-weighing -changes-allies-object-spying-140030023—politics.html.

58. Jack Goldsmith, "Skepticism About Supposed White House and Intelligence Committee Ignorance About NSA Collection Against Allied Leaders," Lawfare, October 29, 2013, www.lawfareblog.com/skepticism-about -supposed-white-house-and-intelligence-committee-ignorance-about-nsa-col lection.

59. Mark Landler and Michael B. Schmidt, "Spying Known at Top Levels, Officials Say," New York Times, October 29, 2013, www.nytimes.com/2013/10/30 /world/officials-say-white-house-knew-of-spying.html.

60. Editorial Board, "The White House on Spying," New York Times, October 28, 2013, www.nytimes.com/2013/10/29/opinion/the-white-house-on-spy ing.html.

61. Landler and Schmidt, "Spying Known at Top Levels."

6. A Time of Testing Limits

1. Elias Groll, "The United States Has Outspent the Marshall Plan to Rebuild Afghanistan," Foreign Policy, July 30, 2014, foreignpolicy.com/2014/07/30 /the-united-states-has-outspent-the-marshall-plan-to-rebuild-afghanistan.

2. Richard A. Clarke, "Why You Should Worry About the NSA," New York Daily News, June 12, 2013, www.nydailynews.com/opinion/worry-nsa-article-1 .1369705.

3. Paul Wagensell, "NSA Mass Surveillance Useless, Former Bush Official Says," Tom's Guide, February 26, 2014, www.tomsguide.com/us/rsa-nsa-spy-pro gram-useless,news-18384.html.

4. Sandy Fitzgerald, "NSA Panel Member: Edward Snowden Guilty of 'Treason, High Crimes,'" Newsmax, December 21, 2013, www.newsmax.com /Newsfront/edward-snowden-treason-white-house-panel/2013/12/21/id/543177.

5. Chris Arthur, "Laser Spying: Is It Really Practical?," The Guardian, August 22, 2013, www.theguardian.com/world/2013/aug/22/gchq-warned-laser-spy ing-guardian-offices.

6. Ed Pilkington, "New York Times Says UK Tried to Get It to Hand Over Snowden Documents," The Guardian, October 15, 2013, www.theguardian.com /world/2013/oct/13/new-york-times-snowden-nsa-files.

7. Ibid.

8. Charlie Savage, "U.S. Knew Britain Planned to Erase Data at The Guardian," New York Times, July 11, 2014, www.nytimes.com/2014/07/12/world/europe /us-knew-britain-planned-to-erase-data-at-the-guardian.html.

9. Emily Schultheis, "Arguing with Michael Hayden in Aspen," The Atlantic, July 2, 2014, www.theatlantic.com/politics/archive/2014/07/arguing-with-mi chael-hayden-in-aspen/373822.

10. Sheryl Gay Stolberg, "Senators Left Out of the Loop Make Their Pique Known," *New York Times*, May 19, 2006, www.nytimes.com/2006/05/19/wash ington/19scene.html.

11. Ibid.

12. Shane Harris, "NSA Veterans: The White House Is Hanging Us Out to Dry," *Foreign Policy.com*, October 10, 2013, foreignpolicy.com/2013/10/11 /nsa-veterans-the-white-house-is-hanging-us-out-to-dry.

13. Ibid.

14. Eun Kyung Kim, "Edward Snowden: 'I'd Volunteer for Prison' to Return to US," Today.com, August 13, 2014, www.today.com/news/edward-snowden -tells-wired-magazine-i-would-volunteer-prison-return-1D80056514.

15. Transparency International Germany, "Whistleblower Prize 2013 for Edward Snowden," press release, July 25, 2013, www.transparency.org/news /pressrelease/transparency_international_germany_whistleblower_prize_2013 _for_edward_snow. I have discussed "lawfare" in *Killing Machine: The American Presidency in the Age of Drone Warfare* (New York: The New Press, 2013), 138–39.

16. "Edward Snowden Nominated for Nobel Peace Prize by Fans in Norway," *New York Daily News*, January 31, 2014, www.nydailynews.com/news/world /edward-snowden-nominated-nobel-prize-article-1.1596270?.

17. The following paragraphs are largely based on two articles by Scott Horton, "Justice's Vendetta Against a Whistleblower: Six Questions for Jesse-lyn Radack," OpEdNews.com, February 4, 2010, www.opednews.com/articles /Justice-s-Vendetta-Against-by-Scott-Horton-100224-156.html; and "Traitor: Six Questions for Jesselyn Radack," blog, *Harper's*, June 1, 2012, harpers.org/blog /2012/06/_traitor_-six-questions-for-jesselyn-radack.

18. Horton, "Traitor."

19. Ibid.

20. Steve Nelson, "Edward Snowden Endorses D.C. Protest Against NSA in Rare Public Statement," *U.S. News & World Report*, www.usnews.com/news /articles/2013/10/24/edward-snowden-endorses-dc-protest-against-nsa-in-rare -public-statement.

21. Tom Gjelten, "First Strike: US Cyber Warriors Seize the Offensive," *World Affairs*, January/February. 2013, www.worldaffairsjournal.org/first-strike -us-cyber-warriors-seize-offensive.

22. Ed O'Keefe, "McCain Wants Special Counsel to Investigate Recent Leaks to Media," *2chambers* blog, *Washington Post*, June 5, 2012, www.wash ingtonpost.com/blogs/2chambers/post/john-mccain-wants-special-counsel-to -investigate-national-security-leaks/2012/06/05/gJQAZU4kGV_blog.html.

23. Gordon Lubold, "Obama's Favorite General Stripped of His Security Clearance," *Foreign Policy*, September 24, 2013, foreignpolicy.com/2013/09/24 /obamas-favorite-general-stripped-of-his-security-clearance.

24. "Binney: 'The NSA's Main Motives: Power and Money,'" *Deutsche Welle*, August 18, 2014, www.dw.de/binney-the-main-motives-power-and-money /a-17862571.

25. Gjelten, "First Strike."

26. "Edward Snowden Christmas Message: End Mass Surveillance," BBC News, December 25, 2013, www.bbc.com/news/world-us-canada-25516081.

27. James Vincent, "Nude Photos of Strangers a 'Fringe Benefit' for NSA Employees, Says Snowden," *The Independent*, July 18, 2014, www.independent .co.uk/life-style/gadgets-and-tech/nude-photos-of-strangers-are-a-fringe-benefit -for-nsa-employees-says-snowden-9614097.html.

28. James Bamford, "Why NSA Surveillance Is Worse Than You've Ever Imagined," Reuters, May 11, 2015, blogs.reuters.com/great-debate/2015/05/11/if -youre-not-outraged-about-the-nsa-surveillance-heres-why-you-should-be.

29. Cheng Li and Ryan McElveen, "NSA Revelations Have Irreparably Hurt U.S. Corporations in China," Brookings Institution, December 8, 2013, www .brookings.edu/research/opinions/2013/12/12-nsa-revelations-hurt-corporations -china-li-mcelveen.

30. Barton Gellman and Ashkan Soltani, "NSA Infiltrates Links to Yahoo, Google Data Centers Worldwide, Snowden Documents Say," *Washington Post*, October 30, 2013. The following paragraphs are largely based on information from this article.

31. John Napier Tye, "Meet Executive Order 12333: The Reagan Rule That Lets the NSA Spy on Americans," *Washington Post*, July 18, 2014, www .washingtonpost.com/opinions/meet-executive-order-12333-the-reagan-rule-that -lets-the-nsa-spy-on-americans/2014/07/18/93d2ac22-0b93-11e4-b8e5-d0de8076 7fc2_story.html.

32. Nicole Perlroth and Vindu Goel, "Internet Firms Step Up Efforts to Stop Spying," *New York Times*, December 5, 2013, www.nytimes.com/2013/12/05 /technology/internet-firms-step-up-efforts-to-stop-spying.html?pagewanted =all.

33. Ibid.

34. "Inside TAO: Documents Reveal Top NSA Hacking Unit," *Der Spiegel* Online, December 29, 2013, www.spiegel.de/international/world/the-nsa-uses -powerful-toolbox-in-effort-to-spy-on-global-networks-a-940969.html; and John Callaham, "NSA Intercepting PC Shipments to Install Spyware," Neowin .net, December 29, 2013, www.neowin.net/news/nsa-intercepting-pc-shipments -to-install-spyware.

35. Edward Wyatt and Claire Cain Miller, "Tech Giants Issue Call for Limits on Government Surveillance of Users," *New York Times*, December 9, 2013, www.nytimes.com/2013/12/09/technology/tech-giants-issue-call-for-limits-on -government-surveillance-of-users.html?pagewanted=all.

36. The information on Klayman's career is taken from the Wikipedia biographical entry.

37. Ellen Nakashima, "U.S. Reasserts Need to Keep Domestic Surveillance Secret," *Washington Post*, December 22, 2013, www.washingtonpost.com/world /national-security/us-reasserts-need-to-keep-domestic-surveillance-secret/2013 /12/21/9d2b4538-6a7e-11e3-a0b9-249bbb34602c_story.html.

38. Marcy Wheeler, "This Is Why You Can't Trust the NSA. Ever," *The Week*, August 22, 2014, theweek.com/articles/444348/why-cant-trust-nsa-ever.

39. Spencer Ackerman, "FISA Judge: Snowden's NSA Disclosures Triggered Important Spying Debate," *The Guardian*, September 14, 2013, www.theguardian .com/world/2013/sep/13/edward-snowden-nsa-disclosures-judge.

40. Philip Bump, "Federal Judge: NSA's 'Almost Orwellian' Data Collection Likely Violates Constitution," *The Wire* (*The Atlantic* news site), December 16, 2013, www.thewire.com/politics/2013/12/federal-judge-nsas-almost-orwellian -phone-data-collection-likely-violates-constitution/356207.

41. Ibid.

42. Jens F. Laurson and George Pieler, "Fourth Amendment Quartet: Edward Snowden, Judge Leon, Barack Obama, and the NSA," *Forbes*, January 21, 2014, www.forbes.com/sites/laursonpieler/2014/01/21/rational-bias_richard-leon _4th-amendment_phone-meta-data-survaillance.

43. "Bad Times for Big Brother," *New York Times*, December 21, 2013, www .nytimes.com/2013/12/22/opinion/sunday/bad-times-for-big-brother.html.

44. Michael Morell, "Correcting the Record on the NSA Recommendations," *Washington Post*, December 27, 2013, www.washingtonpost.com/opinions /michael-morell-correcting-the-record-on-the-nsa-recommendations/2013/12/27 /54846538-6e45-11e3-aecc-85cb037b7236_story.html.

45. Lawrence Wright, "The Al Qaeda Switchboard," *New Yorker*, January 13, 2014, www.newyorker.com/magazine/2014/01/13/the-al-qaeda-switchboard.

46. Matt Sledge, "White House NSA Panel Undermines Key Defense of Phone Surveillance Program," *Huffington Post*, December 18, 2013, www.huffing tonpost.com/2013/12/18/nsa-review-panel-report_n_4468958.html.

7. A House Divided Against Itself

1. Andrea Peterson, "Patriot Act Author: 'There Has Been a Failure of Oversight,'" *The Switch* blog, *Washington Post*, October 11, 2013, www.washington post.com/blogs/the-switch/wp/2013/10/11/patriot-act-author-there-has-been-a -failure-of-oversight.

2. Darren Samuelsohn, "Stone: White House Viewed Surveillance Report as 'Liberal,'" *Politico*, January 14, 2014, www.politico.com/blogs/under-the -radar/2014/01/stone-white-house-viewed-surveillance-report-as-liberal-181849 .html.

3. Michael Isikoff, "NSA Program Stopped No Terrorist Attacks, Says White House Panel Member," NBC News, December 20, 2013, www.nbcnews.com /news/other/nsa-program-stopped-no-terror-attacks-says-white-house-panel-f2D 11783588.

4. Paul Wagenseil, "NSA Mass Surveillance Useless, Former Bush Official Says," *Tom's Guide*, February 26, 2014, www.tomsguide.com/us/rsa-nsa-spy-pro gram-useless,news-18384.html; Brandan Blevins, "Richard Clarke: NSA Revelations Show Potential for Police State," *TechTarget*, February 24, 2014, search security.techtarget.com/news/2240214986/Richard-Clarke-NSA-revelations-show -potential-for-police-state.

5. Ellen Nakashima, "NSA Phone Record Collection Does Little to Prevent Terrorist Attack, Group Says," *Washington Post*, January 12, 2014, www

.washingtonpost.com/world/national-security/nsa-phone-record-collection-does
-little-to-prevent-terrorist-attacks-group-says/2014/01/12/8aa860aa-77dd-11e3-89
63-b4b654bcc9b2_story.html.

6. Alan Rusbridger and Ewen MacAskill, "I, Spy: Edward Snowden in Exile," *The Guardian*, July 19, 2014, www.theguardian.com/world/2014/jul/18/-sp
-edward-snowden-interview-rusbridger-macaskill.

7. Ibid.

8. Ibid.

9. NSA, "Statement in Response to Recent Allegations Regarding Contact with the NSA Office of General Counsel," May 29, 2014, www.nsa.gov/public
_info/speeches_testimonies/29may14.shtml.

10. Mike Brunker and Matthew Cole, "Snowden Strikes Back at NSA, Emails NBC News," NBC News, May 30, 2014, www.nbcnews.com/feature
/edward-snowden-interview/snowden-strikes-back-nsa-emails-nbc-news-n118821.

11. Amy Davidson, "Did Edward Snowden Break His Oath?," *New Yorker*, January 5, 2014, www.newyorker.com/news/amy-davidson/did-edward-snowden
-break-his-oath.

12. Nicholas D. Kristof, "A War Hero or a Phony?," *New York Times*, September 18, 2004, www.nytimes.com/2004/09/18/opinion/18kristof.html. Kristof concludes that while Kerry's campaign exaggerated some of his feats in the Vietnam War, his decorations were earned, and he was respected by members of his crew.

13. Kerry interview with Savannah Guthrie, *Today Show*, May 28, 2014.

14. Denise Oliver Velez, "Ellsberg: 'Kerry's Challenge to Snowden' Is 'Either Disingenuous or Simply Ignorant,' " *Daily Kos*, May 30, 2014, www.dailykos
.com/story/2014/05/30/1303083.

15. See the recent book by Michael MacDonald, *Overreach: Delusions of Regime Change in Iraq* (Cambridge, MA: Harvard University Press, 2014), for a discussion of the Lockean assumptions of American foreign policy that came apart in Gulf War II.

16. Sean Wilentz, "Would You Feel Differently About Snowden, Greenwald, and Assange If You Knew What They Really Thought?," *New Republic*, January 19, 2014, www.newrepublic.com/article/116253. Quotations that follow are taken from this article.

17. With such a sweeping statement at the outset, Wilentz risked invoking the Facebook trap: whatever embarrassing thing one did in years past could be called up with the touch of a few keys on a computer to ruin chances in a job interview or even a marriage proposal. But the larger question here was about the underlying assumption that "deepest beliefs and true motives" are set in stone. If that were true, then liberals would have to give up on the idea, for example, that Justice Hugo Black had evolved from a Ku Klux Klan beginning into a powerful voice for many liberal causes on the Supreme Court. Black himself later wrote that he used the Klan's support to get elected—nothing more. But the record shows that many of his early views were in tune with its views, particularly anti-Catholicism. He wrote a concurring opinion on the 1971 Pentagon Papers case that seems an apt commentary at a time the Obama administration has set out

to use the Espionage Act against leakers: "In the First Amendment the Founding Fathers gave the free press the protection it must have to fulfill its essential role in our democracy. The press was to serve the governed, not the governors. The Government's power to censor the press was abolished so that the press would remain forever free to censure the Government. The press was protected so that it could bare the secrets of government and inform the people. Only a free and unrestrained press can effectively expose deception in government. . . . The word 'security' is a broad, vague generality whose contours should not be invoked to abrogate the fundamental law embodied in the First Amendment."

Hugo Black also demonstrates the fallacy of assuming that a person is an either/or creature without the usual crosscurrents and reconsiderations that fill a lifetime. However that may be, Wilentz felt he had to use strong words to describe the true motives and reveal the goals of the leakers. "Where liberals, let alone right-wingers, have portrayed the leakers as truth-telling comrades intent on protecting the state and the Constitution from authoritarian malefactors, that's hardly their goal. In fact, the leakers despise of the modern liberal state, and they want to wound it." Apparently, all leakers share such views. If not, then Wilentz does not tell us which of the many do not. Nor does he account for those, like Jesselyn Radack and James Risen, who have resisted loss of employment and threats of imprisonment rather than violate their conscience by cooperating with investigations.

18. Peter Eisler and Susan Page, "3 NSA Veterans Speak Out on Whistle-Blower: We Told You So," *USA Today*, June 16, 2013, www.usatoday.com/story/news/politics/2013/06/16/snowden-whistleblower-nsa-officials-roundtable/2428809.

19. Michael Kinsley, "Eyes Everywhere," review of Glenn Greenwald's *No Place to Hide: Edward Snowden, the NSA, and the U.S. Surveillance State* (New York: Metropolitan Books/Henry Holt, 2014), *New York Times Book Review*, May 22, 2014. The review didn't actually appear in print in the Sunday *Book Review* until June 8, 2014. By that time, it had been around the world and back again several times on the Internet, and the debate was in full swing. Later quotations from Kinsley are taken from this source.

20. This is the point made by Barry Eisler in "Prioritizing Personalities over a Free Press," blog, Freedom of the Press Foundation, May 27, 2014, freedom.press/blog/2014/05/prioritizing-personalities-over-free-press.

21. Conor Friedersdorf, "A Liberal Moderate's Critique of Snowden and Greenwald," *The Atlantic*, May 28, 2014, www.theatlantic.com/politics/archive/2014/05/the-establishment-critique-of-edward-snowden-and-glenn-greenwald/371678. This clear-headed essay is actually a critique of the pro-surveillance pundits, who often attack the leakers "as if *they* are the ones who pose an ongoing threat to what is right and good."

22. George Packer, "The Errors of Edward Snowden and Glenn Greenwald," *Prospect*, June 2014, www.prospectmagazine.co.uk/features/the-errors-of-edward-snowden-and-glenn-greenwald.

23. Rory Carroll, "Ecuador Says It Blundered over Snowden Travel Document," *The Guardian*, July 2, 2013, www.theguardian.com/world/2013/jul/02/ecuador-rafael-correa-snowden-mistake.

24. See, for example, the debate between Jack Goldsmith and Rahul Sagar, in Goldsmith, "Critical Comments by Rahul Sagar on My Post on Kinsley," *Lawfare*, June 2, 2014, www.lawfareblog.com/critical-comments-rahul-sagar-my-post -kinsley. Sagar, the author of *Secrets and Leaks: The Dilemma of State Secrecy*, argues at several points that Greenwald and others "who value privacy and royalties above all else may continue to insist that secrecy is illegitimate, but democrats at least can safely discount such extreme views." The reference to libertarians and their views on state secrets—like Kinsley's allusion to Adam Smith—is unmistakable.

25. Joe Kloc, "NSA-Leaker Snowden Shares 'Truth-Telling' Award with Journalist Who Helped Him," *Newsweek*, April 8, 2014, www.newsweek.com/nsa -leaker-snowden-shares-truth-telling-award-journalist-who-helped-him-244491.

26. Aaron Blake, "Welcome to the Post–Edward Snowden Era," *Washington Post*, September 11, 2014, www.washingtonpost.com/blogs/the-fix/wp/2014 /09/11/welcome-to-the-post-edward-snowden-era.

27. Greg Miller and Adam Goldman, "A Hard-Edged Defender of Spy Agencies," *Washington Post*, January 12, 2014, www.washingtonpost.com/world /national-security/2014/01/12/43841ac6-7a34-11e3-af7f-13bf0e9965f6_story.html.

28. Polo Rocha, "Sensenbrenner NSA Reform Bill Faces Competing Proposals," University of Wisconsin–Madison *Badger Herald*, May 8, 2014, badger herald.com/news/2014/05/08/sensenbrenner-nsa-reform-bill.

29. Ibid.

30. Charlie Savage, "Changes to Surveillance Bill Stoke Anger," *New York Times*, May 20, 2014, www.nytimes.com/2014/05/21/us/politics/changes-to-sur veillance-bill-stoke-anger.html.

31. Steve Vladeck, "The USA Freedom Act and a FISA 'Special Advocate,' " *Lawfare*, May 20, 2014, mail.lawfareblog.com/usa-freedom-act-and-fisa-special -advocate.

32. Andrea Peterson, "NSA Reform Bill Passes House, Despite Loss of Support from Privacy Advocates," The Switch blog, *Washington Post*, May 22, 2014, www.washingtonpost.com/blogs/the-switch/wp/2014/05/22/nsa-reform-bill -passes-house-despite-loss-of-support-from-privacy-advocates; and Patrick Tucker, "Snowden's Legislative Legacy: A Bill That No One Likes," *Defense One*, June 6, 2014, www.defenseone.com/technology/2014/06/snowdens-legislative -legacy-bill-no-one-likes/86032.

33. Tucker, "Snowden's Legislative Legacy."

34. Ibid.

35. Spencer Ackerman, "NSA Review Panel Casts Doubt on Bulk Data Collection Claims," *The Guardian*, January 14, 2014, www.theguardian.com /world/2014/jan/14/nsa-review-panel-senate-phone-data-terrorism.

36. John Napier Tye, "Meet Executive Order 12333: The Reagan Rule That Lets the NSA Spy on Americans," *Washington Post*, July 18, 2014, www .washingtonpost.com/opinions/meet-executive-order-12333-the-reagan-rule -that-lets-the-nsa-spy-on-americans/2014/07/18/93d2ac22-0b93-11e4-b8e5-d0de 80767fc2_story.html.

37. Ibid.

38. Benjamin Wittes, "Yeah, But Is It a Good Bill? Thoughts on the Leahy FISA Reform Proposal," *Lawfare*, July 30, 2014, www.lawfareblog.com/yeah-it-good-bill-thoughts-leahy-fisa-reform-proposal.

39. Cyrus Farivar, "The Executive Order That Led to Mass Spying, as Told by NSA Alumni," *Ars Technica*, August 27, 2014, arstechnica.com/tech-policy/2014/08/a-twisted-history-how-a-reagan-era-executive-order-led-to-mass-spying.

40. Ibid.

41. Kate Tummarello, "Senator 'Within Inches' of NSA Reform Deal," *The Hill*, July 22, 2014, thehill.com/policy/technology/213030-leahy-administration-within-inches-of-surveillance-reform-deal.

42. "ISIS Calls Obama 'More Foolish' than Bush in Purported Recording," NBC News, September 22, 2014, www.nbcnews.com/storyline/isis-terror/isis-calls-obama-more-foolish-bush-purported-recording-n208591.

43. Dustin Volz, "Is ISIS Stalling NSA Spying Reform?," *National Journal*, September 10, 2014, www.nationaljournal.com/tech/is-isis-stalling-nsa-spying-reform-20140910.

44. Melissa Clyne, "NSA Director Says Snowden Hasn't Hurt Agency's Work," *Newsmax*, September 17, 2014, www.newsmax.com/US/National-security-agency-ISIS-cybersecurity-Snowden/2014/09/17/id/595166; and Justin Sink, "Intelligence Chief Says Snowden Leaks Created 'Perfect Storm,'" *The Hill*, September 18, 2014, thehill.com/policy/technology/218155-intelligence-chief-says-snowden-leaks-created-perfect-storm.

45. Spencer Ackerman, "Senate Republicans Block USA Freedom Act Surveillance Reform Bill," *The Guardian*, November 19, 2014, www.theguardian.com/us-news/2014/nov/18/usa-freedom-act-republicans-block-bill.

46. James Bamford, "Israel's N.S.A. Scandal," *New York Times*, September 16, 2014, www.nytimes.com/2014/09/17/opinion/israels-nsa-scandal.html.

47. Ibid.

8. Afraid of Our Shadow (Government)?

1. Orin Kerr, "Public Support for the NSA Greater Among Those Under 30," *Volokh Conspiracy* blog, *Washington Post*, January 25, 2015, www.washingtonpost.com/news/volokh-conspiracy/wp/2015/01/25/public-support-for-the-nsa-greater-among-those-under-30.

2. Kimberly Dozier, "Spy General Unloads on Obama's ISIS War Plan," *Daily Beast*, January 27, 2015, www.thedailybeast.com/articles/2015/01/27/ex-pentagon-spy-chief-blasts-white-house-paralyzed-by-radical-islam.html.

3. Melissa Clyne, "Ex-CIA Chief Michael Hayden: 'Torture' Report Will Cripple Agency," *Newsmax*, December 8, 2014, www.newsmax.com/Newsmax-Tv/torture-report-al-Qaida-CIA/2014/12/08/id/611736.

4. Floyd Brown, "Any Potential for NSA Reform Dies in Paris," *Capitol Hill Daily*, January 13, 2015, www.capitolhilldaily.com/2015/01/nsa-patriot-act-charlie-hebdo.

5. Colin Campbell, "Sen. Richard Burr Wants CIA Torture Report Copies Returned," *Under the Dome* blog, *Raleigh* (NC) *News & Observer*, January 21,

2015, www.newsobserver.com/news/politics-government/politics-columns-blogs/under-the-dome/article10228955.html.

6. Julian Hattem, "Leahy Eyes NSA Reform as Crowning Glory," *The Hill*, November 14, 2014, thehill.com/policy/cybersecurity/224136-leahy-eyes-nsa-reform-as-crowning-glory.

7. Michael V. Hayden and Michael B. Mukasey, "NSA Reform That Only ISIS Could Love," *Wall Street Journal*, November 17, 2014, www.wsj.com/articles/michael-v-hayden-and-michael-b-mukasey-nsa-reform-that-only-isis-could-love-1416268847.

8. Charlie Savage and Jeremy W. Peters, "Bill to Restrict N.S.A. Data Collection Blocked in Vote by Senate Republicans," *New York Times*, November 18, 2014, www.nytimes.com/2014/11/19/us/nsa-phone-records.html.

9. Amar Toor, "NSA's Internet Surveillance Faces Constitutional Challenge in Court," *The Verge*, December 17, 2014, www.theverge.com/2014/12/17/7407535/nsa-eff-court-challenge-upstream-internet-data-collection-surveillance.

10. Zach Miners, "Judge Questions Evidence on Whether NSA Spying Is Too Broad," *Computerworld*, December 20, 2014, www.computerworld.com/article/2861424/judge-questions-evidence-on-whether-nsa-spying-is-too-broad.html; and Cory Bennett, "NSA to Defend Internet Collection in Court," *The Hill*, December 16, 2014, thehill.com/policy/cybersecurity/227283-nsa-heads-to-court-to-defend-internet-collection.

11. "NSA's Water, Power Supply Under Threat in State Legislatures," *U.S. News & World Report*, January 29, 2015, www.usnews.com/news/articles/2015/01/28/nsas-water-power-supply-under-threat-in-state-legislatures.

12. Lauren Fox, "GOP Senators: Paris Shooting Justifies NSA Powers," *National Journal*, January 7, 2015, www.nationaljournal.com/congress/republicans-on-capitol-hill-paris-shooting-shows-congress-can-t-hamstring-nsa-20150107.

13. Matt Sledge, "Obama Gets an Incomplete on NSA Reform," *Huffington Post*, January 30, 2015, www.huffingtonpost.com/2015/01/30/obama-nsa-reform_n_6580702.html.

14. Dustin Volz, "Marco Rubio Wants to Permanently Extend NSA Mass Surveillance," *National Journal*, January 27, 2015, www.nationaljournal.com/tech/marco-rubio-wants-to-permanently-extend-nsa-mass-surveillance-20150127.

15. "Attorney General Nominee: NSA Surveillance Is 'Constitutional and Effective,' " *Democracy Now!*, January 29, 2015, www.democracynow.org/2015/1/29/headlines/attorney_general_nominee_nsa_spying_program_is_constitutional_and_effective.

16. Steven Mufson, "Six Years Later, Political Debate Over CIA Interrogations Hasn't Gone Away," *Washington Post*, December 9, 2014, www.washingtonpost.com/business/economy/six-years-later-political-debate-over-cia-interrogations-hasnt-gone-away/2014/12/09/6e1be114-7fd4-11e4-81fd-8c4814dfa9d7_story.html; and Lloyd Gardner, *Killing Machine: The American Presidency in the Age of Drone Warfare* (New York: The New Press, 2013), 212ff.

17. Michael Crowley, "John Brennan's Zigzag on Torture," *Politico*, December 9, 2014, www.politico.com/story/2014/12/john-brennan-cia-torture-113456.html.

18. "Transcript: Sen. Dianne Feinstein Says CIA Searched Intelligence Committee Computers," *Washington Post*, March 11, 2014, www.washingtonpost.com /world/national-security/transcript-sen-dianne-feinstein-says-cia-searched-intel ligence-committee-computers/2014/03/11/200dc9ac-a928-11e3-8599-ce7295b685 1c_story.html.

19. Ibid.

20. Gardner, *Killing Machine*, 187–88, 236–38.

21. Carl Hulse and Mark Marzetti, "Obama Expresses Confidence in C.I.A. Director," *New York Times*, August 2, 2014, www.nytimes.com/2014/08/02/us /obama-expresses-confidence-in-cia-director-brennan.html.

22. Josh Rogin and Eli Lake, "White House Must Decide Who Will Be Named in the CIA 'Torture Report,' " *Daily Beast*, August 7, 2014, www.thedaily beast.com/articles/2014/08/07/white-house-must-decide-who-will-be-named-in -the-cia-torture-report.html.

23. Greg Miller, Adam Goldman, and Ellen Nakashima, "CIA Misled on Interrogation Program, Senate Report Says," *Washington Post*, March 31, 2014, www.washingtonpost.com/world/national-security/cia-misled-on-interrogation -program-senate-report-says/2014/03/31/eb75a82a-b8dd-11e3-96ae-f2c36d2b1245 _story.html.

24. Amy Davidson, "Who's 'Emotional'—Feinstein or the C.I.A.?," *New Yorker*, April 6, 2014, www.newyorker.com/news/amy-davidson/whos-emotional-fein stein-or-the-c-i-a.

25. Mark Mazzetti, "Ex-Chief of C.I.A. Shapes Response to Detention Report," *New York Times*, July 25, 2014, www.nytimes.com/2014/07/26/world /george-tenet-ex-chief-of-cia-is-set-to-defend-actions-on-interrogation-program .html.

26. Crowley, "Brennan's Zigzag."

27. Ibid.

28. Rebecca Kaplan, "CIA Director: True Value of Enhanced Interrogation 'Unknowable,' " CBS News, December 11, 2014, www.cbsnews.com/news /cia-director-john-brennan-addresses-senate-torture-report/.

29. Agence France Presse, "CIA Torture Report Revealed 'Inexcusable Crimes': Edward Snowden," NDTV, December 11, 2014, www.ndtv.com/world-news /cia-torture-report-revealed-inexcusable-crimes-edward-snowden-711406.

30. Peter Baker, "Bush Team Approved C.I.A. Tactics, but Was Kept in Dark on Details, Report Says," *New York Times*, December 9, 2014, www.nytimes .com/2014/12/10/world/cia-kept-bush-ill-informed-on-interrogation-tactics-tor ture-report-says.html.

31. Ibid.

32. Mark Mazzetti, "Panel Faults C.I.A. Over Brutality and Deceit in Terrorism Interrogations," *New York Times*, December 9, 2014, www.nytimes.com /2014/12/10/world/senate-intelligence-committee-cia-torture-report.html.

33. John Heilprin, "UN Expert Calls for Prosecution over US Torture," AP, December 10, 2014, www.huffingtonpost.com/2014/12/10/un-us-torture_n _6300864.html.

34. Spencer Ackerman, "CIA Lied to the Public and John Brennan Must Quit, Says Outgoing Senator in Fiery Speech," *The Guardian*, December 10, 2014, www .theguardian.com/us-news/2014/dec/10/cia-director-john-brennan-quit-mark-udall.

35. Sarah Damian, "John Kiriakou on CNN—Says 'Crimes Were Committed' by CIA," Government Accountability Project blog, December 17, 2014, whistleblower.org/blog/111117-john-kiriakou-cnn-%E2%80%93-says-crimes-were -committed-cia-daily-whistleblower-news.

36. Matt Apuzzo and Mark Mazzetti, "Investigators Said to Seek No Penalty for C.I.A.'s Computer Search," *New York Times*, December 19, 2014, www.nytimes .com/2014/12/20/us/politics/panel-to-advise-against-penalty-for-cia-computer -search.html; and Mark Hosenball, "Exclusive: CIA Says Its Inspector General Is Resigning at End of Month," Reuters, January 5, 2015, www.reuters.com /article/2015/01/05/us-usa-cia-inspector-exclusive-idUSKBN0KE1BO20150105.

37. Adam Liptak, "Supreme Court Rejects Appeal from Reporter," *New York Times*, June 2, 2014, www.nytimes.com/2014/06/03/us/james-risen-faces-jail-time -for-refusing-to-identify-a-confidential-source.html.

38. Hadas Gold, "Eric Holder Meets with Media over New Guidelines," *Politico*, May 27, 2014, www.politico.com/blogs/media/2014/05/doj-meets-with -media-over-new-guidelines-189254.html.

39. David Uberti, "Why Obama's Statement on Reporters' Arrests in Ferguson Is Hypocritical," *Columbia Journalism Review*, August 14, 2014, www.cjr.org /the_kicker/obama.php.

40. Stephen Z. Nemo, "James Risen vs. the Security State," Communities Digital News, August 20, 2014, www.commdiginews.com/politics-2/james -risen-vs-the-security-state-24229.

41. Quoted in Matt Apuzzo, "C.I.A. Officer Is Found Guilty in Leak Tied to *Times* Reporter," *New York Times*, January 26, 2015, www.nytimes .com/2015/01/27/us/politics/cia-officer-in-leak-case-jeffrey-sterling-is-convicted -of-espionage.html.

42. Quoted in Conor Friedersdorf, "Michael Hayden's Hollow Constitution," *The Atlantic*, January 2015, www.theatlantic.com/politics/archive/2015/01 /former-cia-and-nsa-director-nsa-doesnt-just-listen-to-bad-people/385007.

Conclusion: Defending the Republic?

1. Matt Apuzzo, "C.I.A. Officer Is Found Guilty in Leak Tied to *Times* Reporter," *New York Times*, January 26, 2015, www.nytimes.com/2015/01/27/us /politics/cia-officer-in-leak-case-jeffrey-sterling-is-convicted-of-espionage.html.

2. Jesselyn Radack, "The Shocking Court Case That Proves the Government's Shameful Petraeus Hypocrisy," *Salon*, May 10, 2015, www.salon.com /2015/05/10/the_shocking_court_case_that_proves_the_governments_shameful _petraeus_hypocrisy.

3. Apuzzo, "C.I.A. Officer Is Found Guilty,"

4. Norman Solomon, "CIA Leak Trial: 'This Case Is Not About Politics' [sic]," *Huffington Post*, January 26, 2015, www.huffingtonpost.com/norman -solomon/cia-leak-trial-this-case_b_65446666.html.

5. Philip Giraldi, "Obama's War on Leaks Skirts the Constitution," *American Conservative*, February 12, 2015, www.theamericanconservative.com/articles /obamas-war-on-leaks-skirts-the-constitution; and Matt Zapotosky, "Former CIA Officer Convicted in Leak Case," *Washington Post*, January 26, 2015, www.wash ingtonpost.com/local/crime/ex-cia-officer-convicted-in-leak-case-sentenced-to-3 -12-years-in-prison/2015/05/11/fc5427a6-f5a0-11e4-84a6-6d7c67c50db0_story.html.

6. "Overkill on a CIA Leak Case," editorial, *New York Times*, May 13, 2015, www.nytimes.com/2015/05/13/opinion/overkill-on-a-cia-leak-case.html.

7. Apuzzo, "C.I.A. Officer Is Found Guilty."

8. Matt Zapotosky, "Prosecutors: Ex-CIA Officer in Leak Case Is Different from Petraeus, Others," *Washington Post*, May 7, 2015, www.washingtonpost.com /local/crime/prosecutors-ex-cia-officer-in-leak-case-is-different-from-petraeus -others/2015/05/07/f78c04bc-f4fd-11e4-84a6-6d7c67c50db0_story.html.

9. "Obama Admin Could Have Been Much Tougher on Whistleblowers, Leakers—Holder," RT, February 19, 2015, www.rt.com/usa/233551-holder-obama -whistleblowers-leakers.

10. Catherine Taibi, "*New York Times*' James Risen Blasts Eric Holder as 'Enemy of Press Freedom,' " *Huffington Post*, February 18, 2015, www.huffington post.com/2015/02/18/james-risen-eric-holder-obama-free-press-white-house_n _6705078.html.

11. Margaret Sullivan, "Why a Reporter's 'Epic Rant' on Twitter Gets No Argument Here," *Public Editor's Journal* blog, *New York Times*, February 19, 2015, publiceditor.blogs.nytimes.com/2015/02/19/why-a-reporters-epic-rant-on-twitter -gets-no-argument-here.

12. Benjamin Wittes and Jack Goldsmith, "The New York Times Public Editor Backs James Risen's 'Truth-Telling,' " *Lawfare*, February 19, 2015, www .lawfareblog.com/new-york-times-public-editor-backs-james-risens-truth-telling.

13. Apuzzo, "C.I.A. Officer Is Found Guilty."

14. Ben Kamisar, "McCain Weighs In on NSA Ruling: 'People Seem to Have Forgotten 9/11,' " *The Hill*, May 7, 2015, thehill.com/policy/technology/241329 -mccain-weighs-in-on-nsa-ruling-people-have-forgotten-about-9-11.

15. Lawrence Wright, "The Al Qaeda Switchboard," *New Yorker*, January 13, 2014, www.newyorker.com/magazine/2014/01/13/the-al-qaeda-switchboard.

16. Charlie Spiering, "Chris Christie Blasts Edward Snowden, Hollywood, for Culture of Fear Surrounding Government Surveillance," *Breitbart*, May 18, 2015, www.breitbart.com/big-government/2015/05/18/chris-christie-blasts-edward -snowden-hollywood-for-culture-of-fear-surrounding-government-surveillance.

17. David Sanger and Nicole Perlroth, "Obama Heads to Tech Security Talks amid Tensions," *New York Times*, February 12, 2015, www.nytimes .com/2015/02/13/business/obama-heads-to-security-talks-amid-tensions.html.

18. Dominic Rushe, "Obama Responds to Hacks and Silicon Valley with 'Emerging Cyber Threat' Plan," *The Guardian*, February 13, 2015, www.the guardian.com/us-news/2015/feb/13/president-obama-cyber-threat-plan-hacks -silicon-valley; and James Vincent, "Apple Targeted by CIA Spies for Years, Say New Snowden Documents," *The Verge*, March 10, 2015, www.theverge .com/2015/3/10/8181531/cia-targets-apple-xcode-encryption.

19. Jeremy Scahill and Josh Begley, "iSpy: The CIA Campaign to Steal Apple's Secrets," *The Intercept*, March 10, 2015, firstlook.org/theintercept/2015/03/10 /ispy-cia-campaign-steal-apples-secrets.

20. Ibid.

21. Rory Carroll, "Hillary Clinton: People Felt Betrayed by NSA Surveillance," *The Guardian*, February 24, 2015, www.theguardian.com/us-news/2015 /feb/25/hillary-clinton-people-betrayed-nsa-surveillance-edward-snowden.

22. "Activists Spent Year Planning Snowden Bust in Brooklyn Park," *New York Post*, May 7, 2015, nypost.com/2015/05/07/activists-spent-year-planning-snowden -bust-in-brooklyn-park; "NYPD Returns Edward Snowden Bust to Activist Artists," *Sputnik*, May 7, 2015, sputniknews.com/us/20150507/1021802742.html; and John Biggs, "Print Your Own Bust of Edward Snowden," *TechCrunch*, May 12, 2015, techcrunch.com/2015/05/12/print-your-own-bust-of-edward -snowden.

23. Conor Friedersdorf, "The Vindication of Edward Snowden," *The Atlantic*, May 11, 2015, www.theatlantic.com/politics/archive/2015/05/the-vindication -of-edward-snowden/392741.

24. Kate Vinton, "Edward Snowden Calls Ruling on NSA Mass Surveillance 'Extraordinarily Encouraging,' " *Forbes*, May 8, 2015, www.forbes.com/sites/kate vinton/2015/05/08/edward-snowden-calls-nsa-mass-surveillance-ruling-extraor dinarily-encouraging.

25. Scott Shane, "Snowden Sees Some Victories, from a Distance," *New York Times*, May 20, 2015, www.nytimes.com/2015/05/20/world/europe/snowden-sees -some-victories-from-a-distance.html.

26. Benjamin Wittes and Jodie Liu, "So What's New in the Freedom Act, Anyway?," *Lawfare*, May 14, 2015, www.lawfareblog.com/so-whats-new-usa -freedom-act-anyway.

27. Julian Hattem, "ACLU, Tea Party Take On Federal Spying: 'They've Gone Too Far,' " *The Hill*, May 19, 2016, thehill.com/policy/national-security/242502 -aclu-tea-party-run-anti-nsa-ads-in-dc-iowa-new-hampshire.

28. Kevin Boyd, "Conservative Republican Changes Mind About the Patriot Act, Thanks to Edward Snowden," *Rare*, May 15, 2015, rare.us/story/conservative -republican-changes-mind-about-the-patriot-act-thanks-to-edward-snowden.

29. Anthony Zurcher, "US States Take Aim at NSA over Warrantless Surveillance," BBC News, April 27, 2015, www.bbc.com/news/world-us-canada -32487971.

30. Nicole Perlroth, "Tech Giants Urge Obama to Reject Policies That Weaken Encryption," *New York Times*, May 20, 2015, www.nytimes.com/2015 /05/20/technology/tech-giants-urge-obama-to-reject-policies-that-weaken-encryp tion-technology.html.

31. Mike Masnick, "After Claiming USA Freedom Would Be a Boon to ISIS, Ex-NSA Director Now Mocks How Weak USA Freedom Is," *Techdirt*, June 18, 2015, www.techdirt.com/articles/20150618/06521231384/after-claiming-usa-free dom-would-be-boon-to-isis-ex-nsa-director-now-mocks-how-weak-usa-freedom -is.shtml.

32. Maya Rhodan, "White House Responds to Petition Urging Obama to Pardon Edward Snowden," *Time*, July 28, 2015, time.com/3974713/white-house-edward-snowden-petition.

33. Chelsea E. Manning, "We're Citizens, Not Subjects. We Have the Right to Criticize Government Without Fear," *The Guardian*, May 7, 2015, www.theguardian.com/commentisfree/2015/may/06/were-citizens-not-subjects-we-have-the-right-to-criticize-government-without-fear.

INDEX

ABOUT THE AUTHOR

Native of Ohio and recipient of a PhD from the University of Wisconsin, Lloyd C. Gardner taught American history at Rutgers University from 1963 until 2012. During that time he published more than a dozen books and received numerous awards and fellowships, including a Guggenheim and two teaching Fulbrights, to England and Finland. He is a past president of the Society of Historians of American Foreign Affairs and has received the American Historical Association's award for lifetime achievement in the writing of American history. He is also a member of the Society of American Historians. Beginning with his book *Economic Aspects of New Deal Diplomacy*, he has written widely on twentieth-century and twenty-first-century foreign policy, including *Architects of Illusion: Men and Ideas in American Foreign Policy, 1941–1949* and *Safe for Democracy: The Anglo-American Response to Revolution, 1913–1923*, as well as two books on the Vietnam War, *Approaching Vietnam: From World War II Through Dienbienphu, 1941–1954* and *Pay Any Price: Lyndon Johnson and the Wars for Vietnam*. His most recent books—*The Killing Machine: The American Presidency in the Age of Drone Warfare*, *The Road to Tahrir Square: Egypt and the United States from the Rise of Nasser to the Fall of Mubarak*, *Three Kings: The Rise of an American Empire in the Middle East After World War II*, and *The Long Road to Baghdad: A History of U.S. Foreign Policy from the 1970s to the Present*, all published by The New Press—have been on U.S. policy in the Middle East since World War II, with all its conflicts and controversies. He lives in Bucks County, Pennsylvania.

Publishing in the Public Interest

Thank you for reading this book published by The New Press. The New Press is a nonprofit, public interest publisher. New Press books and authors play a crucial role in sparking conversations about the key political and social issues of our day.

We hope you enjoyed this book and that you will stay in touch with The New Press. Here are a few ways to stay up to date with our books, events, and the issues we cover:

- Sign up at www.thenewpress.com/subscribe to receive updates on New Press authors and issues and to be notified about local events
- Like us on Facebook: www.facebook.com/newpressbooks
- Follow us on Twitter: www.twitter.com/thenewpress

Please consider buying New Press books for yourself; for friends and family; or to donate to schools, libraries, community centers, prison libraries, and other organizations involved with the issues our authors write about.

The New Press is a 501(c)(3) nonprofit organization. You can also support our work with a tax-deductible gift by visiting www.the newpress.com/donate.